THEORY AND THE PREMODERN TEXT

MEDIEVAL
CULTURES

SERIES EDITORS

RITA COPELAND
BARBARA A. HANAWALT
DAVID WALLACE

*Sponsored by the Center for Medieval Studies
at the University of Minnesota*

Volumes in this series study the diversity of medieval
cultural histories and practices, including such
interrelated issues as gender, class, and social
hierarchies; race and ethnicity; geographical
relations; definitions of political space; discourses of
authority and dissent; educational institutions;
canonical and noncanonical literatures; and
technologies of textual and visual literacies.

Theory
and the
Premodern
Text

Paul Strohm

Medieval Cultures, Volume 26
University of Minnesota Press
Minneapolis
London

Chapter 4 originally appeared in *Art and Context in Late Medieval English Narrative,* ed. Robert R. Edwards (Cambridge: D. S. Brewer, 1994), 163–76; reprinted with permission from Boydell & Brewer Ltd. Chapter 8 originally appeared in *Journal of British Studies* 35 (1996): 1–23; copyright 1996 by the North American Conference on British Studies, all rights reserved; reprinted with permission of *Journal of British Studies* and the University of Chicago Press. Chapter 11 originally appeared as "Chaucer's Lollard Joke: History and the Textual Unconscious," *Studies in the Age of Chaucer* 17 (1995): 23–42; reprinted with permission of the New Chaucer Society.

Published by the University of Minnesota Press
111 Third Avenue South, Suite 290
Minneapolis, MN 55401-2520
http://www.upress.umn.edu

Library of Congress Cataloging-in-Publication Data

Strohm, Paul, 1938–
    Theory and the premodern text / Paul Strohm.
       p.   cm. — (Medieval cultures ; v. 26)
    Includes bibliographical references and index.
    ISBN 0-8166-3774-1 (acid-free paper) — ISBN 0-8166-3775-X (pbk. : acid-free paper)
    1. English literature — Middle English, 1100–1500 — History and criticism — Theory, etc. 2. Chaucer, Geoffrey, d. 1400 — Criticism and interpretation. 3. Literature and history — England — History — To 1500. 4. Literature and history — England — History — 16th century. 5. Historical drama, English — History and criticism. 6. Shakespeare, William, 1564–1616 — Histories. 7. Civilization, Medieval, in literature. 8. London (England) — In literature. 9. Kings and rulers in literature. 10. Rhetoric, Medieval. I. Title. II. Series.
    PR275.H5 S77 2000
    820.9'358 — dc21

Printed in the United States of America on acid-free paper

The University of Minnesota is an equal-opportunity educator and employer.

11 10 09 08 07 06 05 04 03 02 01 00   10 9 8 7 6 5 4 3 2 1

To
David Wallace

Contents

Acknowledgments

Our enterprise is finally social and collective. Not invariably, but most often, it is conducted with astounding generosity and within presuppositions of goodwill. Perhaps I may illustrate my point by listing a diverse company of fellow scholars who have supplemented these essays, or provoked their elaboration, by after-lecture or written queries, by suggestions, by information freely volunteered. Some are dear friends, some are virtual strangers... and that, after all, is the point, isn't it? They include David Armitage, Caroline Barron, Derek Brewer, John Burrow, Chris Cannon, Linda Charnes, Andrew Cole, Rita Copeland, Susan Crane, Carolyn Dinshaw, Diane Elam, Dyan Elliott, Jonathan Elmer, Stanley Fish, Tom Foster, Vanessa Harding, Robert Hasenfratz, Gareth Stedman Jones, David Kastan, David Lawton, Sheila Lindenbaum, Derek Pearsall, Andrew Prescott, Matthew Reynolds, Miri Rubin, Fiona Somerset, John Watts, and Karen Winstead.

The dedication for this volume is reserved for the discussant, provocateur, and friend who has helped it most: David Wallace. His intellectual generosity, gift for inquiry, and practical acumen have greatly enriched my life and work.

Introduction

I recently attended a lecture by Bruno Latour in which he discussed a Chinese proverb, the gist of which was "Show a fool the moon and he looks at your finger." The folly in question overemphasizes the interpretative framework or strategy that renders the phenomenon visible (the pointing finger) at the expense of the phenomenon itself (the moon). Obviously, a balance is to be sought, in which the role of theory in identifying a problem is acknowledged, yet the object of study is also respected. Needless to say, this balance is threatened by overmuch indulgence in "theory" for its own sake, resulting in an estrangement from the object it seeks to illuminate.

In my view, a solution to this dilemma rests in the area of what I would consider engaged or "practical" theory. Its hypothetical opposite— "pure" theory, uncorrected or unchastened by sustained contact with a particular text—does not command or hold my attention. But if theory away from the text eludes me, theory *with* the text enjoys my fullest attention and respect. What I have in mind here is voluntarily "impure" theory: project oriented, aimed at explaining the text rather than its own vindication, uninsistent about its own status as a total explanatory system. Such theory need not currently be in fashion, or even have originated in France. It might occasionally be angular or difficult, if the concepts in question require it, but it should normally be susceptible to clear articulation, in the ordinary language of women and men.

The phrase "practical theory" is a deliberate reminiscence of that salutary volume, I. A. Richards's *Practical Criticism,* an early edition of which still occupies a respected place on the shelves of my college library.[1] First published in 1929, Richards's work did not reach North America with full force until the 1950s and the heyday of New Criticism, and I am old enough still to remember the bracing impact of his insistence on "making out the plain sense of poetry," unencumbered by personal associations or stock responses. For all its common sense, I no longer regard Richards's proposal as feasible — although I think it still enjoys a *place* within a feasible project.

His is the activity that Derrida has since described as the "respectful doubling" of a text's statements and assumptions about itself.[2] I hasten to say that I have no quarrel with intelligent description or thoughtfully arranged repetition of a text's contents or apparent designs. Nor do I doubt that this descriptive enterprise can itself be theorized, as can any enterprise that takes the time to reflect on its own practices; this point was settled long ago by the writings of the Prague school of linguistics, the Russian formalists, the early American New Critics, and brilliant individualists like William Empson in *Seven Types of Ambiguity*. The intelligent description of the work of art in its own terms is the endeavor of which Derrida speaks when, in one of his least frequently repeated comments, he describes "doubling commentary" as that essential "recognition and respect" without which criticism "would risk developing in any direction at all and authorize itself to say almost anything." Whatever its limitations with respect to opening (as opposed to protecting) a reading, such commentary offers (he says, in a phrase that must surprise many of his critics) an "indispensable guardrail" against interpretative disrespect.

But why, then, does not "doubling commentary" suffice? My reply is that it would be found adequate *if* texts were never evasive, never silent about their own suppressions and omissions, never misleading or forgetful about their own sources and origins, always fully candid and articulate about themselves and their own prehistories and the circumstances of their composition, always able to "close" themselves by specifying their own objectives and unifying principles. Yet texts are rarely candid in any of these ways. The textual condition is more normally one of nontransparency, of inherent and obdurate recalcitrance. I use words like "inherent" because I believe texts not only to be unwilling but unable to tell us all they know — everything about their antecedence, their suppressions and evasions, the uses and appropriations to which they are, or will be, exposed.

This is why "the text itself," as the New Critics used to say, can indeed be centralized as the object of study, but cannot be spared all the perturbations from which Richards sought to protect it. The unperturbed text will, in respects made apparent by contemporary theory, remain partially unanalyzed, will remain in possession of possibilities and experiences that it cannot or will not articulate. A necessary task of theory is precisely to provoke a text into unpremeditated articulation, into the utterance of what it somehow contains or knows but neither intends nor is able to say. Still, in a sense, the text "itself"—but not finally the text *by* itself (since I often place a text in dialogue with a theory that questions its very assumptions) or even *for* itself (since my interest extends to what Said would call the "affiliated text," or the text in its relations with history and the world).[3]

One *respects* a text by granting it a certain "selfhood"—by framing careful statements about what it is saying and by verifying those statements against its language and the circumstances of its utterance. Such respectful treatment is, and must remain, the sine qua non of interpretation. But one must also, at times, treat a text with what I have elsewhere called a "strategic *disrespect*" (see chapter 11), or, in another current parlance, a kind of "tough love." This form of disrespect is abetted by literary theory. It is theory, as elaborated by Barthes and others, which has so powerfully reminded us of texts' irreducibility to paraphrase, their inability to close or finish themselves or to reveal their secrets.[4] One may even suggest that the "text" as an object of study, with all that this designation implies about indeterminacy and inconclusion, is a creation of theory. The intimate relationship of textuality and theory may partly explain the extent to which the term *text* remains something of a red flag to literary scholars who would regard bounded "works" as stable productions of authorial intent and also to historians who seek empirical information from "sources" and "documents." Any piece of writing called "text" is already at least partly freed from the oversight of any single discipline, has already been identified as a provisional object of interpretation.[5]

Refusing an easy assimilation to the text's self-representations, theory justifies itself, and even some of the difficulties it occasionally presents, by offering a standpoint of appraisal grounded somewhere outside that range of possibilities afforded by the text's internal or authorized commentary. Theory thus enjoys a role that need not be understood as one of minimization or reduction, but rather of augmentation. Its promise, that is, involves supplementing the text, enriching its meaning by unearthing its tacit knowledge and its implicit or canceled opinions. Thus, my persistent attraction to Freud, and the bold entry he affords into the issue of what the text "represses," the possibility that the text possesses an unconscious, comprised by what it has repressed or declines to say.

So, too, am I drawn to Macherey and other more contemporary theorists of textual silence and evasion, who consider the rejected or un-
stated materials at the text's boundaries to be part of its total meaning.
The concomitant of Macherey's position, and mine — in fact, the consequence of theory and what it has taught us — is that a text cannot fully
reveal itself, unless pressured by questions formed somewhere outside
its own orbit of assumptions.[6] I therefore argue that *theory is any standpoint from which we might challenge a text's self-understanding.*[7] Or, to put
the same thing differently, as I do in chapter 11, I am interested in theory
to the extent that it underwrites the claim to know more about a text
than it knows about itself.

The analyst who asks hard questions or "springs" questions from
somewhere outside the text's own orbit of assumptions should be ad-
versely judged only if the effect of the analysis is to override or silence
the text as a complicated articulation. Certainly, any deployment of a
theory to overbear a text, to reduce it to "more of the same," to predes-
tined conclusions already borne within the theory's initial assumptions,
must be deplored. The outcome of "strategic disrespect" must be a new
and amplified form of respect: for the text as a meaning-making system, for its conceptual power and its unpredictable effects in the world.

The theoretical enterprise, as I am describing it, is frankly and in-
escapably pluralist, and unrestricted pluralism is not without its problems. I allude to what David Aers has termed "magpie theory": hyper-
mobile and opportunistic theory that operates across different systems
with potentially opposed claims and objectives, blinding itself to con-
flicts among and between the theoretical models it employs.[8] One of my
own precautions is simply to tread with care, to attempt not to conclude
too quickly that two different systems are compatible simply because they
enjoy a few words or concepts in common.[9]

Most crucially, though, the initial decision to centralize the text as
the object of analysis exerts its own form of control over the theories I
use and the ways in which I use them. The text as the center of analysis
ultimately escapes or exceeds any single critical system that is aimed at
it. Properly respected, the text itself becomes a center of resistance to
inappropriate theory or theory inappropriately applied. With its embrace of meanings that no single theorization can pretend to exhaust,
the text itself offers a standpoint (or numerous standpoints) from which

a theoretical insufficiency or an overliteralization can be revealed. Something in the text is liable to — can be expected to — remain inviolate, in the sense of withstanding this or that theory's attempted reduction to its own terms.[10] I am thus most attracted to those theories which allow the impossibility of the text's exhaustion, the mystery or inexpressibility of its most private center.

Nevertheless, I must allow some legitimacy to Aers's critique of cobbled or polyglot systems with elements in one way or another pitted against themselves. As a check against unwieldy improvisations, I look for certain very broad consistencies among and between the theories I employ. Skeptical as I am about the practice of "theory away from the text," I should nevertheless step back from particular cases for a moment, in order to say what some of these consistencies are. They include the following:

The centrality of the text. The text itself is always centralized, with its self-assertions, deployments, reticences, and contradictions always allowed to set the agenda for discussion. Theory is of interest as an interrogative standpoint, implicated in the framing of questions from somewhere outside the text's own network of assumptions. Theory is employed to identify and investigate the text's exceptionalities, but never — I hope — to override them.

Provisional neglect of "the literary." As I was writing this introduction, an essay appeared by a respected critic who deplored "a historicism which excludes attempts to differentiate between writing that was once regarded as literary, of aesthetic value, and all other contemporary documents."[11] I certainly admit to this presumed barbarism. Perhaps my experiences with medieval writing, in which so much interesting writing takes no pains to insert itself in a "literary" register, influence my view. More important, though, are the procedural gains fostered by ignoring the literary/nonliterary divide: a vastly enlarged field of consideration, an appreciation of the social "work" of the text, a more generous assignment of creativity across a larger range of written productions.

Textual/extratextual dialogue. The text is found always to exist in intimate dialogue with the external/extratextual world. Whether registered by direct acknowledgment, telling silence, symptom, or other distortion, the material world exerts a constant pressure on the text, and may be considered (borrowing terminology from Jameson) the text's "absent cause."[12] Attending to the dialogue of text and world, or *texte* and *hors-texte* (as opposed, say, to looking only for signs of the text's internal self-elaboration), seems to me the critic's highest calling.[13]

The textual unconscious. Believing that texts are constituted partially by silences and repressions, I treat these repressed materials as comprising an effective "textual unconscious." Although I stop well short of embracing the entire Freudian system, I am nevertheless a believer in the reality of both social and psychological "repression," and believe that Freud's writings contain the most comprehensive account of repression, its mechanisms, and the relation of repression to the formation of the unconscious and the preconscious.

Shared meaning. "Meaning" is treated as a phenomenon always shared out or held in common. The meaning of a particular text exists somewhere in the range between broad tradition and unique articulation, between authorial intent and a broadened diversity of uses and appropriations, between the work's meaning to its intended and actual and subsequent audiences. Never unitary, a meaning's history and status (when? to whom? for what?) must always be specified.

Differing considerably among themselves, the theorists most important to this volume are likely to share the foregoing propositions. Especially prominent are some theorists who have found, or whose work suggests, ways of merging previously separate aesthetic and social and psychological domains; writings of Pierre Bourdieu, Michel de Certeau, and Slavoj Žižek recur with particular frequency. Obviously, I make no claim to engage all, or even very much of, the currently exciting theoretical work germane to my interests. Some of the most productive recent inquiries — including queer and postcolonial theory — receive little or inadequate discussion in the following pages. Regarding "theory" less as a settled matter and more as a set of evolving practices, I take some consolation from my belief in the futility of any attempt finally or conclusively to survey its terrain.

The brevity of this introduction may give the impression that I am packing awfully "light" for the rigors of the journey ahead. As I have said, though, I consider myself a practical theorist, which means that only now, with actual texts and real textual problems, does the serious work of this book begin.

PART I

SPACE, SYMBOLIZATION, AND SOCIAL PRACTICE

1

THREE LONDON ITINERARIES

AESTHETIC PURITY AND THE COMPOSING PROCESS

THE SYMBOLIC CHARACTER OF LATE MEDIEVAL SPACE

The mixed character of social self-representation emerges in "street-level" narratives by three writers who chart itineraries within the medieval city of London. The writers and writings in question are Chaucer in Friday Street, Usk making his way to Willingham's tavern, and Hoccleve returning home via the Thames to the Privy Seal. In the course of these descriptions, each writer draws, variously, upon established urban resonances; upon the organizational expectations of non- or extraliterary genres, and also upon analogies and precedents drawn from the most prestigious possible literary sources.

Before turning to the texts in question, however, some note must be taken of their specifically *medieval* character. A number of influential theoretical texts have recently addressed questions of urban space and the dynamics of urban self-definition, and I am interested in gaining such assistance from them as I can. Nevertheless, even if elements of a problematics of space remain constant from historical period to historical period, each period offers different issues and instantiations. Henri LeFebvre thus argues, correctly, in *The Production of Space* that "each society offers its own peculiar space,"[1] and one would not wish to commit so fully to the persistence of certain spatial issues as to ignore the distinctive problems to be confronted within a particular cultural configuration.

In my view, the peculiarity of medieval space involves the extent to which it is already symbolically organized by the meaning-making activities of the many generations that have traversed it. Which is to say that, as a typical late medieval city, London incorporated a noticeably durable and complicated set of *presignifications.* Any wayfarer defines himself or herself in relation to preconstituted choices; this is true for the medieval wayfarer, moving through the rich symbolic terrain of the medieval city—only, one might say, "more so."

Every urban walker—medieval or modern—makes choices that amount to what Pierre Bourdieu calls "regulated improvisation."[2] Current theory maximizes the zone of improvisation, allowing the postmodern rambler to remake the city, to rearrange it according to his or her whim or perception. Encountering little resistance from the city's own loosened symbolic structure, the postmodern walker, in the words of Michel de Certeau, "transforms each spatial signifier into something else."[3] Yet, with the *pre*modern walker, the balance shifts from improvisation toward regulation and a lessened freedom with respect to established social signifiers. Vagabondage and goliardic transgression notwithstanding,[4] the medieval walker may not be seen as a free rambler or "flâneur," an improviser within a decentered or nonexistent set of urban rules.[5] Rather, discovering himself or herself within presecured space, the medieval walker renegotiates an itinerary through an especially densely marked terrain.

This is not to confine the medieval walker in a strict symbolic straitjacket. For one thing, the space of the late medieval city was never as ordered, hierarchical, or serene as some commentators used to imagine it. Boundaries overlap, temporalities jostle together, spatial claims and counterclaims abound and proliferate within the Guildhall Letter-Books and Plea and Memoranda Rolls and other civic records. Overlapping jurisdictions, discontinuous social circles, and other political and vocational cacophonies meant that the medieval walker's place within the medieval city's universe of social possibilities was never entirely self-evident or foregone. Occasionally, and most remarkably, the late medieval walker or wayfarer might even be found alone—a status so exceptional as already to mean something, as already to presuppose some kind of reconsideration.

Each of our three urban itineraries does indeed involve a walker who finds himself, or sets out, alone. Along with itinerants and night-

walkers and others who even briefly eschew customary corporate identity, the medieval solitary enjoys a situation of some liminality or at least
vulnerability. Yet solitude, in the medieval text, is a temporary condition,
consequential less in its own right than for what it foresees: the itinerant's own renegotiated relationship with a presymbolized city and with
other urban inhabitants. Thus, Hoccleve's troubled dreamer in the *Regement* responds to his situation of intellectual turmoil by arising the next
morning and betaking himself "into the feld" where he can indulge his
"seekly distresse."[6] Almost immediately, however, a "poore olde hore
man," discovering him walking alone, approaches him with a set of socially defining questions, central to which is his celebrated "What man
art thou?" The solitary state is, in this sense, merely preliminary to the
defining encounter. New knowledge will not be delivered to the solitary
as solitary: it will be dialogic in form, a result of social exchange. The lone
dreamer of the vision-poem, the solitary penitent, the solitude-seeker of
the chanson d'aventure—all lay themselves open to, or in fact place
themselves in the way of, unusual opportunity. Should they however
briefly experience anything like a twentieth-century "identity crisis,"
they will not experience it alone: their transformation will occur as a result of a visitation, a conversation, a shared task, or other socially inflected
exchange. This exchange will, in turn, lead to a mixed denouement—at
once *artistic* and *social*—and this denouement will be expressed as a
personal repositioning within a complexly rendered social order.

Three Urban Itineraries

Chaucer on Friday Street

Chaucer describes his stroll in Friday Street in a deposition given in a
celebrated heraldry dispute.[7] This is the extended dispute in the court
of chivalry between Sir Richard Scrope and Sir Robert Grosvenor over
the awkward discovery that they bore identical arms. Chaucer was among
the numerous witnesses for Scrope, the eventual winning side, and the
central part of Chaucer's testimony, appropriately enough, finds him
telling a story.

It seems (as recorded from testimony before the presiding judge)
that he was once in Friday Street ("il estoit une foitz en Fridaystrete en

Loundres"), when he saw a pertinent sight. Now Friday Street was no mere backdrop or tabula rasa. At the time of Chaucer's deposition and for several centuries before and after, Friday Street existed as a secondary thoroughfare some 240 yards long, running on a north-south axis from Westcheap, beginning just west of Cheap Cross, bisecting Watling Street and Maiden Lane, and terminating at Fish Street (later, Thames Street), just east of the fishmarket. Friday Street may have received its name from a long-superseded craft connotation. Stow explains its name as deriving from "fishmongers dwelling there, and seruing Fridayes market."[8] In any case, as with Bread and Milk and other streets of the fourteenth century, this connection with a specific trade had already become vestigial in the highly organized and big-money trading practices of Chaucer's own day. More vividly knowable to the fourteenth-century stroller would have been its current political and religious affiliations, as exemplified by its ward and parish divisions. It bisected the Bread Street Ward, the power base of recent mayor—and pro-Ricardian factionalist and sometime overseer of Chaucer's career—Nicholas Brembre.[9] No less evident to the stroller of 1386 was the parish structure invisibly touching and transecting the street. A short walk down Friday Street traversed three parishes, each then represented by a flourishing and visible church: Saint Matthew's Friday Street, leading south to Saint John the Evangelist, thence to Saint Margaret Moses.[10]

These divisions may be understood as invisible lines of force, as symbolic concentrations, and each possesses its own temporality. The street name itself (if Stow is to be believed) evokes LeFebvre's "space of accumulation" or workspace, an aggressive temporality marked by what LeGoff calls "merchant's time."[11] The ward represents political space, the space of faction, of contention, punctuated by aldermanic elections, council meetings, and other by-products of political organization. Though by no means wholly unpolitical, the parish represents an aspiration toward vertical space:[12] supramundane space, the space of ceremonial repetition. Together, these spaces constitute an ensemble—an orchestration of different ways of thinking and experiencing an urban life.

Against which Chaucer now sounds an additional and discordant note. For, within this densely organized urban space, Chaucer encounters a blazon or *signe*, exemplified by the public display of arms by a knight resident in an inn on Friday Street. This sign mounts a claim to yet another temporality, not yet seen on Friday Street. This sign exemplifies slow time, backward-looking time with an anachronistic and outdated feel on this bustling city street. It is the time of (if this word means anything at all anymore)[13] feudality, of ancient privilege, a symbol that, like all the symbols at issue in the Scrope-Grosvenor trial, claims its origins in "time out of mind": "When he came into the street he saw hanging outdoors a new sign made of the said arms [arms in dispute] and he asked what inn ['herbergerie'] that was which had hung these arms of Scrope." In the first instance, the surprise is not that a lord has come newly to town or that he has displayed his arms, but that a new inn has sprung up, or an existing building has begun to accommodate such guests. The *herbergerie* in question was presumably not a permanent dwelling, like the bishop's palaces and dwellings of other prominent lords, all of which were marked in some such way. Most of these structures lay along the river or in the open fields on the west or east ends of town, and were already familiar features of the London landscape. This *herbergerie* would seem to represent a phenomenon noted by Caroline Barron in her study of aristocratic town houses: the fourteenth- and fifteenth-century development of "commercial inns," serving the needs of the lesser aristocracy and gentry, at a lower cost.[14] And Chaucer's initial interest seems to have been that a new establishment, in a somewhat unexpected part of town, has joined this trade.

But the greater surprise is to come — the sign, and *then* the discovery that these arms do not belong to Scrope (as he had supposed) at all: "And the other person replied to him and said, not at all, sir [nenyl sieur],[15] they are not hung out as the arms of Scrope ... nor painted there as his arms, but they are painted and placed there for a knight of the county of Chester who is named Sir Robert Grosvenor." A newcomer has staked his claim; first territorial and then seigneurial and genealogical. Surprising, in other words, is not the mere fact of Grosvenor's accommodation, or even its ostentatious announcement, but its encroachment — both upon this street and upon the symbolic terrain of the Scropes.

LeFebvre describes the later medieval city as the place of a fated encounter, with "Urban space ... fated to become the theatre of a compromise between the declining feudal system, the commercial bourgeoisie, oligarchies, and communities of craftsmen" (269). Here, in effect, the "declining feudal system" weighs in — though, if declining, still with enough life to sustain a quarrel! And so feudality and feudal pride show themselves in an unaccustomed place.

Usk at Willingham's Tavern

In a testimony of another sort, Thomas Usk appeared before a special session of the king's Council at Reading in August 1384, armed with a predrafted "appeal," or accusation, against his one-time ally, former mayor John Northampton. Northampton was now in trouble with his successor, Nicholas Brembre, and Usk had been persuaded to change sides and to assist in the indictment. His appeal therefore sets out to incriminate Northampton of treasonous designs against Brembre's rival candidacy and the common good of the city of London. He explains that some of these designs were hatched during meetings he attended together with John Northampton and other key conspirators. These meetings occurred in a place of private resort, a space evidently owned by an intriguer and suited to intrigue: "in John Willynghames tavern in the Bowe."[16] Or, in the slightly more intact Latin of the jury presentment based on Usk's testimony, Northampton invited representatives of the guilds that supported him "per diversas vices congregare . . . apud tabernam Iohannis Willyngham in the Bowe."[17] Whether his trajectory originated in a neighborhood in which he may have lived — Queenhithe[18] — or elsewhere in the city, Usk is one of the persons making his way to this central (and suspect) place.

John Willingham's tavern was apparently located in the heart of the heart of the City, in the Parish of Saint Mary le Bowe, in Cordwainer Ward. The much frequented and symbolically central church of Saint Mary le Bowe rested on the site of the present church (rebuilt by Wren after the Fire) at the southwest corner of Cheapside and Hosier Lane. Hosier Lane was, in turn, the northern extension of Cordwainer Street, and was informally known as Bowe Lane — a name that it had officially assumed by the eighteenth century.[19] "The Bowe" was the scene, not only of this group's meetings, but also its most significant agitations. It was "to the Bowe" that Northampton sent Usk to address a protest meeting and to display an indictment drawn against him. Sections of Westcheap adjacent to the Bowe were the site of civil agitations when John Constantine and others protested Northampton's arrest by closing their shop windows. John More's house in the Bowe was another hot spot, and the Bowe is identified as the site of continuing conspiracies after Brembre was sworn in as mayor. In heading for "the Bowe," Usk was inserting himself in a zone of political volatility, a place where careers and reputations rose and fell with heightened rapidity.

Hoccleve, "Homeward Bound"

Writing in his *Male Regle*, Thomas Hoccleve describes his excessive tavern life at "Westmynster yate," when, presumably after work in the offices of the Privy Seal, he paused to disport himself before returning home to sleep in his quarters on the Strand. Afflicted by the summer heat (and, he goes on to tell us, equally afflicted in the winter by "deep" or sodden streets), he (sometimes) decided to walk to the "brigge" and to take a boat:

> Whan I departe sholde & go my way
> Hoom to the priuee seel so wowed me
> Heete and vnlust and superfluitee
> To walke vn-to the brigge & take a boot.[20]

Hoccleve tells us that he is heading "hoom" to the Privy Seal. But exactly what sort of journey is to be imagined? Hoccleve says he walked to the "brigge" to catch a boat. There was only *one* bridge in London at that time, and its use makes no particular sense. His place of work was the Privy Seal, in Westminster. He had been drinking in a Westminster tavern, on King Street.[21] His home was indeed to the east, at a hostel maintained for clerks of the Privy Seal, located on the Strand, roughly between Westminster and London. But he would have gained nothing from a journey all the way to London Bridge—at least twice as far to the east as he wanted to go—in order to get there. The resolution of this apparent dilemma rests in the nature of Hoccleve's "brigge." Relevantly, as Vanessa Harding has shown in her study of the medieval London waterfront, *pons* or *brigge* was in the fourteenth and fifteenth centuries at least as likely to mean "jetty" or "dock" as to indicate the river-spanning structure of our modern imagination.[22] Several such "bridges" existed in Westminster, and Hoccleve could conveniently enough have walked (or staggered) down to one of them. At the other end of his imagined journey, Tempelbrygge abutted the Thames just south of Hoccleve's dwelling on the Strand. Thus, we may imagine him heading downriver: "hoom to the priuee seel."

THE SYMBOLIZATION OF
SOCIAL ENCOUNTER

It happens that all three protagonists are writers — and the fact that each was adept in writing as a form of self-symbolization, and as an instrument of personal and legal and political expression, is obviously connected with our possession of these "memoirs" in any form. But Chaucer gives us no reason to suspect that he was headed down Friday Street to a poetry reading, and Usk certainly had nonliterary fish to fry at Willingham's tavern, and Hoccleve's Thames boatmen were unlikely to have known him as a poet at all. Each was, rather, on his way to a less vocationally specific kind of social encounter. This need not surprise us. Even twentieth-century writers have lives . . . But, measured against the not-yet-existing standard of the eighteenth- or nineteenth-century "man of letters,"[23] the lives of Chaucer and Usk and Hoccleve displayed less, rather than more, exclusivity of focus on "writerly" experiences and activities. However aesthetically shaped, the writings in question all finally turn on some question of *social redefinition* that finds the protagonist outside his usual circle or circles and that cannot be confined to the category of the aesthetic.

An impending occasion of social redefinition is, in fact, signaled by all these taverns lurking in and around our three narratives. Grosvenor's upstart move is mounted from his *herbergerie* or inn on Friday Street. (An *herbergerie*, or inn, may have been exclusively a dwelling place; yet food and drink were sometimes available, and the inn's status as what Barbara Hanawalt calls "permeable domestic space" associates it with taverns and less reputable alehouses.)[24] Usk and his co-conspirators do business at Willingham's tavern;[25] Hoccleve is solaced and emboldened with a stop after work at the King Street taverns.

Thus, with a bit of license, much of the activity of these three narratives may be seen as "tavern related."[26] The tavern as a locus or touchstone of action in each of these three narratives of social transformation is hardly coincidental. Within a city so extensively subdivided according to class, vocation, and activity, the tavern constituted a kind of neutral zone, a place where reconsideration and redefinition of social status might occur. Whether considered as unorganized space or as space organized but more ambiguously and inclusively than most, the tavern seems a natural place for any work of social redefinition. Hanawalt imagines the diverse clientele of the tavern potentially to include "honest peasants and artisans, respectable merchants and their factors, pilgrims, clerics of various sorts, royal officials, nobles, knights, robbers, prostitutes, and con men."[27] Whereas so diverse a band was no more likely to have gathered at a single tavern than Chaucer's characters to have undertaken a single pilgrimage,[28] some widened range of possible attachment might be supposed for the alehouse.

The tavern would seem to operate on more than one front, as a fact of social life and a stimulus to the imagination. As one of the few places where social remobilization might be envisaged, the tavern occurs in these narratives as an emblem of potential social transformation.

MOVEMENT IN SOCIAL SPACE

My subject is self-representation within the symbolic space of the medieval city, but "space" persistently reveals itself in a figurative, as well as literal, sense. For the space traversed in these three narratives is not only the physical distance between, say, Westcheap and Fish Streets, or Queenhithe and the Bowe. Additionally traversed in each of these narratives is a more figurative and less distinct "social" space, the invisible space that separates city residents according to considerations of rank and status. Even as the walker in the city moves from one of its locations to another, so does he continually renegotiate his own place within a less tangible (but still implicitly felt) positioning based on vocation together with other forms of earned and unearned recognition.

To return for a moment to Chaucer's discovery of the sign outside the *herbergerie* on Friday Street. Incidental or surplus social meaning is generated in the microdrama of Chaucer's encounter with the unnamed stranger — "un autre" — whom he interrogates about the display of what he takes to be Scrope arms there on Friday Street, and who replies, "not at all, *sieur*," and says that they are actually the arms of one Grosvenor. Of course, just by giving testimony in the Scrope-Grosvenor trial at all, Chaucer was playing a small part in an expansive social drama. With its lengthy list of deponents and its laborious gathering of depositions from hundreds of aristocrats and gentry in a number of locations under the auspices of the court of chivalry, the trial created an occasion for chivalry to perform itself and to reiterate and reconfirm its values. (This was what anthropologists, when I was in college, would have called "a rite of intensification.") As an esquire among lords, Chaucer was already among the most marginally situated among the beneficiaries of this rite;[29] the trial was thus an opportunity to "perform" his own gentility by joining his views to those of his most securely situated patrons, reaffirming his own armorial tenure, and having his own arms described and recorded as part of his testimony.[30]

But Chaucer's testimony also accomplishes an additional bit of status enhancement. His encounter with the stranger brings him into the company of an "autre" who knows enough to recognize him as a man of substance. One aspect of this recognition might be his address by the term *sieur*. If we take *sieur* as the legal, Anglo-Norman equivalent of the Middle English *sire*, it might not mean all that much; consider the Miller's familiar "Now, sire, and eft sire" in Chaucer's *Canterbury Tales* I.3271, or the "good day, syre" with which the old man greets the disheveled and distraught Hoccleve in the *Regement of Princes*, line 123.[31] On the other hand, *sire* suggests considerable respect in Palamon's address to Theseus in the "Knight's Tale," line 1715, or in Constance's address to the Constable in the "Man of Law's Tale," line 570. The most balanced account of Chaucerian usage has been provided by John Burrow, who suggests that "it can mean 'master,' 'husband' or 'father'; and it is also frequently used as a form of polite address."[32] What it apparently no longer suggests is special deference for a chivalric class, except satirically, as in the often iterated reference to "sire Thopas."[33] Yet the counterpossibility nevertheless remains that, within the context of the records of the court of chivalry, and in more conservative Anglo-Norman usage, the term suggests a bit more standing than its Middle English equivalent. Its abbreviation, as *sr* with an overline, is theoretically expandable as *seigneur*, or "lord," although I follow the judgment of Nicholas and Crow in adopting the slightly more modest "monsieur" and "sieur" as its expansions. In the Scrope-Grosvenor manuscript, knights are normally called "monsieur," esquires "esquier," civic officials "meistr," and lords either by title ("Le Conte") or simply as "Le Sire de . . ." Within the manuscript as a whole, Chaucer would merely be "esquier," the variants of "sieur" being reserved for his superiors. But here, in an unusual situation of direct address, he claims (or is scribally awarded) what amounts in context to a mark of honor. Furthermore, whether or not much is to be made of *sieur*, the anonymous interlocutor certainly approaches Chaucer with deference, treating him as a person entitled by demeanor and knowledge to discuss the points of heraldry.

Discovered and rendered visible via Chaucer's encounter and modestly conveyed in his testimony is Chaucer's own status, as a gentleman. Temporarily admitting Grosvenor's banner to display on Friday Street, London opens itself to "slow time," to the faintly anachronistic rhythm of the declining feudal system. And so does Chaucer renegotiate his own sense of time and social place, in which this merchant's son and customs official turns out to possess more knowledge than might have been supposed about this traditional order of society on whose fringes he lived.

In the case of Thomas Usk's visits to the Bowe, a spatial trajectory likewise leads to a social possibility. Usk initially showed up at these meetings in his professional capacity, "to write thair billes." He seems, in other words, not to have been an active conspirator in his own right, but to be present in his capacity as a literate practitioner, a member of the scrivener's guild.[34] But Usk had always shown an interest in building upon his literate skills. Scriveners, according to their common papers, were normally engaged to write wills, charters, and deeds and to record transactions involving the grant of lands, tenements, and rents.[35] For his part, Usk seems to have learned how to put such documents to work; evidence of the Plea and Memoranda Rolls suggests that he acted from time to time as attorney,[36] and his Appeal of John Northampton suggests a certain mastery of legal forms. (Caroline Barron has described him as one of "the small fry who lived in, and by, the fringes of the legal world.")[37] He was elsewhere known as "sometime clerk of the sheriff of London" and as secretary of John Northampton,[38] and even, ambiguously, as *clericus* in Northampton's household.[39] He interests us largely in yet another capacity, as a literary figure, author of the fluent and learned and often eloquent *Testament of Love*.

Usk's own tendency to expand and diversify his role is already apparent in the meetings at Willingham's. For example, he soon advanced from the position of draftsman and note-taker to active provocateur, accepting an assignment to electioneer among the commons for the selection of Northampton supporters to the next parliament.[40] He accompanied Northampton to the Goldsmith's Hall to recruit the loyalty of certain common council members for the next mayoral election; he was a member of the pro-Northampton delegation that met with John of

Gaunt in his manor to protest Northampton's defeat; and also agitated among other potential followers in the Bowe. This trajectory—from note-taker to one of the half dozen key conspirators—positioned Usk to become Northampton's principal accuser during his trial at Reading and led ultimately to his royal appointment as undersheriff of Middlesex with its accompanying title of sergeant at arms of King Richard.[41]

Usk's trips to the Bowe thus were not only concrete itineraries but also culminated in another sort of social trajectory repeated in several different forms throughout his career: a movement from outside to inside, from periphery to center. Here rendered visible is an instance of rather considerable social mobility, in which a scrivener and fringe legalist and person of inauspicious birth becomes an intimate, first of the sitting mayor, and then (turning coat) his successor Brembre, and finally receives a royal appointment and apparent title of sergeant at arms . . . as well as, unfortunately, the more ominous and career-ending notice of the aristocratic appellants, enemies of Brembre and the king.

Hoccleve knows the meaning of his own itinerary well enough, and he impresses his interpretation upon us: he gives us a spiritual—or, more accurately, a moral—drama, cast in the mold of the "riotous prentice," in which a dissolute civil servant yields to temptations of ease and excessive expenditure. But—inevitably, since it traverses a route within a late medieval city—it does not escape a secondary, social drama as well.

This social drama is conducted with considerable awareness on all sides. At its heart is the boatmen's mutual practice of calling Hoccleve "maistir"—not quite "sieur," but nevertheless a considerable promotion for this middling bureaucrat.

> Othir than "maistir" callid was I neuere,
> Among this meynee, in my audience.
> Me thoghte I was y-maad a man for euere.

Maister might apply to "an official appointed to be in charge of a place, a department of household, government, etc." *(Middle English Dictionary)*, and Hoccleve, by no means the head of his office, is naturally flattered by this interpretation of his status. He is undoubtedly called *maister* with some ironic awareness.[42] He clearly understands that he is being mocked, and yet plays the role, terming the boatmen his "meynee" in the sense

of a "following" or an "entourage." This is, of course, a disloyal following, for, as he notes, their respectful address will persist only in his hearing, in "audience." Nevertheless, as he observes with caustic self-irony,
he enjoys the temporary fantasy of himself as a "made man." He is so
enamored of this pretense that he overpays, to sustain the illusion:

> So tikelid me that nyce reuerence,
> That it me made larger of despense
> Than that I thoght han been.

Hoccleve's confession that he was "tickled" into excessive largesse acknowledges a moral flaw, but also indicates a social process. It proceeds
from a dream of advancement, energized by a situation of social difference, in which he is perceived (as was Chaucer, also by a social inferior,
or Usk, by his social superiors in Willingham's tavern) as something beyond his station, as something closer to what he would like to be.

CONCLUSION: THE INDIVISIBILITY OF SYMBOLIZING PRACTICES

In discovering a social drama at the heart of each itinerary, I do not
mean simply to reduce complicated texts to social "data." For these texts
are neither the innocent reportage of the details of urban life on the one
hand, nor outright literary inventions on the other. Rather, they issue
from complex processes, in which are presumed and put to work (1) the
city's own previous investment in its symbolization; (2) various discursive conventions, appropriate to the genre or kind of writing; and (3) a
number of characteristically "literary" ways of deploying material.

So does Chaucer, in the first place, rely upon and incorporate a number of *pre*workings of his material, such as a street name marked by
commerce, the symbolic vocabulary of an aristocratic *signe*, and the spatial and gestural language of aristocratic assertion. Additionally, he observes the requirements of a deposition, including a good deal of specificity about time and place. And finally, in turn, these materials are
realized with the assistance of typically literary techniques. We are offered a timebound narration, punctuated by unanticipated developments,
a fortuitous encounter, reported speech, and something of a denouement.

Moreover, Chaucer's encounter with the talkative stranger retains elements of his literary persona's encounter with the talkative guides of his dream visions, as for instance the abruptly available interlocutor of his *House of Fame*: "With that y gan aboute wende, / For oon that stood ryght at my bak, Me thoughte, goodly to me spak" (lines 1868–70). Furthermore, the narrative of Chaucer's deposition is managed via the consistent deployment of what Lee Patterson describes as an "experiencing subject."[43]

Usk's narrative likewise draws upon varied resources. First, in respects not entirely visible within my tiny quotation but evident in the "Appeal" as a whole, is the development of Usk's testimony within the previously developed and extrinsically available language of urban conflict, as embodied in the vernacular petitions and proclamations and other strife-saturated documents that first appeared in the city at this time.[44] This language is, in turn, shaped in accordance with the effectively generic requirement that a properly drawn legal "appeal" should be highly specific about time and place, a requirement that he meets by identifying a known tavern as a center of conspiratorial intrigue. Many of the decisions underlying choices of detail in his incriminating narrative track the requirements of treason law and present simple electioneering as an insurrectionary activity.[45] Finally, although I would not claim much in the way of a "literary" register for Usk's "Appeal," he stood ready to re-present this same material in the explicitly literary art-prose of the first book of his *Testament of Love*. Among its other argumentative motives, the elaborate and allegorically framed art-prose of that ambitious composition recasts Usk's decision to turn informer/appellant against his former friends by associating him with a series of literary and spiritual antecedents drawn from classical epic and the historical books of the Old Testament. Here, for instance, is a representative mingling of religious allusion, classical reference, and autobiographical detail:

> "Lady," quod I, "ye remembre wel, that in most laude and praysing of certayne seyntes in holy churche, is to reherse their conuersion from badde in-to good; and that is so rehersed, as by a perpetual mirrour of remembraunce, in worshipping of tho sayntes, and good ensample to other misdoers in amendement. How turned the Romayne Zedeoreys fro the Romaynes, to be with Hanibal ayenst his kynde nacion; and afterwardes,

him seming the Romayns to be at the next degre of confusion,
turned to his olde alyes. . . . Wherfore, to enfourme you, lady, the
maner-why I mene, see now. In my youth I was drawe to ben
assentaunt and (in my mightes) helping to certain conjuracions
and other grete maters of ruling of citizins. . . . Now than tho
persones that suche thinges have cast to redresse, for wrathe of
my first medlinge, shopen me to dwelle in this pynande prison,
til Lachases my threed no lenger wolde twyne."[46]

Usk in his prison, brooding on Lachesis's intentions with regard to the
thread of his destiny, is entirely a creature of London faction, trying to
divine the consequences of his factional allegiances, and no less a protagonist acting within an interpretative structure offered by the hyper-
literary milieu of example and precedent derived from Hesiod, Livy, and
the classical pantheon as known and deployed by Jean de Meun, Boccaccio, Chaucer, and other influential near-contemporary and contemporary authors.

    By the same token, Hoccleve's Thames voyage begins with a com-
mercially established practice and a group of histrionic rivermen who
may be presumed to have developed their own persuasive patois, of which
hailing him as "master" is undoubtedly an example. These tradesmen
also "tug him to and fro," and they are thus behaving like good Westminster tradesmen. As Gervase Rosser wryly observes in his study of
the medieval city, "The economy of medieval Westminster was based primarily upon the entrapment of the consumer."[47] Yet, ultimately, Hoccleve's discovery of significance within this material occurs within the
ambit of a moral recital—that being the particular genre of his *Male
Regle*—which he employs to allegorical, as well as autobiographical, effect. Hoccleve represents himself as weakened by his own excesses,
falling under the ominous dissuasions of three dubious personae: not
just Heat, but also "vnlust" or Disinclination and superfluity or Excess.
The first of this dangerous trio is external to our poet, but "vnlust" and
"superfluitee" are internal adversaries (just as the avaricious merchants
are spiritually dangerous flatterers) in a personal psychomachia of scant
virtue overwhelmed by vice. So complete, in one sense, is this allego-
rization of his experience that Hoccleve represents himself (like Jealousy in the *Fairie Queene*) as transmogrified into his attribute: given to
riot, the free-spending Hoccleve is wholly stormed and invaded on this

unfortunate upriver voyage; in fact, *becoming* riot and emptying his own
purse:

> For riot paieth largely eueremo;
> He styntith neuere til his purs be bare.

He travels a known river to a customary destination, yet, as in the case
of Usk, his journey is simultaneously structured by, and amplified within,
the fullest resources afforded by western literary tradition. For example,
he imagines himself coextensively with the more successful "Vlixes" who
successfully restrained his desires and resisted the "meermaides . . . song."

These three narratives therefore suggest daily experience itself as
one compositional horizon. By "daily experience" I do not mean the activities of a delineated and preformed self, but the realization of a self
within a social setting already delineated and written over by collectively
devised symbolizations. A second compositional horizon is provided by
the requirements and promptings of legal and moral and other associated discourses. And, finally, even though two of my narratives are legal
and functional and thus "nonliterary" in nature, all of them draw upon
existing literary practice and the set of expanded possibilities associated
with a third, "literary" register.

Speaking of different expressive registers, I find myself separating
for analytical purposes things that cannot really be separated in the end.
Each of my three registers draws upon common practices of symbolization, and the ostensibly literary concept of genre is no less useful when
applied to different kinds of legal documents or even to guild records or
parish-names. My rather paradoxical enterprise is, actually, that of separating these registers in order to argue that they cannot be separated,
that they are finally tumbled together in representations that cannot help
but be mixed. Concerning itself with space, and with movement in physical and social spaces, this essay concludes with the most completely
"mixed" space of all: compositional space, a space within which seeming differences and prohibitive decorums are overridden in the interest
of more complete representation.

To assert the interpenetration of compositional levels is not to deny
them any difference at all. A decision to allude to an activity or an individual or a day of the week by naming a thoroughfare "Friday Street"
(or the retrospective invention of an etymology for Friday Street) has only

the most distant kinship to an allusion to the trials of Odysseus—or, for that matter, to the composition of the Odyssey in the first place! But I do mean that each writer engages a broad spectrum of *symbolizing activities* within compositional practice: some activities so unassuming and collective as hardly to be recognizable as symbolization at all; others drawing their prestige from their utility in political and judicial activities; and yet others self-consciously employing literary registers and genres supported by the most prestigious of ancient examples. These expressive registers have different histories and enjoy different conditions of enunciation. Nevertheless, the successful writer draws freely and diversely upon them, and refashions them into a new creation into which they are inextricably bound.

The interpenetration of different symbolizing activities demands of the critic a certain openness of response. It also argues against the elevation or hierarchization of some representational strategies and regimes at the expense of others. This essay actually began as my rebuttal of an attempt to hierarchize social categories and kinds of writing, as represented by a panel at Kalamazoo, Michigan, two years ago.[48] In my view, the critic deciding among or between several courses or procedures of textual analysis must stop and decide: what are the gains? what are the losses? I conclude that the conceptual gains all rest with the refusal to separate or hierarchize a single register—such as the literary—at the expense of those other varieties of symbolization with which it coexists and by which it is constantly refreshed.

We need the most *inclusive* interpretative and disciplinary models, if we are to pursue meaning up and down Friday Street, discover it among connivers at Willingham's tavern, or accompany it to an unsteady landing on Temple Bridge.

2

WALKING FIRE

SYMBOLIZATION, ACTION, AND LOLLARD BURNING

The 1401 burning of Lollard ex-priest William Sautre was the first of its kind in England. Whatever insulation the passage of time might be hoped or imagined to offer, that event raises issues of the most urgent present importance. This essay was written in the year of Yitzhak Rabin's assassination, murderous assaults on doctors at abortion clinics, and shortly before the murder of an African American in Texas by chaining and dragging behind a pickup truck and the crucifixion of a gay student, left dangling on a wire fence in Wyoming. Nor are the files of Amnesty International lacking in further instances of more formally sponsored violence, during brief ascendancies in the states of the former Yugoslavia, in breakaway provinces of the former Soviet Union and Indonesia, in the doubtful equities of the American death penalty.[1] In each of these modern instances, ensuing commentary has involved the relation between stigmatizing speech and hateful actions, between violence depicted or described and its actual occurrence. This linkage is natural enough, since prior aggressive words and subsequent physical or corporeal deeds seem to constitute an intuitively obvious continuum. Everyone has surely witnessed sidewalk encounters in which an exchange of taunts precedes a physical scuffle; I saw one just a few nights ago, outside a pub, in my new and highly civilized place of residence. Yet, conceptually speaking, a chasm still divides speech from action; an awkward near-relative of Zeno's Paradox seems to prevent us from understanding exactly how it is that a line is crossed, that a verbal assault becomes a physical one. My purpose in this essay is to reflect upon this divide—so regularly crossed in deed yet so resistant to explanation—as a modest and historically based contribution to our understanding of "hate speech" and its implications. I will rely upon speech-act philosophy, and some of its subsequent elaborations, in order to narrow the perceived difference between speech and action by emphasizing the "action-seeking" elements of speech and the "symbolic" elements of action. Throughout, the plight of William Sautre will be my case in point, although I will seek not to lose sight of its painful specificities, even while deploying it as a broader example.

WRITING AS PERFORMANCE

A step so drastic as burning a dissenting neighbor is taken only within various authorizing and acquiescing structures. With respect to authorization, several scholars have painstakingly explored the legislative and statutory stages by which canon and civil law, sacerdotal authority and lay power joined forces to identify and discipline the Lollard heresy in the first years of Lancastrian rule.[2] But another precondition for public burning was its rehearsal in speech and writing. Aided by learned rhetoric, pulpit invective, and everyday talk, a society that had not customarily burned heretics somehow found itself imaginatively able to contemplate so extreme a practice. The initiative of Arundel and Henry IV, come suddenly to power and disposed to its use, cannot be ignored; but Sautre could probably not have been burned were it not for a period of some twenty years in which anti-Lollard sentiments were consolidated and burning emerged as a natural and even inevitable penalty for lapsed heretics among the clergy and, ultimately, for all categories of Lollard believers among the laity of the land.

The Lollards were placed at a discursive disadvantage from the outset when first branded as "Lollardi." This term's complicated etymology laid them open to a range of stigmatizations, including association with false mendicants and implication in proscribed Continental heresies.[3] Moreover, through easily available jibes and puns based on the similarity of Middle English "Lollard" to Latin *lolium/lollium* (cockle or tare), a vista was opened upon yet another and potentially even more damaging form of linguistic mayhem within anti-Lollard discourse. Cockles and tares, as pollutants of good grain, had long provided an obvious, and highly suggestive, metaphorical vehicle for orthodox distress over invasive and unwelcome doctrines. As early as 1179, Peter of Blois, hearing of a heresy in the see of York, wrote to the archbishop to remind him that he was a steward of the "vines of the Lord," responsible to watch over them and to do whatever was necessary, so that "ne degenerent propagines vineae in labruscam, *frumenta in lolium*, aurum in scoriam, oleum in amurcam" (the shoots of the vines would not degenerate to wildness, *grain to cockle*, gold to slag, the pressing of oil to its residue).[4] These associations were easily enough, in turn, pressed into service against a domestic Lollard movement. In the early fifteenth century, for example, we find Adam of Usk lamenting the pernicious consequences of Lollardy for orthodox faith: "Among other evils... there arose errors and heresies in the catholic faith on account of the seeds sown by a certain Master John Wyclif, whose noxious doctrine contaminated the faith as if by tares" ("pestifere doctrine uelud lollio eandem fidem corrumpentis"; 6–7).

The extent of this metaphorical contamination was boundless, in its suggestion that *lollii* or cockles might even threaten debasement of Christ's pure sacrifice. A network of associations widely represented in art and sermon literature in and after the twelfth century portrayed Christ as good grain, as spiritual food, ground and milled in the crucifixion and offered for the salvation of mankind in the figurative bread of the eucharistic host. This is the motif of Christ as the "mill of the host," often paired with the "mystical winepress" in treating Christ's body as the true, and pure, substance of the bread and wine. The corruption of good grain by heresy thus had an added consequence, disastrous in the thirteenth and fourteenth centuries, during which the Corpus Christi service was composed and the sacrament of the Eucharist was celebrated with increasing fervor. In polluting the symbolic body of Christendom with its weedy growth, heresy threatened the purity of the Host itself. Accusing the Parson of Lollardy, Harry Bailly complains that "He wolde sowen som difficulte, / Or springen cokkel in our clene corn" (II.1183–84). In compromising the purity of the "clene corn" that issues in the eucharistic Host, the heretic attacked the very foundation of Christian community. Threatening the Host's sacramental conversion into the body of Christ, the heretic was estranged from, and became dangerous to, the larger community of the orthodox.[5]

The spread of this corrupting growth could only be halted as one halts other weedy invasions, by "extirpation" or "uprooting." Again, the language of extirpation was already well secured in ecclesiastical discourse. Innocent III's tirades against heresy in the early thirteenth century invoked the satanic pollution of the Lord's harvest by *zizania*, or tares.[6] Inveighing against the Beghards and Beguines in the early fourteenth century, Clement V had insisted upon the extirpation of such sects ("exstirpare ab ecclesia catholica necessario habeamus").[7] Thus in his prompt assault against native heresy, we find Thomas Arundel, as bishop of Ely in 1382, inveighing against heretical preaching and wishing for its perpetrators to be extirpated ("extirpari").[8] The same remedy is enjoined by the chronicler Knighton, in his retrospective account of the events of 1382. Lollards are identified by name as a *secta nefanda*, observing tenets and educational practices that estrange them from the populace at large. Complaining that their conspiracy is all the more cursed for its intransigence, he invokes God in their destruction: "Accursed be their pertinacious assembly! May God destroy them, and tear them out, and drive them from their tabernacles and uproot them from the land of the kingdom! ... confound them, and let them perish with their doctrine into eternity."[9] Although figurative and subjunctive, this talk of uprooting and destruction quickly came to typify the anti-Lollard discourse of the later 1380s and 1390s. Expressed as a desired condition rather than one that has come to pass, such talk initiates a process in which an action, however hypothetical, is imagistically entertained. To be sure, talk of extirpation will resurface, crucially, in King Henry's order that Sautre be burned, when he notes that among his royal responsibilities is to uproot ("radicitus extirpare") heresies and errors.[10]

More to the point, and a good deal more ominous in the light of future events, is that language which contemplates destruction of heretical adversaries by fire. This association, together with that of tares polluting good grain, is to be found as early as the parable of the sower and his enemy in Matthew 13:24–30. There the sower's enemy oversows *zizania* in his good wheat; the sower recommends that nothing need be done until harvest time, when he will say to the reapers, "First gather the tares and bundle them for burning" ("colligite primum zizania et alligate ea in fasciculos ad conburendum"). Christ's explanation of the parable is that the gatherers are angels at the end of time (13:39–40), but this nuance is a good deal less important than the primary association: the thing to do with tares is to gather them up and destroy them by burning. (These verbal connections were not lost on anti-Lollard polemicist Thomas Netter, when he rather wittily entitled his collection of incriminating writings *Fasciculi Zizaniarum*. The point is that these fascicles are for prosecutorial motives; they represent evidence that facilitates the separation of tares from wheat — and, ultimately, their bundling and burning.)

The discursive availability of this connection (together, of course, with well-known and influential Continental precedents) meant that the *threat* of burning was constantly available and might easily be brought to bear. An example in which discourse outruns concrete action (even while paving its way) occurs in Knighton's discussion of the heretic Swinderby, who, he says, having been publicly convicted of heresies and errors, deserved to be food for the flames ("pabulum ignis digne effici meruit").[11] Similar ideas and images waxed in the later years of the century. Boniface IX, declaiming against the Lollards in 1395, wished them destroyed, so that not even a hidden spark should remain among the ashes ("sic quod nec favilla cineribus operta remaneat").[12] Responding, like Boniface, to the Lollard provocations of 1395, Roger Dymmok pondered the precedent of Joshua, who did away with malefactors and who destroyed idol worship in his kingdom, burning the idolatrous priests upon their altars ("et sacerdotes ydolorum super aras combussit").[13]

Caught up in so highly aggressive a network of symbolizations and imaginings, the Lollard victims naturally enough took note of their predicament — first simply as acknowledgment, and then in a variety of other ways. Most obviously, they sought the grim consolation of victimage, describing their plight in language that seeks to rally sentiment against their oppressors. The "Leaven of Pharisees," for example, presents mendicant aggression against Lollards in this way:

> Yif thei pursuen pore prestis to prison and bodily deth, as hangynge, drawynge or brennynge, for thei [the poor priests] techen trewely and frely the gospel of ihesu crist and techen men wiche ben false prophetis and ypocritis . . . , thanne ben thei perilous ypocrites and heretikis agenst worschipe and sauynge of cristene soulis.[14]

The trials of Lollards or "poor priests" are first noted, as well might such sufferings be noted, and then additionally deployed to generate sympathy for the Lollard position and to stigmatize orthodox clergy as "false

prophetis and ypocrites." Finally, in a move always available within discourse — but ironically, in the sense that the Lollards are here "playing
with discursive fire" — an ultimately unsuccessful attempt is made to
reverse the poles of the orthodox argument, in order to brand the established church as fraught not only with hypocrisy but with heresy as well
("thanne ben thei...heretikis").

The attempt to reverse the politically authorized meanings of orthodoxy and heresy could not have succeeded, in the absence of sufficient influence and numbers to make it succeed, but the presence of a
certain Lollard "counteraggression" cannot be gainsaid. This Lollard response normally took what might be considered more deferred or ac-
ceptably displaced forms, relative to the hotheaded imperatives of orthodox discourse. Consider, in this regard, a Lollard sermon on Matthew
13, with its own ideas about "tares":

> and thanne schal he seye to the reperis "Gedre ye furst thes tarys to-
> gydre, and byndeth hem in knychys to brenne; but gedre ye the goode
> corn to my berne." Tyme of this repyng is cleput the day of doom
> or ellis tyme nyh hit, and these reperis ben goode aungelis...
> and these goode aungelis schullen bynde Cristis enemyes in
> kyncchenys, and aftyr thei schulle brennen in helle by the right-
> ful doom of God.[15]

Perhaps Lollards are no better than the rest of us; in any case, they do
not deny themselves the satisfaction of imagining their tormentors on
fire. Yet this might be considered a socially authorized, or at least bibli-
cally authorized, imagining. It adheres to the original sense of Matthew
13 by deferring the punishment of the wicked until the Last Judgment...
and then, in the spirit of law-abiding sheriffs in Western movies, es-
chewing vigilante justice in favor of the operations of the sanctioned
(divine) "justice system."

The Lollard response thus remains somewhat displaced — an effect,
if not of ethical superiority, then of discourse detached from political
and social power. Even in its displaced form, however, it shows how the
aggressive imaginings of the sanctioned religious system were powerful enough to effect a partial enlistment of its principal victims. And the
full force of this power is yet to be revealed, in the extent to which these
same aggressive speeches constitute a prelude to action, a rehearsal of

aggressive action itself. With respect to speech as a rehearsal for action, let me return to just one speech: Knighton's written wish that the Lollards may be confounded and perish with their doctrine unto eternity: "Confundantur et pereant cum doctrina eorum in eternum."

As J. R. Austin and John Searle and others have shown us, an act is already performed by this writing itself, *in* the act of speaking.[16] It falls into the category of illocutions, or performative utterances, and the act in question is one of stigmatization: the writer performs his dislike, attaches opprobrium to the Lollards. Thus, already, a certain common denominator between writings and actions is established: in so couching his views, Knighton has "done something." Moreover, this written utterance is also, at least to some extent, action seeking:[17] an injunction to action. The passive and hortative subjunctive "confundantur" wishes that they "may be confounded," and the hortative subjective "pereant" urges that they "may perish." Writing some years after the fact, Knighton may not exactly be enjoining vigilante action. Nevertheless, at the very least, his words contain a potential or occluded element of real-world action-seeking. Let me put it this way: his words include what Austin and Searle call a "propositional content" — in this case, something imagined to happen, the disruption of the Lollards' hopes and then their actual destruction. And Knighton is, in fact, pleased to report the partial fulfillment of the first of these two propositions. But the main proposition — Lollard destruction — is allowed to remain hypothetical, as merely a wish, held temporarily in a kind of abeyance.

The failure of Knighton's words, and other like words, to achieve enactment in the 1380s and 1390s — failure, in Austin's formulation, to achieve "uptake"[18] — may be attributed to several causes. One is a certain curtailment of what speech-act theorists would call the "force" of the utterance. One aspect of this curtailment might be irresolution or division on the part of the speaker. Perhaps Knighton does not really expect his program to achieve enactment; perhaps the expression of a hostile wish, and a veiled warning, is all he seeks at this time. Perhaps, given the generally unaggressive attitude of Richard II to anti-Lollard campaigning, oral threats and dissuasions represented the outermost aspiration of the Lollard haters in the 1390s.[19] But, in the presence of the right external conditions, a hostile speech might itself be sufficient to achieve "uptake." The intentions of the speaker are by no means sufficient to control the ramifications of an utterance, in the sense that a moment of inadvertence with a cigarette butt (even in the absence of an antipathy for trees) can cause a forest fire. The right external conditions might simply be a volatile public mood, of a sort likely to lead to mob violence. Or they might involve institutionalization — the existence of external means to assure the verbal invitation's acceptance. And this is, of course, what was to happen in 1401, when an ecclesiastical council, and Parliament, and above all a determined king would assure verbal attacks on William Sautre all the "uptake" they could possibly use.

Knighton's words remain nearly pure illocution, are self-performing, and seek no perlocution or consequence in action. This being said, his words nevertheless do contain a latent or shadowed action orientation. He imagines Lollards destroyed or dead, and his hortative subjunctives constitute an open invitation to action in the larger community. His and other words like them would, in effect, be consummated, once external and institutional conditions were right.

ACTION AS SYMBOLISM

The official utterances that finally sped William Sautre to the pyre are perfect performatives, in that they say something and, in saying it, do something that irrevocably alters the subjects' status in the real world (as in the case of, "I pronounce you man and wife," or "I name this ship the *Queen Mary*"). First we have his ecclesiastical degradation ("degradamus et deponimus"),[20] which really degraded him. And then we have King Henry's writ, issued in order the root of heresy *extirpare:* "coram populo publice Igni committi, ac ipsum in eodem Igne realiter comburi fac' ... Cristianorum exemplum manifestum,"[21] and this writ "really" ("realiter") made him "as good as dead" — finished him off, in the Lacanian formulation, with respect to his first death or death in the symbolic, leaving to be consummated only his second death or death in the body. Reconfirming these illocutions were subsequent written enactments: the parliamentary act *De heretico comburendo* and the king's affirmative response and the ensuing statute.[22] Here we encounter the smooth and concerted functioning of several different agencies, all designed to reconfirm what Austin would call the "felicity" of the Council's, and then the king's, utterances (as opposed to Austin's madman who jumps into the christening ceremony with "I name this ship the *Generalissimo Stalin,*" falling short of any institutionalization of his act).[23] In the parliamentary act, and its endorsement by the king and its acceptance as a statute, we have those very institutionalizations lacking in Knighton's original hostile wish. These institutionalizations secure "uptake" of Sautre's condemnation, to alter the king's illocution (or act performed *in* saying) to a perlocution (or act performed *by,* or as a result of, saying).[24] The role of authoritative figures and bodies in securing the propositional content of an action-seeking utterance is well captured by the *Eulogium* continuator, who arrays his account in mention of the archbishop's role in the degradation and Parliament's consent in the punishment: "During this parliament ['In hoc parliamento'] the archbishop of Canterbury degraded a certain heretic, who said that accident is not without a subject in the sacrament of the altar and that bread remains; who was burned at Smithfield ['qui Smythfeld combustus est']."[25] Because of the authority of the speaker (now the king) and the force of his utterance (in explicit favor of burning) and its context (underwritten by the highest ecclesiastical bodies), sufficient momentum was generated to propel the king's wish into a completed deed.

Between everything leading up to the deed, on the one hand, and the deed itself, on the other, lies what we may see as either a great chasm or a tiny fault line; hardly every difference in the world or hardly any difference at all. Here I want to diminish difference, to speak on the side of virtually no difference at all. Contributing to this diminution of difference is the extent to which the marked *performative content* of the verbalizations of the 1380s and 1390s found its counterpart in the extensive *symbolic content* of the burnings of the early fifteenth century. Of course, one has difficulty imagining a "pure" deed, a deed devoid of inadvertent or advertent symbolization. But the first Lollard burning seems unusually symbolically saturated. This saturation may be seen as a consequence of the deed's own prehistory: so extensively preworked and presymbolized was this deed during its decades of intensive rehearsal that a divorce from its own prehistory could hardly be expected on the occasion of its enactment.

Previous discussions of the Lollard threat had emphasized its affront to the church, and the kingdom, and the dignity of the king; these aspects of the complaint against the Lollards are summed up in *De heretico comburendo,* as when the king provides for the avoidance of "dissensions, divisions, hurts, slanders, and perils" by the utter destruction of this evil sect or "nephande secta" (*Statutes,* 126). A division or wound having been opened in the kingdom, and the dignity of the king having been impaired, any project of repair must emphasize public display, the demonstration before the offended populace that the king's momentarily injured sovereignty is now reconstituted.[26] With regard to this element of public display, consider the language of Henry's own order for burning (italics mine): "[Sautre is to be] committed to the flames in a *public and open place, publicly, before the populace,* in detestation of this kind of crime, and as a manifest example ['exemplum manifestum']."[27] Consistent with the publicity-seeking nature of the punishment is the sense that it must symbolize or mean something in excess of itself— that it must provide an impressive "example" for its beholders. The idea of *exemplum manifestum* is of course pervasive in a culture where words and deeds, characters in written narrative and real people, were found constantly to engage in meaningful performance for the edification of all beholders.[28] But its appearance here, and in other writings related to the execution, suggests that the isolated deed is justified only by its wider penumbra of symbolic implication.[29]

Other symbolic aspects of Sautre's fate might also be discussed here: the barrel in which he was burned as a practical means of his "utter destruction" but also as a Dantesque suggestion of his heretical isolation, the choice of Smithfield as a site of particularly charged public semiosis, and the like.[30] Sautre's agonies exist in a realm of personal cataclysm separate from any of its symbolizations, and any attempt wholly to resubsume his death into a symbolic structure would obviously be misguided. Nevertheless, recognition that his execution occurred within a very amply symbolized frame places his fate on a continuum with decades of previous utterance about the wish for, and implementation of, Lollard burning.

MERGING SYMBOLISM AND ACTION: THE FAGGOT BADGE

During the early sixteenth century, the punishment of choice for Lollards or those harboring Lollard sentiments became the penitential bearing of a bundle of faggots, or else the wearing upon the outer garment's left sleeve of a faggot badge, consisting of "the representation of a burning

faggot."[31] This punishment may be considered a continuation of the fifteenth-century practice of threatening suspected persons with emblems
of burning, in a metaphoric, part-for-whole, allusion to the act itself.
Thus, the monks of Canterbury threatened Margery Kempe with a cartful
of thorns and a burning barrel: "Then she went out of the monastery,
they following and crying upon her, 'Thou xalt be brent, fals lollare. Her
is a cartful of thornys redy for the & a tonne to bren the wyth.'" So, too,
did a woman of Lambeth compass her death, saying "I wold thu wer in
Smythfeld, & I wold beryn a fagot to bren the wyth."[32] The display of
thorns and barrel at ready, the allusion to Smithfield as a place of puni-
tion, the expression of willingness to carry wood for the pyre—all gesture toward the act. Yet a further step is taken when the heretic is himself or herself required to bear faggots in procession or to wear a faggot
badge upon his or her body.

When the Fool in *Lear* sights the torch-bearing Gloucester and cries,
"Look! here comes a walking fire" (3.4.111), he is literally remarking the
fact that Gloucester carries a torch against the darkness of the night.
But he is also referring to figurative fire, to the torch as an external exemplification of that lord's manifest and widely known lechery. So does
the marked criminal (as in Foucault's description of bodily or external
punishment)[33] display a sign of an inner life already known and pro-
claimed, a crime decided upon and its guilt externalized for all to see, a
walking illustration of the truth of the inquisitorial procedure. The faggot badge is a multiple symbol in this sense: of the coincidence of inner
guilt and outer appearance, of the triumph of the process of discernment
and punishment it represents, of the separation of the heretic from the
believing/punitive community. Whether the Lollard ultimately lives or
dies has become immaterial, because the authority of the procedures of
condemnation has been demonstrated, as has the power to impose their
will. The badge-bearing Lollard is *as good as dead*. He or she is, to return
to Lacan's formulation, "between two deaths"—already judged and dead
to the order of the symbolic, stranded short of (but liable to) the second
death, the death of the body.

In other words, as with Stars of David and pink triangles in 1930s
Germany, something has already been *done* to the wearers of these faggot badges—something ominous, invasive, and impermissible. Stanley Fish informs me that the preeminent discourse of symbolism and
action is sponsored by First Amendment law. The debate there (often

employing the terms of speech-act philosophy) is between those who would enlarge the area of speech (in order to extend First Amendment protections) and those who would enlarge the area of action (in order to facilitate control). Fish's response is to step out of this debate, and to argue instead that the issue rests between those speeches which are innocuous and those which are dangerous; those actions which are inconsequential and those with malign consequences. I find considerable merit in this position, when applied to the matter of the faggot badge. It is both a form of compelled speech or symbolization and an action, something already "done." This is a case in which the difference between symbolization and action pales before sheer "eventfulness," and eventfulness of the most actively disturbing sort. Without even pressing the distinction between symbolism and action in the case of the faggot badge, we can say that it is a case in which something has already been *done,* and in which the community has announced its right to do more if it so desires. The infringement, the transgression, could hardly be more complete.

HISTORY AS REPETITION

With the burning of Sautre in 1401, the prehistory of threats and malicious imaginings and symbolic extirpations previously directed against members of this sect retroactively becomes what it always was: a history of homicide, homicide's necessary precondition. The effect of these anticipations and rehearsals of the act is constitutive, in that they constitute the potential Lollard burner *as* a Lollard burner. The Lollard burner "overtakes himself"[34] — achieves a previously announced, but uncompleted, intention — when the first faggot is lit. The original, hostile intent has thus been accomplished through its rehearsal, through a form of repetition. Without the opportunity for repetition afforded within the relatively free environment of jest, argumentation, and polemic, the burning might never have occurred.

In the light of their consequences, even jests like Harry Bailly's subsequently canceled response to the Parson ("I smelle a Lollere in the wynd" [II.1173]) assume an unintended retrospective weight. Certainly, Harry's jibe already contains a hostile charge, in its implication that Harry has performed a kind of "street discernment," is capable of reading off the Lollard's inner state in an informal anticipation of the role of an interrogator in a heresy trial or an inquisitor in the decades to come. But, in the 1380s, consequences far short of mayhem are surely implied. In a recent and persuasive analysis, Anne Middleton explores the consequences of Harry's remark as they pertain to the practice of vernacular theology and to emergent and unproven forms of authorial vocation. She suggests that, in addition to other meanings of Lollardy in the 1380s, Harry might be accusing the Parson of a want of propriety or decorum, a Lollard tendency to practice "religion out of place."[35] Even granting Middleton's point, though, I would want to add that the discovery of Lollardy out of place bears its own ominous implication when read in citational relation to Mary Douglas's equation of matter out of place and uncleanness.[36] For uncleanness invites cleansing, just as (Douglas reminds us) disorder invites order. Among others, techniques for restoring order include elimination of the offending phenomenon, strengthening of approved definitions, and the discovery that disorder spells danger for the community.[37]

The Parson's resistance to swearing is out of place in its trespass against secular good fellowship, and as theology out of place it enters into a continuum that eventuates, not just in more discourse, but in action. Something about the Parson's intrusion doesn't smell right to Harry; there is something fetid about it. Like tares or cockles among good plants and grains, it pollutes its discursive "field." And the discovery that discourse, or belief, or persons might pollute the community can play out in serious consequences. However innocent its ostensible aims, the anti-Lollard speech of the 1380s and 1390s possesses disturbing affinities and continuities with the early-fifteenth-century atrocities that followed in their train.

I am not proposing that we indict Chaucer for what can only be unforeseen consequences of his passage — it is a canceled passage anyway (and perhaps even a passage that he canceled in the light of increasing anti-Lollard acrimony in the 1390s). Nevertheless, we are reminded that a constituted discourse, such as the discourse of anti-Lollardy, is open to permutations and unforeseen applications. Moreover, that discourse is performative in ways always implicitly allied with the world of material consequences — an alternative or bizarro-world always impossibly remote, and always imminently and urgently at hand.

3

CORONATION AS LEGIBLE PRACTICE

ANTIDISCIPLINARITY

We medievalists are more complacent about our cross-disciplinarity than we have any right to be. To be sure, we are unique among academic fields in the extent to which our journals (such as *Speculum*) and our conferences (Medieval Academy, Medieval Institute) foster cross-disciplinary encounter. But such encounters are more often shoulder to shoulder than face to face. We most often read the article or attend the paper in "our field" without actually leaving the security of our disciplinary home. Such are the emotional and material comforts of the disciplinary home that little explanation need be offered for the academic reluctance to leave it or, leaving it, the disposition for a prompt return. The question, rather, is how the more adventurous (but more fraught and less rewarding) state of interdisciplinarity is to be sustained against the constant temptation of a return to more familiar environs and more immediate rewards.

The liminal and fragile state of interdisciplinarity is to be sustained only by adopting the most active and aggressive means; by resolving, not just to be interdisciplinary, but actively to oppose disciplinary complacencies. To be, in a word, "antidisciplinary." To be antidisciplinary is to interest ourselves — and actively to prefer — precisely those knowledges which are underrecognized or unrecognized within existing disciplinary terms. A discipline constitutes itself in and through the kinds of knowledges it seeks and endorses, and equally through those its methodologies render unpresent or invisible. As a result, the processes of disciplinary analysis are likely to — in fact are bound to — leave a "remainder," a residue of phenomena unvoiced or uncommented upon. Antidisciplinarity enlists and deploys new procedures—or at any rate procedures introduced from outside a customary disciplinary range—in order to probe this remainder, to render visible aspects of a text or a situation that would otherwise remain unseen.[1]

Antidisciplinarity begins with a sense of our respective fields' constructedness, a sense of where their unspoken boundaries operate to highlight objects for disciplinary notice and to exclude others from view. Because a field's contours cannot be viewed from within, a standpoint outside its boundaries is required to bring them to view. This is the standpoint of theory—with "theory" understood to constitute an analytical vantage point too powerful or versatile fully to be contained or exhausted by any one discipline or field of study. Often accused of promoting self-enclosed discourse, theory, when properly employed, does precisely the opposite: its task and the test of its effectiveness reside precisely in the external but unnoticed objects and effects it opens to view.

Several contemporary theories share this exterior or even antic relation to the more codified disciplines, this knack for disciplinary defamiliarization, this gift to expose subjects that accepted disciplinary procedures leave unseen.[2] If disciplinary boundaries result from phobic incapacity for disorder, extradisciplinary theory retains, as observed by Diane Elam of feminist deconstruction, its capacity to precipitate a disciplinary anxiety attack![3] No doubt an affection for boundaries and a phobic dislike of boundary crossers has something to do with the fury that conventional critics can still muster over the mention of theoretical bogeyman-practitioners. Somehow, the anger and anxiety roil around Derrida or Lacan, the anxiety around the practice of deconstruction or the Lacanian split subject. I don't recall anybody becoming angry about Bourdieu or practice theory. Yet if capacity for disciplinary subversion were to be fairly measured, then practice theory must be allowed its own ruckus-raising potential.

Theories of practice are by no means giddily new. A determinate point of origin would be the work of Bourdieu and Giddens in the 1970s, with the appearance of Bourdieu's *Outline of a Theory of Practice* in English in 1977 and Giddens's *Central Problems in Social Theory* in 1979. Disciplinarily, its origins are appropriately vague, but are indebted more or less equally to anthropology and sociology, with reasonably early pickups in political science and literature. In its inception, practice theory posed a welcome alternative to the unwelcome binary in which human behavior was seen either as rational, purposive, and agent driven or as a wholly agentless product of synchronous social structure.[4] As a theory founded in resistance to simplifying binaries, it has proven highly resistant to disciplinary appropriation, and it flourishes twenty years after the fact precisely by virtue of its capacity to subvert or override the very simplifications (textual versus extratextual, temporal versus atemporal) by which disciplines once closed themselves.

At the heart of practice theory lies an understanding of human activity as what Bourdieu calls "regulated improvisation,"[5] as activity occurring within structure, but not structurally determined. Or, to put it slightly differently, practice theory offers an analysis of activity as conceived, and made intelligible within, a set of tacit rules, but not as wholly predetermined by those rules. Even so short a summary suggests the advantage of practice theory over its adversaries in the 1970s: over, that is, a residual humanism that admitted no obstacles to individual self-determination, and a briefly triumphant structuralism that insisted on the subjection of individuals to rules. But what conceptual advantages does practice theory, twenty years after, continue to allow to its practitioners? What disciplinarily specific binds does it nullify or elude? For my answer I return to the concept of the extradisciplinary "remainder," those shadow events or accompaniments which remain undisclosed in traditional disciplinary analyses. Practice theory proves its worth by enlarging the circle of discussion, by clustering objects and experiences previously thought to have little in common, by discovering zones of volition and choice left unrecognized by previous or competing analytical standpoints.

Here is my own shortlist of descriptive advantages gained through application of practice theory:

Expands the field of analysis. Immediately striking within practice theory is its refusal to differentiate objects of analysis. A text, a symbolic object, a performance, a ceremonial or pageant, an event may all be found to unfold equally within structure, to be subject to "practical" analysis. A more specific observation, bearing on a particular problem of my discipline, is that practice soars over the imagined chasm between the symbolic and the material, or (to put it slightly differently) the textual and the historical. This particular achievement is enabled by Bourdieu's introduction of a powerful concept that identifies the goal of all practice as the accumulation of "capital," that is, social leverage, and then argues that capital may be variously symbolic or material or both at once (see 183). Bourdieu's analytical flexibility has a payoff of its own, in that it permits him to recognize the varied motives from which participants engage in a practice, the differential rewards they seek from it, the multiple meanings a practice can produce. He thus escapes aestheticism by exposing the underlying materiality of "symbolic" effects, and escapes functionalism by emphasing the varied forms in which "profit" can arise.

Rejects the tyranny of structure. Practices manifest abstract (and hence timeless) structure, but the process of *structuration* occurs in time, with meaning subject to modification by temporal arrangement and duration or "tempo" (8–9). The vantage point of practice theory thus allows the analyst of actions and events to recognize the synchrony or atemporality of the structures within which they are conceived, and to reconnect these actions and events to the diachrony or temporality of their unfolding. An action released into time necessarily becomes unpredictable, as its differential reception and possible self-modification rebound upon or modify the circumstances of its original production. This is what Ian Hacking calls a "looping effect," in which an object of study can change as a result of what we think we know about it, or (in the case of people) what they have now come to believe about themselves.[6] I certainly do not want to deny either social scientists or humanists the ability to describe "looping effects," but I would say that they remain invisible to any practitioner of either discipline unable to enter the current of time, to view events as mobile and self-transforming within constantly shifting circumstances.

Outflanks the question of intent. Despite occasional emancipatory attempts, literary studies constantly revert to the concept of "authorial intent" to guarantee its interpretations. The potential circularity of this gesture need hardly be mentioned: the most far-fetched interpretations are routinely but bogusly secured by the claim that they represent the author's wishes, or the discovery of an authorial "spokesperson" within a text. The advantage of practice theory is that it permits a text or an event to be perceived as strategic, whether or not it is the product of what Bourdieu calls a "strategic intention" (73). Without ignoring people's sense of what they think they are doing, practical analysis finally bets on observed behavior, on what they may be seen to do.[7] Freeing the act or event from the dominion of any given participant's sense of his or her motives permits a more expansive view of its causes and consequences.

Opens a theory of resistance. Much as literary studies have learned from Foucault, criticism conducted under his aegis has had difficulty breaking the circuit in which practices are seen merely to reproduce the structures of which they are a product. Hence, the unlikelihood of an opposition that cannot somehow be recontained by the structures of power within which it originated, or of which it might even be considered an epiphemenon. Still, in Bourdieu's conception, practices always open the possibility of symbolically manipulating the very power relations out of which they are produced (165). Even good-faith attempts at reproduction can involve such manipulation. Independently from Judith Butler's theory of the imitative "swerve," Ortner and Sahlins were employing elements of practice theory in their observation that social change may be a paradoxical result of good-faith failure; that is, change may result from "failed reproduction."[8]

I do not mean that practice theory is always trying to do all these things. They might be located among its incidental derivatives, as effects of its implementation. For it is, above all else, an "applied" theory, a "hands-on" theory, which is why I want to move as quickly as possible to some illustrative applications. As my title suggests, I will concentrate on several late medieval English coronation events, seen as occasions of "ritual practice."

RICHARD II: BAD TIMING AS BAD LUCK

Social practices — including those relative formalizations which Bourdieu calls "ritual practice" — manifest structure, but in their own way: not in static arrest, but as a process of structuration or realization, occurring in time. Time is, in this sense, not only the proper element of practice, but also one of the ways in which it makes meaning. Bourdieu observes of the slightly different case of exchange relations, "Even the most strictly ritualized exchanges, in which all the moments of the action, and their unfolding, are rigorously foreseen, have room for strategies: the agents remain in command of the *interval* between the obligatory moments and can therefore act... playing with the *tempo* of the exchange" (15). Similarly, considerations of temporal order, timing, and tempo are centrally important within rituals of coronation, where the *ordo* of coronation (*ordo* referring in this case not to stratum or rank but to sequence) was of sufficient importance to be written down, revised, argued over, and learnedly commented upon.

The objective of the coronation ritual, as with most ritual practices, may be understood as what Bourdieu calls the "euphemization" of a boundary crossing (120–24). The passage from late king to present king, old king to new king, presents a relatively elementary boundary crossing, but nevertheless a crossing to be euphemized, by insistence upon legitimacy, continuity, rebirth, divine sanction, and other means. Whichever of these strategies is pursued, practice theory locates its chances for success in its manipulation of time. Analysis of coronation, not as an abstract pattern but as a practice unfolding in time, reveals the orchestration of these and other legitimizing effects, and also highlights those moments when the process breaks down, when the gears and wheels of the ritual's smooth euphemizations are revealed for all to see. One such moment is the ill-timed coronation appearance of Richard's own champion.

In the process of claiming his hereditary role as king's champion, John Dymmok showed a clear enough sense of his moment in time: that the responsibility of the champion is to "come ... the day of the coronation, and ride before the king in the procession ['chiuacher deuant le Roi al procession'] and ... say and cry to the people three times together ... that if there be any man high or low who will deny that his liege lord Sir Richard, kinsman and heir to the King of England, Edward, now lately dead, ought not to be crowned King of England, that he is ready with his body to adventure now ... that he leith as a false traitor" (141, 160).[9] The notion that he should defend Richard's title on the morning of the coronation, in procession to the abbey, makes perfect sense, for, were a defense of Richard's right to be required, it should obviously occur before rather than after the coronation ceremony.

Yet, according to anti-Ricardian Walsingham, this is not what happened.[10] As he tells it, the coronation was under way behind the closed doors of the abbey when John Dymmok, splendidly arrayed on a charger with two attendants, arrived at the doors of the abbey to await the end of the coronation mass. First issuing from the abbey doors was Marshall Thomas Percy, who abruptly addressed the king's champion, say-

ing that he ought not to have come at this time but should have postponed his arrival until the coronation banquet ("dicens non debere eum
ea hora venire, sed quod usque ad prandium Preis distulisset adventum
suum"). Percy then, in what seems a peremptory way, instructed him to
go take off his heavy armor and to await that time for his return ("mo-
nuit ut rediret, et, deposito tanto onere armorum, quiesceret ad illud
tempus"). Walsingham says that—unsurprisingly, given Percy's authority and tone—Dymmok took his advice and withdrew. Twenty-three
years later, when Dymmok's nephew performed the role of champion
on the occasion of Henry IV's coronation, he does indeed seem to have
entered the king's hall in the course of the banquet ("in medio prandio . . .
aulam intravit"), fully mounted and ready to sustain the king's right
against any challenger.[11]

Dymmok's withdrawal, and presumed humiliation, is the moment
at which a tacit and barely visible, but nonetheless vital, system of reci-
procity begins to break down. The king's champion customarily received
his horse and harness as payment for his services—though this payment is couched as the king's gift, lying within the "volonte" of the king
(Legg, 141). Thus, Dymmok's gift of loyalty was reciprocated by the king's
gift of a horse: loyalty for horse, horse for loyalty. Yet records suggest
that Dymmok, having never fought for the king, and perhaps in disfa-
vor besides, received no gift.[12] Here suggested in miniature is a rending
of the tissue of obligations that left Richard, in 1399, with few supporters in a time of need.

Also revealed through these alterations of sequence—first from
the coronation procession to the abbey doors and then to a ceremonial
cameo at the coronation banquet—is a more general decline of the king's
champion's role to derisory status. Although superficially conflictual in
nature, the champion's appearance may be viewed more accurately as a
euphemization, in the way it collects and stages potential conflict in a
manageable form, transposing potential civil unrest into a temporal ceremony with a finite conclusion. The shunting of this ceremonial to a less
consequential (and in fact redundant) moment incidentally reveals everything about the coronation that the coronation is designed to conceal.
The coronation seeks, not only to elide a boundary crossing, but even
more ambitiously to perform an act of "social alchemy" by which participants are encouraged to misrecognize interested gestures (magnate control, dynastic perpetuation) as disinterested or consensual in nature, and

hence as voluntary and legitimate rather than constrained (Bourdieu, 192). Derogation of the champion's role is a telltale indication of the coronation not as a consensus-building event, but as a "done deal"—a consequence of backroom brokerage within a magnate elite.

The scene in which Richard's elaborately harnessed champion is told to go away and come back later has a certain Monty Pythonesque quality... or at least I can imagine what the Pythons would have done with it. But such minor slips and transpositions need not amount to much, unless somebody wants to make something of them; unless, that is, they are caught up in some larger signifying network. Walsingham's comments on Dymmok's untimely appearance would seem to derive from a willingness to see Richard embarrassed, but perhaps no more than that. The real scandal, which Richard's enemies were not soon to forget, was next to ensue.

It involves, in certain respects, a charming moment. The celebrants now issuing in confused tumult from the abbey, amid a rout of mounted lords and preceded by a great number of minstrels ("praecedente magno numero diversi generis histrionum"), the young Richard was carried from the abbey to the royal palace on the shoulders of a knight ("portatus est in humeris militum usque ad regale Palatium"). Although Walsingham leaves the matter there, it is pursued by the Westminster chronicler (who, via his association with the abbey and its privileged relation to ceremonies of coronation, and his chapter's responsibility to keep the coronation regalia, has a great deal more to say about the matter). Writing in 1390, the chronicler redescribes the circumstances and informs us that the knight in question was the young Richard's tutor, the now reviled—and two years dead—Simon Burley. Moreover, he tells us about a grievous blow to the ceremonial security of the coronation, a blow resulting from carelessness, but even more from failure to observe the proper order of things:

> It is generally accepted that immediately after his coronation the king should go into the vestry, where he should take off the regalia and put on the other garments laid out ready for him by his chamberlains before returning by the shortest route to his palace, but at the coronation of the present king the contrary was done, with deplorable results; for when the coronation was

over, a certain knight, Sir Simon Burley, took the king up in his arms, attired as he was, in his regalia, and went into the palace by the royal gate with crowds milling all round him and pressing upon him, so that on the way he lost one of the consecrated shoes ["sotularibus regalibus benedictis"] through his carelessness ["incuria"].[13]

Surely one could forgive the ten-year-old king's carelessness in this matter, but the monk of Westminster's actual grievance seems to be against not the young Richard or his tutor Burley, but the violation of order, of good ritual sequence.[14] Already by Richard's time the regalia were regarded as highly venerable, with written record connecting many of the items to the reign of Henry III (Legg, 54–56) and with common report connecting them with the coronation of Edward the Confessor (Legg, 191–192). Yet antiquity alone is not at issue here; the reason for keeping Richard's ritual failure alive was its relevance to a pro-Lancastrian project of delegitimization, proceeding (among numerous other stratagems) by means of a deconstruction of its ritual basis. Among the avalanche of pro-Lancastrian portent and rumor and innuendo launched between Richard's deposition and death was this analysis by Adam of Usk:

> At the coronation of this lord three ensigns of royalty foreshadowed for him three misfortunes. First, in the procession he lost one of the coronation shoes; whence the commons who rose up against him hated him ever after all his life long; secondly, one of the golden spurs fell off; whence the soldiery opposed him in rebellion; thirdly, at the banquet a sudden gust of wind carried away the crown from his head; whence he was set aside from his kingdom and supplanted by King Henry.[15]

Adam here deconstructs or unbinds the ordered significances that make the ritual of coronation "work" as a metaphor of ordered transference. No slipper, no metaphor; no metaphor, no transference. And thus, without the stately and ordered progress through the signs by which the royal *dignitas* is invoked and secured, no smooth euphemization of the passage from one reign to the next. Disregard of sequence opens a rift or rent in the symbolic fabric, and this rift is the place where an argument for a different king can take hold and flourish.

HENRY IV AS SOCIAL ALCHEMIST

"Officializing strategies," according to Bourdieu, transmute private and particular interests into disinterested, collective, publicly avowable interests. Thus, the "capital of authority" works by solemnizing and thus universalizing private incident, and also (in reverse) by disowning a person "who, failing to identify his particular interest with the 'general interest,' is reduced to the status of a mere individual" (40). We have seen this process of demotion applied to Richard's coronation, where Lancastrian interests made much of Richard's small failures to observe temporal, and hence ritual, coherence. Not only deofficializing but also desacralizing the coronation, they performed something akin to the ceremony of clerical degradation, in which the effects of time are reversed and run backward, with the people finally "holding him not for king, but for a private person, Sir Richard of Bourdeaux, a simple knight."[16] But officializing (and, in the case of coronation, sacralizing) strategies more often run forward than backward, and the Lancastrians may most often be seen as masters of ritual transmutation, invoking those processes of "social alchemy" which encourage the misrecognition of power relations as relations of broad consent, of compelled relations as elective ones.

Perhaps this is why Henry IV enjoys such an affirmative and Kennedyesque reputation today: his genius was to use power ruthlessly, but to encourage its misrecognition as a participatory exercise. The "participation" of which I speak is by no means to be understood (à la Bishop Stubbs) as precocious parliamentarianism. The participation encouraged by Henry IV's ceremonies of acclamation and assertions of free election was less parliamentary than ritualistic and spectacular.[17]

Henry, for example, appears to have wrought significant changes, as measured against previous practice, in the crucial element of the coronation ceremony, that of unction or anointment with holy oil.[18] According to normal practice, as described in the fourteenth-century *Liber regalis*, the loosening of the king's garments and his anointment is to occur while a *pallium* or canopy is spread over him to conceal him from view ("pallio supra dictum principem extenso"; Legg, 92). Yet in the detailed, sponsored description of MS Julius B.II, the *pallium* is unmentioned. We are told that "Kyng Herry lay vpon a cloth off golde before the hyh awter in Westm'. Chirche. And there in ffoure parties off his body his

clothes weren opyn, and there he was anoynted."[19] Furthermore, according to the account of Julius B.II, this anointment was followed by another apparent innovation, in which the anointed monarch, rather than
transporting himself from place to place, is borne to the place where
crowning is to occur: "And affter this anoyntyng his body was leffte vp
into another place" (Legg, 49). These two alterations might be found superficially discordant, with the former a gesture of accessibility or popular access and the latter a deliberate elevation of the king's supramundane status. Yet the two alterations possess a common denominator,
which is the king's enactment of a willingness to pacify and subordinate his own volition, first as an object of his subjects' gaze and then as
the vessel of God's will. In each case, he is the object of regard — first
by his subjects and then by God (whose gaze the principal prayer invites:
"Prospice omnipotens deus serenis obtutibus hunc gloriosum regem";
Legg, 92). Invited is a gaze that consents in his elevation, that instates
and beholds Henry as "glorious king." Having recently seized the throne
by magnate alliance and force of arms, Henry was in a position to demand compliance; yet, condescending to his subjects' (and God's!) gaze,
Henry solicits consent and transmutes an occasion of forceful seizure
into a seemingly voluntary and elective one.

Since we are looking not only at an "officializing" moment but also
at a "sacramental" one, a ratifying miracle would do no harm. Henry's
coronation was indeed not to happen without a divine miracle ("sine di-
vino miraculo"; Walsingham, 2:239), and we might pause to view this
miracle within the lens of practice theory. The interesting thing about
practice is that it manifests rules, but the rules need not be rigorously
followed. In fact, practice is annihilated precisely in those analyses which
insist that rules are *always* followed, since the meaning-making edge of
practice consists in difference and departure. In the case of unction, the
"rule" is that there must be an oil, but the source of the oil, and the stories told about it, remain open to improvisation. Why should it not, for
an exceptional king, be an exceptional oil?

Accounts of such an exceptional oil, an oil presented to Saint Thomas
à Becket by the Blessed Virgin, had been long in circulation before the
accession of Henry IV. Edward II, for example, sponsored an account of
such an oil, informing Pope John XXII that he had considered coronation with it, but had decided to content himself with the customary oil

("unctione consueta contentus"; Legg, 71), but that now, as a result of reversals in his reign, he was considering a second ceremony of anointment. Among the properties of this oil, the fifth king from the one then reigning (a slot occupied by Richard II) would, by virtue of this oil, recover the Holy Land from the heathen. Taken up by the Lancastrians, this older legend was first stripped down for use by omission of the "fifth king" in favor of a "rex futurus" who, anointed with this oil, will recover "sine vi," not the Holy Land, but the lost lands of Normandy and Aquitaine (Legg, 169).[20] Now, stripped of its previous, inopportune association with Richard II and crusades, this legend lay open to new inscription. We reencounter it in Walsingham as a fully Lancastrian "miraculum." Walsingham gives it a specific Lancastrian genealogy: it is now discovered by Henry, first duke of Lancaster; passed by him to the Black Prince (who, had he lived, would have been a worthy recipient and the fifth king), then placed in the Tower only to be rediscovered accidentally ("inopinate"; Walsingham, 239) by Richard II in 1399 as he was randomly rooting around in relics of his ancestors. The insertion of Richard in the chain might seem strange, until we see how he is used: as an unwitting, and hence innocent, vehicle of Henry's felicity. Learning of the oil's properties, he seeks a renewal of his unction, but is refused. He then (pathetically) carries the ampule around with him, along with other items of regalia, until handing it over to the archbishop of Canterbury, observing (in words assigned him by the Lancastrians) that it was not the divine will that he should be so anointed but that this noble sacrament was intended for another.[21]

In the Arundel manuscript of Walsingham, a later (presumably Yorkist) commentator marginally debunked this account, inserting "unguentum fictitium" adjacent to the oil's discovery. But such fictions have their uses, one of which is to open new forms and modes of belief for the larger circle of the ceremony's participants. Speaking of the means by which difference may be consecrated as common consent, Bourdieu observes that "for ritual to function and operate it must first of all present itself and be perceived as legitimate, with stereotyped symbols serving precisely to show that the agent does not act in his own name . . . but in his capacity as delegate."[22] Here Henry IV, as when he permitted himself to be lifted and carried about the altar, offers himself as delegated sovereign and agent of God's plans for England—in a form conducive to ratification by all those who believe that a *miraculum* has indeed occurred.

JOANNE OF NAVARRE AS LIQUID ASSET

Shortly after her arrival in England and her marriage to the widowed Henry IV at Winchester in 1403, Joanne's leading role was solemnized in a formal ceremony of coronation, with invitations broadly distributed among the lords, ladies, and knights of the realm. This was, to judge from such indications as its ambitious guest list,[23] a sumptuous affair, conducted (in the view of one chronicler) with due honor and festivity ("satis honorifica et festiva").[24] An illustration of the event (British Library, Cotton MS Julius E.iv, fol. 202) shows Joanne instated with the contradictory symbols of majesty and subjection typical of late medieval queenly coronation: on the one hand, enthroned in majesty; on the other, her hair loosely tressed, symbolically suggesting her supplementary role as the king's virginal bride.[25] The point of difference from tradition that measures the esteem in which she was held is that, along with the traditional *virga,* or rod, in her hand, she extraordinarily holds an orb surmounted with a cross in her left. Before Philippa in 1330, English queens seem to have held only the *virga.* The fourteenth-century recension of the *Liber regalis* grants queens a scepter, but a lesser one, unequal to that of the king: a small one, gilt, surmounted by a dove ("paruum septrum deauratum in cuius summitate est columba deaurata"; Legg, 100). The orb and cross are unusual, and regal indeed. Additionally, she is shown alone, rather than together with, but at a lesser level than, the king. No formality is spared because of her solitary status, with the archbishop of Canterbury and the abbot of Westminster simultaneously placing the crown upon her head. Behind are various emblems of English and Continental royalty: at her right the Plantagenet lions and fleurs-de-lys, and at her left possibly a more fanciful evocation of the arms of Brittany.

Measurable, against previous coronation practice, is a margin of exceptionality: the exceptions, in this case, underscoring the honor and sumptuousness of this coronation event. Intent here is hard to assign, since different sorts of symbolic capital would appear to accrue to its different participants. The intent may be Joanne's. Daughter of the king of Navarre; fiancée of the dauphin of France; subtle manipulatrix of the quarrelsome John, duke of Brittany; regent of Brittany; architect of an attempted deal to secure her own fortune by selling the city of Nantes; reputed mistress of deception and disguise; survivor of witchcraft charges;[26] politically influential in the reigns of three Lancastrian kings — she was no pushover. Perhaps the sumptuous coronation was her idea, and demand. But — despite the fact that she dominated and outmaneuvered her king in every material respect — Henry IV also had something to gain from her elevation. Bourdieu would locate regal marriages among those extraordinary cases occurring outside normal kinship groupings, in which the woman is treated "as a political instrument, a sort of pledge or liquid asset, capable of earning symbolic profits" (54). And, if Joanne was a liquid asset, convertible to capital, the capital in question was going to have to be symbolic, because that is all the capital Henry was ever going to get.

Joanne was a wealthy heiress, and contemporary commentators supposed that Henry had reaped a financial windfall. In fact, Henry received no dowry, gained no access to her substantial dower from Duke John of Brittany, and paid *her* a massive dower of ten thousand marks annually — a sum amounting to some 10 percent of the royal government's annual income.[27] The immensity of the resources available to Joanne and the autonomy with which she enjoyed them are emblematized by Henry's 10 December 1404 grant to Joanne of the new tower at the entrance of the great gate of the great hall within the palace of Westminster, for management of her councils and business, the auditing of her accounts, and other aspects of her own fiscal self-determination.[28] Seeing all this money so close but unavailable must have greatly pained the ever impecunious Henry. Nonetheless, from the viewpoint of the Lancastrians, as a usurping and ever insecure dynasty, *any* sort of marital tie to the ruling houses of Europe evidently made sense as a symbolic contribution to their legitimization, however exorbitant the cost.

Whose agency or volition is finally exhibited, Joanne's or Henry's, practice theory does not begin to tell. Practice theory merely registers a pressure, an interest, a socially defined desire that Joanne receive more than ordinarily deferential treatment. But it has much to tell us about social process, about a collective preparedness to misrecognize Joanne as things she could never be: a thrice-betrothed, twice-married mother of eight as a virginal bride with untressed hair; a daughter of the ill-reputed Charles "the Bad," king of Navarre, as an important royal alliance; a representative of sectional, and more often personal, interests as a queen and an object of general regard.

THE ANTIDISCIPLINARY REMAINDER

Earlier I suggested that certain antidisciplinary theories highlight things that traditional disciplinary configurations leave unsymbolized, undiscussed, unseen. What, then, has practice theory rendered visible that might otherwise have remained invisible to disciplinarily sanctioned procedures?

A preliminary answer might involve practice theory's capacity to identify, and appreciate the importance of, the exceptional, the aberrant, the symptomatic. Richard's lost slipper, Henry's miraculous oil, Joanne's orb: each is in some way legible as a deviation from an expectation or a norm. Yet practice theory is not alone in its capacity to respond to such exceptions. The rearguard attack on contemporary theory has deplored the extent to which almost *all* currently admired theories return to the exceptional case. This is true of performance theory (with its dexterous movement across, or defiance of, traditional categories). And of queer theory (with its interest in whatever was omitted or thrust from visibility in the process of constructing stable binaries). And of post-Freudianism (with its interest in the symptom, and what the symptom has to tell us about the whole).

Each of these currently productive theorizations offers us a way of grasping the relation of part to whole, incidental detail to larger structure, marginal or exceptional to dominant or central. But, among them, practice theory allows a more specific contribution that is all its own, for practice theory offers us a grasp of the exceptional *at its moment of production*. The exceptional is produced (along with its near relation, the *un*exceptional) by a process of structuration, in which abstract and atemporal structure reproduces itself as concrete and timebound action. Moving between abstract structure and its instantiation via the process of structuration, practice theory sees Richard's lost slipper not just as childish inattention or as a ten-year-old's forgivable resistance to an overly awesome interpellation, but as a telling and potentially exploitable failure in a larger temporal process, by which structure is either affirmed or, in this case, seen as unfortunately altered. John Dymmok's delay is not just confusion or insubordination, but a breakdown in a crucial ceremony of legitimization. Henry's oil and his queen's orb renew coronation structure, but novelly so, with adjustments that assert the exceptionality of their incumbency.

To be sure, practice theory is not alone in attending to the shift from atemporal structure to temporal realization. A similar "reading" of culture occurs in performance theory, as in the performative emphasis of Judith Butler's *Gender Trouble* (although Butler places somewhat more emphasis on the creativity of improvisation),[29] and is also at least implicit in much narrative theory. The moment of structure's realization via "structuration" can be approached and described in several interrelated languages. But this moment is still often elided within existing disciplinary configurations. Social science privileges structure over its instantiations. Narrative history, and the study of literary narrative, favor the nuances of a moment's realization in time over the essential contribution of structure to that same moment's intelligibility. Practice theory assumes a more encompassing obligation, or at any rate an obligation that runs both ways at once: to general structure, and simultaneously to that very particular moment when a structure is newly reproduced as possible difference. Respecting pattern and respecting sequence, practice theory brings us excitingly close to that critical moment—the point of structural difference or the gap or lapse in sequence—which signals a change, a shift of intent, the end of something and the beginning of something else.

PART II

TIME AND NARRATIVE

4

"LAD WITH REVEL TO NEWEGATE"

CHAUCERIAN NARRATIVE AND HISTORICAL
METANARRATIVE

*If elected vice president, Yanayev said, he
would campaign "against the political
bacchanalia which the country is seeing."*
— *San Francisco Chronicle*, 19 August 1991

PERKYN'S REVELRY AND
ITS SYMBOLIC AFFILIATIONS

Whatever might be said of the "Cook's Tale" as a fragment, it embraces
a brief but relatively complete narrative of Perkyn Revelour's emergence,
rebuke, and social descent. The Cook's recital begins with a description
of Perkyn's "gaillard's" temperament and disposition to merriment. It
progresses to a series of interrelated examples of how he earned and
enjoyed his reputation as "revelour" par excellence, including his attendance at festive processions or "ridyngs" (I.4377); his commitment to
dancing (I.4370), hazard (I.4383–87), and "mynstralcye" (I.4394); his
skill at attracting adherents in the form of a loyal "meynee" (I.4381); his
comprehensive tendency to "riote" (I.4414, etc.).[1] It ends with an emphasis upon his previous rebukes, including the fact that he was more
than once "lad with revel to Newegate" (I.4402), and a concluding account
of his worldly descent from the status of apprentice in a prosperous guild
to an underground demimonde of gambling, revelry, and prostitution.

This little narrative, unexceptional in itself, is signaled as important by the superfluity of commentary that punctuates and surrounds it — commentary not only in excess of any immediately apparent narrative necessity but also commentary more than usually heedless of the presumed perspective of its ostensible teller. For the low-life Cook, characterized by his own physical disfigurement (I.386) and churlish inability to separate his own emotional and physiological responses (I.4326) and later to be hailed out for ridicule and rejection in his own right as a debauched figure of fun (in the Manciple's Prologue), here adopts the voice of pulpit moralist and conservative satirist. The Cook's presumed purpose of telling an urban "jape" (I.4343) is pushed to the back burner as he pauses to lecture errant apprentice, indulgent master, and everyone else who will listen.[2]

His surprising and — given his own social station — personally incongruous theme is the failings of revelers and especially those of low degree: "Revel and trouthe, as in a lowe degree, / They been ful wrothe" (I.4397–98). Then, having reported Perkyn's incarcerations, his perspective virtually merges with that of the master, as he partially ventriloquizes the master's reasoning on the advisability of releasing this unruly prentice from his service:

> But atte laste his maister hym bithoghte,
> Upon a day, whan he his papir soghte,
> Of a proverbe that seith this same word:
> "Wel bet is roten appul out of hoord
> Than that it rotie al the remenaunt."
>
> (I.4403–7)

"So fareth it," the Cook adds in amplification of this view, "by a riotous servaunt" (I.4408), and, his voice still effectively paralleling that of the master, he sends Perkyn into the world with a sarcastic "late hit": "Now lat hym riote al the nyght" (I.4414).

The effect of this surplus commentary is to underscore and amplify a narrative curve running from revelry to inevitable rebuke and to imbue it with an importance in excess of any immediately apparent explanation. Chaucer's intentions for this tale and the ultimate effect to which he would have deployed this voice of urgent moralization cannot finally be known. But the short-term effect of the Cook's evocation of Perkyn's revelry and his emphatically negative pronouncements upon it is to invite the repositioning of this account of revelry-and-rebuke within a larger and highly resonant symbolic field.

The imagery of revelry as dangerous and irresponsible excess was widely prevalent within the numerous late-fourteenth-century accounts of the Rising of 1381. Needless to say, a wide gap separates Perkyn Revelour's dice games and petty cash box pilferings from substantial transgressions like the beheading of Sudbury and the burning of the Savoy. If Perkyn is a rebel at all, his insurrection occurs in a register we nowadays have ample precedent for recognizing as less substantive than stylistic. Yet the Cook's brief account of Perkyn's behavior embraces an extraordinary number of historical preconditions and buzzwords and key symbols common to most accounts of the 1381 Rising. Here are just a few of the common terms that permit a resituation of Perkyn's brief bacchanal within this larger symbolic field:

Revelry itself. However innocuous we might find the attraction of this "prentys revelour" (I.4391) to holiday *ridyngs* (I.4377) and to street life and to other sorts of public disport, the imagery of revelry carried a heavy symbolic freight in the later fourteenth century. Accounts of the Rising of 1381 are frequently couched in terms of the outbreak of revelry and its subsequent rebuke and repression, as notably illustrated by the Westminster chronicler's claim that, during the burning of Archbishop Sudbury's Lambeth Palace, the London rebels of 1381 repeatedly exclaimed, "A revelle! A revelle!"[3]

Perhaps the rebels actually employed ideas and occasions of revelry as staging grounds of oppositional action. (This possibility is certainly enhanced by the fact that the burning of Lambeth Palace is usually placed on 12 June, which in 1381 was the eve of Corpus Christi.)[4] Or perhaps the imagery of revelry is simply an aspect of the chronicler's program of stigmatization, effectively burdening the rebels with all the negative associations that revelry bears for its scandalized observers, including the overprivileging of the "low" and insufficient respect for the "high," its broad erasure of the line between spectators and participants, its encouragement of temporary license. Either as incriminating description or as libelous invention, the effectiveness of revelrous imputations in discrediting the rebel program was widely recognized. Walsingham, for example, says that the rebels arranged their executions as if they were a "solemnis ludus."[5] The *Anonimalle* chronicler describes the rebels in a grotesque variant of those same holiday *ridyngs* so esteemed by Perkyn and his fellow apprentices, bearing the severed head of Sudbury "en processione" through the city.[6] The rebels in the Tower are shown lolling on the king's mother's bed, issuing invitations as if she were a common wench, and the lowest of them reversed hierarchy by touching the beards of the "most noble" knights. Tyler himself is said to have mocked limit and ceremony by drinking ale and rudely rinsing his mouth and by playing a menacing boy's game with a dagger before the king. The whole rebellion in Kent, in fact, seems to Knighton a kind of *tripudium*—a festive celebration involving frivolity and dance.[7]

Apprentices as a volatile grouping. Perkyn moves mainly in a subsociety of London prentices that hovers rather ominously at the edge of many accounts of 1381. Andrew Prescott's research into the judicial records of the rebellion has shown conclusively that the majority of London rebels came not from Essex and Kent but from London itself and that, while drawing upon a wide social spectrum, their numbers were disproportionately tilted toward servants and apprentices.[8] An earlier Marxist interpretation of the London Rising sympathetically supposed it to have been an expression of solidarity with the cause of the rural peasantry.[9] In point of fact, the broad spectrum of London apprentices, servants, and journeymen (not to mention the transient and unemployed) had much to complain about in their own right, and evidence of their organizing attempts in the last decades of the fourteenth century suggests that they would have been an unstable group in any case, whatever their views of labor predicaments in the countryside.

Apprentices, together with journeymen and others, must have been on the Westminster chronicler's mind when he suggested that the London officials were paralyzed in the early stages of the revolt by the fear that the urban commons might throw in their lot with the serfs against the remainder of the city and that the whole city would thus be lost as a result of its inner divisions: "formidabat quidem ne si invalescentibus servis resisterent, communes tanquam suorum fautores cum servis contra reliquos civium insurgerent, sicque tota civitas in seipsa divisa deperiret" (*Westminster Chronicle*, 8). We can hardly doubt the affinity of Perkyn and his peers, with their attachment to civic spectacle and propensity for uproar, to those who were in the streets in those June days and nights, nor would any fourteenth-century reader have had cause to doubt the same.

Formation of an illicit "meynee." Perkyn's charisma, if not his organizational gifts, seems to have won him a devoted band of followers, somewhat derisively styled by the Cook as "a meynee of his sort" (I.4381), a band of "compeers" (I.4419) devoted to riotous conduct in the spirit of his own.[10] So, in the chronicle accounts, are the rebels regularly accused of appropriating forms of sworn association normally employed by their betters. The Westminster chronicler says that the rebels on the way to Lambeth forced those they met to swear an oath of alliance to their *contubernium* or band (2), and the jurors at Scarborough claimed that the local rebels constituted themselves as a sort of retinue or sworn association by employing a livery of hoods in order to further their conspiracy.[11]

Control of written records. Perkyn's objective is to regain his "papir" (I.4404) — presumably, an indenture or contract specifying his reciprocal obligations with his master. His master, reflecting on his riotous conduct and its corrupting example to the other "servantz," gives him his release, through ill will rather than good (I.4403–12).[12] So, by analogy, had possession of records bearing on their conditions of service been the most consistent motivation of the 1381 rebels. At Lambeth, for example, the rebels are said by the *Anonimalle* chronicler to have made a point of burning the registers and chancery rolls they found there: "mistrent en feu toutz les livers des registres et rolles de remembrauncez de la chauncellerie illeoqes trovez" (140). And Walsingham notes by way of explanation their determination that court rolls and muniments should be burned so that, the memory of old customs having been rubbed out, their lords would be unable to vindicate their rights over them: "statuerunt omnes curiarum rotulos et munimenta vetera dare flammis, ut, obsoleta antiquarum rerum memoria, nullum jus omnino ipsorum domini in eos in posterum vendicare valerent" (1:455).[13]

Perkyn's commitment to riotous misconduct, his associations with a like-minded "meynee," and his determination to regain control of his "papir" all suggest some relationship between his temporary excesses and the more thoroughgoing transgressions of 1381. But what relation is here tantalizingly implied? The Cook's account of Perkyn is certainly not a "reflection" of 1381 and is not exactly an "allegory" of 1381, either. What we seem actually to encounter here is a more general relationship of mutual participation in a larger representational environment. The particular terms of this participation will be the subject of the second part of this essay. I might simply observe, though, that it has several aspects, including a common reliance by Chaucer and his contemporaries on key symbols of revolt and also their frequent recourse to narrative strategies of palliation and control.

From Symbolization to Narratization

The theoretical problem of establishing a relation between the Cook's after-the-fact narrative of Perkyn Revelour and the events of the 1381 Rising has already been anticipated in certain respects by a spirited debate over the methodological procedures and implications of Robert Darnton's influential essay, "The Great Cat Massacre." In that essay, Darnton recreates an episode of the late 1730s in which a group of disgruntled printer's apprentices taunt their master by practicing various abuses, including guillotining, upon hapless cats and his wife's own favored cat.[14] The essay explores the larger field of meaning within which these events occurred, touching on witchcraft, revelry, and the practices of charivari; additionally implied, though nowhere specified, is a relation between cat-guillotining and events of the subsequent French Revolution. Roger Chartier, at odds with what he sees as Darnton's rather loose concept of symbolization and signing, argues for a more cautious mode of analysis, in which a symbol is "a sign, but a specific, particular sign, which implies a relation of representation—for example, the representation of an abstraction by a figure."[15] Interesting himself in the specificity of the cat massacre, Chartier employs his definition of symbolism to discredit Darnton's assertion that such explanatory contexts as sorcery and charivari may be "revelatory of a totality" (695)—rejecting by implication still looser symbolic affinities to the Revolution itself. In response, Darnton has advanced a more supple description of symbolization, in which the process "works as a mode of ontological participation rather than as a relation of representation."[16]

Admittedly, Darnton may not always successfully enact his view of symbolic polysemousness in practice.[17] And one may indeed question the meaning of so vague a phrase as "ontological participation" at the level of abstraction. But Darnton's concept has considerable value as a procedural tool or tool of practical inquiry. For Chartier's attempt to restrict symbolism to a "relation of representation" does insufficient justice to the status of larger representational fields that embrace many different symbolizations without necessarily specifying the particular relations between them. The cat massacre may, for example, be seen to participate in a larger textual system along with subsequent representations of the Revolution itself—a system in which the deeds and texts of the Revolution play a towering role but by no means the only role. The cat massacre and the Revolution may, that is, exist not in a relation of reference but a relation of participation within a larger system of events and signs.

In the later fourteenth century, one crucial symbolic field was constituted through and around images of revelry and revelrous behavior. Revelry was broadly available to Chaucer and his contemporaries for varied employment as what Bercé would call "un langage gestuel" (77)—a symbolic, behavioral language available for localized enactments and representations. Actual revelers in the streets might draw on this gestural language to produce a variety of actions, some festive and some insurrectionary; litterateurs like Chaucer might use it to create tales; chroniclers might use it to stigmatize rebels and rebellious acts. But all participate in a widely accessible regime for the creation and bestowal of meaning. It is within this relationship of general participation, of reliance upon a commonly held body of socially created symbols, rather than any more particularized cross-reference among and between events, that their commonality is to be found.

Now with Chartier, rather than against him, I find symbolic regimes like that of revelry to be broadly shared within a society and unlikely to be the property of any one social or cultural group.[18] The very ubiquity of a symbol like revelry nevertheless opens another interpretative problem, since all applications of the symbols are not alike. Inherent in the broad distribution of a cluster of symbols bearing on revelry and revelrous behavior is their availability for varied appropriation and use. And this very availability raises a set of coordinate issues: who is eventually to control them and for what purpose? Is, for example, a powerful symbol like revelry to be wielded as a vehicle of social transformation, as a staging ground of oppositional actions and the transgressive and possibly permanent substitution of "low" for "high," or is it to be seen as a device of social containment, a way of confirming hierarchy through temporary but closely delimited inversion?

This debate about the implications of revelry is long-standing but has remained unresolved precisely because it has been argued out in mainly essentialist terms, with the assumption that revelry must be one thing (or the other), must work one way (or the other). In fact, like other such symbols, the symbolizations of revelry can and do mean different things to different participants. Gareth Stedman Jones once put it to me this way in conversation: that all the spectators at a football match are present at the same event but experience the match differently according to whether they are sitting in the owners' box or the cheap seats and according to their different loyalties and affiliations and other factors. So, too, with actions conceived within the symbolic language or "langage gestuel" of revelry; the same set of terms may be wielded to produce oppositional actions or to celebrate their inevitable cessation, menacingly to articulate social hostility or reassuringly to rehearse its ultimate control.

The most conclusive way to gain control of an unruly but powerful symbol is by employing it in a narration, by assimilating it to an exemplary sequence of events that unfolds in time and that, preferably, ends with a determinate conclusion illustrating or vindicating one's claims. "Narration," in the sense in which I am using it here, can occur at the level of action in the world, when one produces a train of events that depend upon and mobilize key social symbols. Or, as in the Cook's treatment of Perkyn's revelrous heyday and ultimate rebuke, it can function textually—in this case, to control a potent and potentially socially destabilizing symbolic cluster.

The larger narrative pattern of the "Cook's Tale," in which revelry is evoked within a controlling frame that guarantees its ultimate chastisement, may be viewed in convenient miniature within the narrator's derisive observation that Perkyn was "somtyme lad with revel to Newegate" (I.4402). On the face of it, the Cook's observation would seem to be a matter of derision pure and simple, supplying the conclusion that Perkyn's devious ways lead to imprisonment and that "this is the kind of revelry he deserves." But actual fourteenth-century practice supplements and complicates the line. Convicted felons and others were subject to public exposure and ridicule, frequently including a procession, either to the pillory or other public display, accompanied by emblems of the misdeed, or to a prison for confinement. In case of procession either to the pillory or to prison (or even, at intervals, procession out from Newgate for public display and then back again), minstrelsy might be supplied in the form of trumpets or other instruments.[19] At the most obvious level, the purpose of the minstrelsy was simply to draw notice to the punishment. But it might also have functioned as a kind of anticeremony, less a harnessing of mirth for purposes of transgression than a subduing of mirth to the aims of civic rectitude.

Perkyn, led with revel to Newgate, is thus accompanied with a reminder of this riotous conduct—but a reminder conveyed through an image of revelry bound over, itself now bent to purposes of chastisement. Our glimpse of Perkyn in procession is, to borrow a narratological term, synchronous, in the sense that we see him in a single moment, caught in arrest on his way to Newgate with minstrels in his party. But this synchrony includes elements of its own diachrony, in its implied sequence: Perkyn, formerly a reveler given to singing and dancing and other disport, is now arrested, and revelry is now aligned with the law and contributory to a critique of its own former devotee. Perkyn's story thus has an implied beginning (in revelry), middle (apprehension by his master and the representatives of civil authority), and end (led off, with the trappings of his former revelry now redirected for purposes of mockery, to prison). The symbolic apparatus of revelry is thus loosed from its original moorings in riotous lowlife and controlled within a closed narrative system that guarantees its ultimate rejection.

The same narrative pattern, moving from revelry to its necessary rebuke, is repeated in what we have of the "Cook's Tale" and is repeated on a much grander scale in the later-fourteenth- and early-fifteenth-century chronicle narratives of the 1381 Rising. Walsingham pauses, for example, after the most ambitious of the recitals of the rise and fall of rebellion and sums up his generic and symbolic accomplishments: "Scripsimus ... historiam tragicam ... de dominatione rusticorum, et debacchatione communium, insania nativorum" (We have now written the tragic history of the lordship of the rustics, and the wild bacchanal of the commons and the madness of the villeins; 2:13). Walsingham's narrative ambitions are large, and he thus claims for his work a literary form; his genre is *historia*, or history, but his form is tragic—not tragedy, that is, in the Greek or classical sense but tragedy in the broad medieval sense that it recites a downfall, with a "falling" plot.[20] (The rebels might in their first heady days, in which resistance failed to materialize or melted away, have fancied themselves in a comedy. But, writing subsequent to the rebels' defeat and dispersion at London and then at Saint Albans, Walsingham knows better.) Still more pertinent to the subject at hand, however, is his description of the Rising itself as a "debacchatio"—a passionate raving with Bacchic overtones. Embedded in Walsingham's final reproof, as indeed in his narration as a whole, this allusion to the rebels' brief carnival or revel makes it seem all the more futile and doomed. The fact that Walsingham has already told of the failure of the Rising and the dispersal of the rebels casts his allusion to the rebels as bacchants in an explanatory capacity. By this descriptive stroke, such known characteristics of the carnivalesque as its inversion of the order of things, its prevailing license, and above all its temporary nature are recruited to account for the ultimate failure of rebellion.[21]

The disciplining of the rebels, as described by Walsingham, proceeded in several stages, the most consequential of which occurred when they resolved upon further sedition after their return to their homes. The king heard, Walsingham tells us, that the Kentishmen were conspiring again and that they had congregated in another profane assembly to the destruction of the whole kingdom (2:14). The king's first impulses toward wholesale slaughter being tempered by the intercession of the Kentish notables, a variety of disciplinary actions was then instituted, along mainly judicial lines. Walsingham portrays a number of the leading rebels taking an additional step toward collaboration in their own rebuke, unlike our apparently unrepentant Perkyn. Alan Treader, one of the murderers of Sudbury, is said to have been seized by the devil and to have run mad in the streets, devising his own exemplary punishment with a naked sword about his neck and an unsheathed dagger at his back: "arreptus a diabolo, insanire coepit, et, domum veniens, nudum gladium a collo suo suspendit ante pectus suum, et cultellum, [quem 'daggere' dicimus] etiam evaginatum, suspendit ad tergum" (2:15). Routinely labeled "insanus" in the chronicle accounts, the rebels are first shown transported by the crazy revelry of their bacchanal, and in the end their insanity is replayed, stripped of illusion, as diabolical possession and frantic guilt.

The narrative evocation of bacchanal or revelry followed by its rebuke may serve varied purposes. The epigraph to my essay is drawn from the recent upheaval in the former Soviet Union, when, just prior to the failed conservative putsch of autumn 1991, the old guard accused the reformers of "political bacchanalia." This representational project bore within it, of course, the seeds of a hoped-for narrative, in which the reform movement is viewed as spontaneous and involving but also as irresponsible and unrooted and — above all — ephemeral and soon to vanish with the appearance of responsible authority figures. The putsch was to be the determinate moment of closure, when the Lenten figures of old authority returned to terminate the brief sway of Mardi Gras. In this case, however, the insurgents in the streets, sticking flowers in gun barrels and otherwise enacting a mythos of spring, had a different narrative in mind — a narrative in which revelry provided a staging ground for open-ended and potentially transformative actions. Unlike the apparently premature rebels of 1381, the Russian reformers were able to link their aspirations to centers of institutional authority (including their own state government with a legitimately elected and highly vocal spokesperson in power) and were able to recruit the urban officials who might loosely be characterized as the Walworths and Brembres of our day. They were thus able to continue the curve of their own narrative, in which revelrous spontaneity and improvisation were open-ended and were linked to ultimate supplantation and apparent political transformation.

Whatever their hopes, the rebels of 1381 remained subject to multiple and interlocking systems of social control. Among these elements of control were such tangible factors as the loyalty of Walworth, Brembre, Philipot, and other key leaders of the London patriciate; the presence of experienced mercenaries like Knolles and the availability of armed elements like the garrison of the Tower; and, eventually, the availability of a judicial system of rebuke and castigation. No less important as elements of control were, however, such intangibles as the rebels' own incomplete ideological program, composed of ill-sorted backward- and forward-looking elements; their persistent deference to the king and their inability to imagine a form of rule that did not involve reliance upon kingship; and the motivation of many of their number to settle finite grudges and scores rather than to instate new social arrangements.[22] Centrally important among these less tangible aspects of revolt is the issue of the rebels' "story" and by whom and for what purposes it is narrated and, in the course of its narration, controlled.

Narration occurs at multiple levels of action and expression. As theorists like David Carr have pointed out, our practical behavior in the world depends on our ability to narratize our own actions. As social actors we inevitably stand in "the story-teller's position with respect to our own actions," with "no elements enter[ing] our experience ... unstoried or unnarrativized."[23] The consequence of Carr's claim is that narrative patterns (such as closure, beginning and end, departure and arrival, means and end, problem and solution; 49) are vitally involved in the production of the most mundane actions, well prior to their analytical or aesthetic uses in written texts. Actions are staged within structure, and existing narrative frames (both nonliterary and literary) constitute a reservoir of relevant structures. Staging their oppositional actions within existing possibilities of structure, the rebels do appear to have drawn upon ideas and images of revelry to produce oppositional actions. Although evidence is limited to accounts that have already been interpretatively overwritten, such as the stigmatizing chronicles, these accounts contain recurrent images of the carnivalesque: most notably, the exclamations of the rebels at Lambeth Palace. These alleged recurrences argue that "revelle" was indeed one of several improvised framings by which the rebels were able to mount actions, even in the absence of a more comprehensively elaborated revolutionary ideology.

Yet actions, once staged, are subject to rehearsal and reconsideration in the written record, with corresponding alteration in meaning. Carr, for example, proposes a distinction between the uses of narrative in, first, producing practical actions and, second, the various forms of written renarration. In these terms, we may see both Walsingham *and* Chaucer as engaged in a socially active and historically important project of written renarration, in which aspects of the Rising of 1381 are retold with a heavy emphasis on closure. Through their renarrations, both Walsingham and Chaucer join a continuing contest over the terms of social understanding, and both join it in ways hostile to the unruly aspirations of the lower strata. Retelling the events of 1381, Walsingham and the other chroniclers draw on such characteristics of revelry as its ephemeral character to underscore the abrupt beginning, unruly middle, and definitive end of rebellion. Chaucer likewise draws upon established images of revelry as revolt—including its disdain for traditional relations of domination and subordination and its disdain for the "papers" in which such understandings are inscribed—in order to suggest the necessity for stern rebuke.

Walsingham's narrative project is a good deal more explicitly related to the events of 1381 than Chaucer's fragmentary tale. Approached as a self-sufficient system, the "Cook's Tale" is only about itself, and its references are meaningful only in relation to its enterprise of constructing a narration about a revelrous apprentice and his past, present, and future rebuke. But it also participates ontologically in a larger system of narratives treating revelry and rebuke in the sense that it draws upon their narrative and symbolic energy and shares a portion of their social work. So seen, Perkyn's story is not an allegory of the 1381 Rising or even necessarily a reference to it, but it participates in the narrative curve of the Rising, a sense of disturbing excitement and inevitable chastisement. It joins other post-1381 narrations in their task of putting a quietus on rising—on the Rising—itself.

THE PROBLEM OF CLOSURE

Historical and literary narratives of revolt and repression offered a premature but highly persuasive rhetoric of closure that encouraged a view of the 1381 Rising as an event with a clear terminus and no afterlife at all.[24] This view influenced contemporaries, constituting one of the many political and cultural forces with which those who sought decisive change had unequally to contend. The effectiveness of such closed narratives, including those founded on a movement from revel to its rebuke, may be measured in a widespread belief that the Rising was unprecedented but unique, discontinuous with other manifestations of social struggle, and was socially and politically *sans issue*. We do not wholly escape these beliefs today.[25]

Narratives of wished-for closure can exert a great deal of influence on the interpretation of an event. But I have perhaps gone as far as I should in implying that a narrative can ever truly close itself or be closed, or that the door can be shut on all its inherent possibilities for continuation or contradiction. As a fragment, Chaucer's tale stands as a particularly suggestive instance of the problems that narratives have in closing themselves. Even granting the particular success of the Cook's account in underscoring Perkyn's moral and social descent, it nevertheless leaves him flourishing underground. He is welcomed by a sympathetic "compeer of his owene sort" (I.4419), a reveler who only pretends to participate in legitimate trade, and by an economically and morally emancipated wife who bleeds the brother-owning patriarchs of the city of their profits by "swiving" on the side.[26]

The fact that Chaucer did not finish Perkyn's story—that he left his prentice *snybbed* (I.4401) or decisively rebuked but still in play—has been discussed by Chaucerians according to all sorts of critical and codicological hypotheses that I will not attempt to summarize here. Let me just conclude by adding another: the energies of 1381 inscribed within Perkyn's brief bacchanal could be thrust from view, but their work was far from done. The aspirations of 1381 were not really brought to an end by the death of Tyler or by the return of the rebels to their homes or by the multiple judicial processes of 1382. Redirected and associated with other arenas of struggle, they resurfaced as parliamentary acknowledgment of the burden of taxation on the working poor, as local impetus for manumission, as religious dissent. Associated through the shared symbolic language of bacchanalia with the most turbulent social energies of its day—with energies, that is, that were by their nature unfinished and not subject to confident closure—Perkyn's story could hardly *be* finished in any satisfactory sense. We leave him as contemporary chroniclers left the rebels of 1381: underground, excluded from the official civil life, associated with illicit small accumulators who shadow and poach upon the sanctioned commercial activities of the day. We leave him, like the social tacticians described by Michel de Certeau, in secure control of no "proper place," still betting on a yet-to-be-narrated time in which his destinies will be revealed.[27]

5

Fictions of Time and Origin

Friar Huberd and the Lepers

Temporal Discontinuity in the "General Prologue"

Texts employ many strategies to extract meaning from time. One vital technique involves the construction of narrative sequences—arrangements of episodes that are diachronic, in the sense that they progress, that one thing follows another. At the highest level of organization these texts are also teleological in the sense that they entertain a destination, or at least "go somewhere." Yet another technique is antisequential, in the sense of supposing that time can be stopped, that an event can be arrested and displayed for static consideration. Yet another stabilizing stratagem secures the text itself in time, supposing that a text comes "from somewhere," that it enjoys a finite source or historical origin.

Naturally, such stabilizing strategies never entirely succeed. Supposedly progressive narratives divagate or tarry and lose sight of their presumed goals. Would-be synchronicities repeatedly bear the marks of time or "fall into" time. Supposed origins reveal themselves as imaginative back-formations or myths of origin. The whole point about texts and time is the inability of writing to prevent the temporal discord imported by the disparate prehistories, and unruly utopianisms, of the verbal materials from which the text is made. Texts are always getting ready to fly apart in time, to decompose into their own heterogeneous materials.

Yet, even if the text's ultimate temporal unruliness always finally trumps its own stabilizing strategies, we should not be indifferent to its attempts to organize time. Even if unsuccessful, such attempts neverthe-less "work," in the sense of accomplishing important meaning-making tasks along the way. Thus, even the discovery of the text as a nonunitary or dispersed temporal event is not simply a form of intellectual mischief-making; in the course of such an analysis, we are likely to draw closer to the work the text accomplishes, and the form of its accomplishment.

Chaucer's "General Prologue" is founded on one stabilizing strat-egy, which imagines, or pretends to imagine, that action can be arrested and relations can be synchronously displayed. Commonality is established by the narrative fact of the pilgrimage, and then further elaborated as the narrator freezes time there at the Tabard Inn in order to permit a di-lation upon his characters' varied identities (he will, he says, stop his "tale" or narration in order to tell the "condicioun" of each).[1] Here, he views his society of pilgrims as a totality and a simultaneity. His descrip-tion of the pilgrims joins a subset of other descriptive texts — including medieval pageants and progresses, sumptuary and other social codes and enumerations, poll tax provisions, portrait galleries, estates satires, and the like — in which time stands still for descriptive purposes. But time does not, of course, strictly stand still; given the historical embedded-ness of language itself, and the different temporal implications of de-scribed actions, any synchronous array quickly resolves itself into a va-riety of temporal perspectives.

So, too, does the seemingly static "Prologue" embrace time's asym-metries. Even while moving from its own beginning to its own end, it abounds in "flash-forwards" (the Miller leading the pilgrims out of town with his bagpipes) or "flashbacks" (the Knight hastening to join the pil-grim band). And so do the pilgrims themselves represent the fullest range of what I will call (after Ernst Bloch) "nonsynchronous temporalities."[2] To be sure, they are all there in one place. But they are far from inhabit-ing a single or synchronized time. Individual pilgrims are revealed as subject to the asymmetrical pressures of ecclesiastical time and mercan-tile time, liturgical time and historical time, traditionality and innova-tion, youth and age, priority and subsequence, the socially residual and the socially emergent. Each pilgrim finally inhabits a temporality all his or her own, not like that of any other. Ultimately, these differences will multiply, as the different pilgrims tell tales with radically varying tem-poral assumptions.

The thing I want to emphasize about the "General Prologue" is how easily and productively it bears these temporal contradictions, acknowledges their inevitability, allows them to proliferate as emblems of the inherent complexity of the Now. These temporal asymmetries are not just by-products of a text's inability to control time. Rather, revealing the complexity of the Now, they are our means of imaginative escape from time's apparent dominion. Concealed within their shifting planes is proliferation of vantage points—some despairing and some hopeful, some satiric and some admiring—on the purported present. Allowed and elaborated and placed in implicit contention, these vantage points generate alternative possibilities and potentially utopian perspectives. Not just aesthetic complexity but (to paraphrase Bloch) societal "gold" lies hidden in the joints and seams and recesses opened when different temporalities fail to cohere.[3]

"Fast Time" and Chaucer's Friar

The "General Prologue" mixes together pilgrims whose time is effectively over and those whose time has not yet come. Some, like the Knight, the Parson, and the Plowman, might be thought exemplars and advocates of "slow time." They do not, to be sure, float entirely free of all later-fourteenth-century social pressures. The Knight must make the most exemplary possible choices from among an array of rather sordid contemporary campaigns, and the ethical slim pickings afforded him by his corrupted field of social choice is what opens him to the "Terry Jones critique." The Plowman is an independent worker taking tempered advantage of a distinctively later-fourteenth-century labor market; in the years following the midcentury plague, his status as independent plowman hiring out his services is the foundation of his economic success.[4] Nevertheless, as so many commentators have recognized, their three portraits rely upon venerable (and partially superseded) values for their moral force.[5] Other pilgrims might be considered devotees or exemplars of "fast time," capitalizing on newly emergent social and institutional possibilities. These are pilgrims who have no stake in earlier values, whose advantage lies precisely in ignoring or suppressing elements of the past.

Among the devotees of "fast time" is Chaucer's Friar (I.208–69). His particular order is, in a sense, immaterial; we might consider him a composite,[6] though — especially because of the centrality of poverty issues in his portrait — I do not feel amiss in treating him as generally Franciscan. Even though the orders in question are now in their second century of existence, his membership in one of them scarcely inhibits his devotion to "fast time." After all, the Franciscan and other orders displayed considerable volatility of their own, devouring their founding doctrine of poverty in nothing flat. From the first approval of their (significantly now lost) rule of 1209, and then Francis's own last rather desperate attempt to reclaim lost ground on the issue of mandatory poverty in his *Testament* of 1225–26, barely two decades elapsed before the definitive subversion of Francis's own founding views with Gregory IX's papal bull *Quo elongati* in 1230, which held, among other things, that the *Testament* had no legal status.[7]

Unencumbered as he is by past history, Friar Huberd nevertheless contributes to its additional erasure, staging himself as the up-to-date and almost oppressively present representative of a thoroughly "presentist" institution. Not only has he the personality of a member of a twentieth-century service club, but he manifests a very specific devotion to the present-time augmentation of his "ordre," giving it his full support ("he was a noble post"), serving as its "licenciat," excelling in collection of silver for "the povre freres."

And so here we have a portrait of a friar utterly devoted to present-time intrigues, told by a pilgrim-narrator who vigorously aligns himself with his subject's point of view. How, in such a portrait — with its subject's own immersion in an ethically depleted present so enthusiastically seconded and narratively secured — is any sense of alternatives to be achieved? Yet alternatives are about to appear, for, to our presumed refreshment and relief, we are about to be cast from an indefensible present into all that the narrator and his Friar would ignore about the larger stream of time.

Huberd is always, in a sense, dogged by time, surrounded by deep mendicant history, which provides a standard against which he can be measured and found wanting. His desertion of Francis's ideals is so complete as, in a sense, to turn him into a kind of anti-Francis... and thus to turn our thoughts to the historical Francis whom he so catastrophically supplants. He is, after all, a deep and constant participant in all those defects which Francis abjured in order to constitute himself as a spiritual exemplar. Francis, brought up vain and proud, strove "to outdo all in the pomp of vainglory, in jokes, . . . in idle and useless talk, in songs, in soft and flowing garments" ("in pompa vanae gloriae praeire caeteros nitebatur, in iocis, in curiosis, in scurrilibus et inanibus verbis, in cantilenis, in vestibus mollibus et fluidis").[8] We now discover Huberd in an advanced state of the very condition the young Francis left behind. Although I would not go so far as to claim that Chaucer deliberately echoed the younger Francis's superseded behaviors, he does touch upon a remarkable cluster of them. Huberd (like his young predecessor) boundlessly develops his own capacity for chatter: "In alle the orders foure is noon that kan / So muchel of daliaunce and fair langage" (lines 210–11). He has a knack for music: "And certeinly he hadde a murye note: Wel koude he synge and pleyen on a rote" (lines 235–36). Whether or not soft and flowing, his garments are indisputably generously cut: "Of double worstede was his semycope, / That rounded as a belle out of the presse" (lines 262–63). Not simply enjoyed as a stage on the way to a more profound development, however, Huberd's vanities are fundamental to his existence; unchastened by the example of the leper, he lacks a way of disciplining or even interrogating his tendencies. Francis and Huberd are, in this sense, mirror images — not in the sense of reflections but in the sense of opposites or reversals: Francis emerges from vainglory into self-critique, even as Huberd cultivates vainglorious and antimendicant ideals.

Nevertheless, Huberd is also more explicitly criticized, by means of a historical marker that exposes him to critique by adding a more pointed perspective from somewhere outside his and the narrator's own rationalizations. I am speaking here of a deliberate depth effect, an effect that casts us out and into time, in this case by raising in a more emphatic way the issue of superseded or suppressed origins. This is the effect of which Roland Barthes so tellingly spoke in his *Camera Lucida,* when, discussing the moment at which history or historical complexity enters an otherwise simultaneous and static photograph, he introduces the concept of the *punctum.* As Barthes has it, the initial experience of the photograph attends to its *studium,* its pretense of simultaneity, an interpretative state enhanced by the picture's own orchestrated self-forgetting, or substitution of real prehistory for bogus or sentimentalized prehistory. But the function of the *punctum* is to "disturb" the tranquillity of the portrait's self-forgetting, to enable the reintroduction of Time and true "re-covery" or "anamnesis" via the rediscovery of the odd or excluded detail.[9]

Here, the *punctum* is unwittingly supplied by the narrator, who en-ters his text to argue in proper voice for Huberd's practice of conducting his tavern life in the presence of hostelers and tapsters rather than asso-ciating with lepers and beggars:

> For unto swich a worthy man as he
> Accorded nat, as by his facultee,
> To have with sike lazars aqueyntaunce.
> It is nat honest; it may nat avaunce,
> For to deelen with no swich poraille.
>
> (I.243–47)

The lazar, or leper, provides the added perspectival, or depth effect, of which I have spoken. One surprise of the leper's appearance is that Chau-cer returns him to the stage at a historical moment when actual lepers were becoming numerically (if not symbolically) less important than in previous centuries. There were, oddly, many fewer lepers in postplague England than in thirteenth-century Italy, with possibilities for lingering in their company correspondingly reduced.[10] For that matter, friars were themselves somewhat less evident on the fourteenth-century scene than the reader of Chaucer might suppose; for all the Wife of Bath's insistence on friars as ubiquitous as motes in a sunbeam, ecclesiastical scholars have long noted the numerical decline of the friars in the decades fol-lowing the Black Death.[11] Less a comment on contemporary history than on the deeper past, the leper's claim on the attention of friars and the dereliction of this friar for refusing the leper's company enter Chaucer's text as a riposte to the present and presentist concerns.

The leper enters the Friar's portrait by denial or negation, via the narrator's assertion that no reasonable person would hang around with trash like that. Accepting that dichotomy of Poet and Pilgrim which proved so powerful an analytical engine in the days of New Criticism, we might say that Chaucer the Poet is the leper's benign sponsor, intro-ducing him via a negative-that-is-really-positive (or, more simply, via irony) and deserving credit for all the havoc this presence must inevitably cause. Chaucer the Poet, in other words, becomes the intending spirit here, deliberately inserting a detail that calls the Friar's present conduct into question by invoking a past ideal. But intentions are hard to ascribe, and the labor of separating the voices of the Poet and the Pilgrim sometimes turns vain when the two voices flow back together again. One scholar who has thought deeply on this matter — Jill Mann in *Chaucer and Medieval Estates Satire* — isn't sure that Chaucer is as critical of the Friar as modern close readers have supposed.[12] Perhaps the simple thing is to say that, *wherever* the leper came from and *whatever* the underlying intent of Chaucer's sponsorship, the text offers him to us; and this is an offer that, once made, cannot be retracted. Once present within the text's bounds, the leper changes everything, leaves nothing as it was before.

The leper as *punctum* is a premier point at which time and history tangibly reenter this portrait, affording us a deep vantage point from which Huberd's present-day activities can be judged against a more complicated, and more historically rich, standard than Huberd's presentist world can afford. The lepers in question do not enter Chaucer's narrative in a unitary way, but are complexly hailed and arrive from more than one direction. They are, most obviously, the present-day lepers with whom Huberd might associate (but does not). They likewise exist outside time, in the sense that they, like Christ's poor, are "always with us," posing a timeless and inexhaustible moral demand. And, drawing more complexly on sedimented history and popular belief about history, they evoke the leper's meaning, or what the leper should have meant to the Franciscan order with its founding ideals.

The leper inhabits a different, and in some ways prior, temporality than that of the Friar, and his presence has the effect of returning the Friar to the criticism of time. Although lepers still existed in the second half of the fourteenth century, the end of the twelfth and the beginning of the thirteenth centuries were the distinctive time of the leper, as well as what might be considered the ethical discovery of the leprosarium. The leper was complexly, and crucially, bound up in the entire subject of mendicant origins — to the extent that, at one earlier moment in time, the two subjects could hardly be disentwined. The merest mention of the leper, in the context of Huberd's portrait, cannot help but return us to the subject of Franciscan origins, with all their unavoidable implications for the present.

Schooled in this matter by Nietzsche and Foucault, we know that origins themselves are never unitary or obvious in their application; multiplicity and contradiction always await us at the point of imagined origin. This leper asks us, in effect, to practice genealogy, in the Nietzschean sense, which is to imagine multiple origins, unfixed origins, origins of diverse import for the future. For Nietzschean genealogy consists in discovery of the event's inevitably discontinuous or heterogeneous core. As Gary Shapiro puts it so well, "*The Genealogy of Morals* insists that there is no single origin but only opposition and diversity no matter how far back we go."[13] The event, subjected to genealogical scrutiny, turns out (now in the words of Foucault) to be "fabricated in a piecemeal fashion from alien forms," to be disparate in origin and meaning, and invariably nonpresent in itself—divided or riven with respect to both external sources and internal chronologies.[14] Twigged by Friar Huberd's neglect, we go looking for a Franciscan origin, for a raison d'être, and we will have much to learn—even if not precisely what I, at any rate, expected. I turn, then, from the textual present to the textual past, in order to ask what the leper meant, or was thought to mean, to Friar Huberd's Franciscan forebears.

THE LEPER AND MENDICANT ORIGINS

The poor, and especially the leper, play what may fairly be called a "constitutive" role in the early history of the Franciscan movement, in the sense that the movement required them for its own self-definition. One could go so far as to say that, without leprosy, the Franciscan movement as we know it could not have occurred. Or at any rate Francis says so, in one of his rare explicitly autobiographical moments:

> This is how God inspired me, Brother Francis, to embark upon
> a life of penance. When I was in sin, the sight of lepers nauseated
> me beyond measure; but then God himself led me into their
> company, and I had pity on them. When I had once become ac-
> quainted with them, what had previously nauseated me became
> a source of spiritual and physical consolation for me. After that
> I did not wait long before leaving the world.[15]

Here the leper is terribly consequential, flaring up at a crucial definitional moment, offering the very pivot upon which Francis turns away from the world and toward an otherworldly standard of conduct. The leper is introduced less in the capacity in which Chaucer's allusion might suppose we should find him, as an occasion of charity, than as a crucial occasion of spiritual ascesis, a test case of whether the movement's early followers can overcome their natural aversion to persons less fortunate than themselves. The leper is, in this sense, a constitutive antagonism, a kernel of aggressive distress, not so much to be eliminated via charity but to be employed as a goad or stimulus to self-mastery on the part of the beholder, who, reining in his disgust, demonstrates a new spiritual capacity.[16]

We are very far here from the reading of the leper as a necessary object of charity, let alone as an object of spiritual imitation in privileged possession of aspects of Christ's own bodily humiliation and suffering. All forms of charity involving gifts of money or coin were, in fact, forbidden to the early friars; this we are told in Thomas of Celano's *Second Life,* in an anecdote even more revealing for its incidentals than its main prescription. Finding a coin on the road near the leper hospital, one brother wishes to misspend it by offering it "to the servile lepers, as financial offerings" ("leprosis pecuniae famulis offerendum").[17] Here presented as inexhaustible wheedlers of funds, the lepers are less occasions of charity than convenient illustrations of whatever points need to be made.

The leper plays a crucial role — an indispensable role, if Francis is to be believed — in his own self-constitution as a particular kind of devotee . . . yet the importance of the leper rests in his value as symbol and provocation, as a form of disgust to be overcome, rather than as an intransigent social problem admissible to any form of solution. Which is to say that the leper provides a tactical occasion, rather than posing a permanent ethical demand. His symbolic, as opposed to more obstinate or tangible, status within the Franciscan text in turn facilitates his swift disappearance. The progression — from literal leper to figurative leper to no leper at all — can be traced in the earliest Franciscan texts.[18] Thomas of Celano's *First Life,* composed around 1228, describes the reformation of Francis's outlook, at an early stage in his life, when he was still clad in secular clothes:

> So greatly loathsome was the sight of lepers to him at one time, he used to say that, in the days of his vanity, he would look at their houses only from a distance of two miles and he would

hold his nostrils with his hands. But now... he met a leper one day and, made stronger than himself, he kissed him. From then on he began to despise himself more and more, until, by the mercy of the Redeemer, he came to perfect victory over himself.[19]

Yet in his *Second Life,* composed circa 1247–48, Thomas of Celano recasts Francis's experience. Again he meets a leper and again finds him abhorrent—naturally ("naturaliter"), Thomas adds. Steeling himself, he gives the leper a kiss, and, when the leper puts out his hand "as though to receive something" ("cum manum quasi aliquid accepturus leprosus protenderet"), money as well. But then we read, "And immediately mounting his horse, Francis looked here and there about him; but though the plain lay open and clear on all sides, and there were no obstacles about, he could not see the leper anywhere" ("leprosum illum minime vidit").[20] A real-world event has become a miracle. In the process, an actual leper has been converted to a figurative one, an epiphenomenon of the miracle itself. The latter version is, incidentally, the version embraced by Bonaventure in his definitive *Legenda maior.* Nor should we be surprised; Bonaventure's work is marked by continuing minimization of the leprous presence, with lepers consistently transformed into poor people and lazar houses into huts, humble dwellings, and the like. Thus, understandably, since Bonaventure's *Legenda* is its primary source, do we find the leper conspicuously absent from the account of Francis's conversion and the early days of the order in the Giottoesque Francis cycle in the Basilica at Assisi.[21]

Nor should we be surprised to find the same process replicated in the Franciscan rule. The rule of 1209 being lost, the earliest extant version is that of 1221, where we read that the friars "should be glad to live among social outcasts, among the poor and helpless, the sick and the lepers, and those who beg by the wayside."[22] Yet, from the 1223 rule, this provision has been expunged. Less a concrete occasion of charity than an abstract emblem of abjection, the actual leper is just as well ignored, as Francis was to do, winning praise by visiting a lazar house and then displaying his sanctity by the extent of his abstraction, paying no more attention to the devotion of its inhabitants than if "he were a lifeless corpse."[23]

So grudgingly present, and disappearing so rapidly from the official Franciscan scene, the leper might in a sense hardly have ever been there at all. Yet the leper still enters the stream of subsequent history—though under collateral, rather than Franciscan, sponsorship. For, with respect to lepers, Francis's was not the only game in town. Concurrently with Francis's own example, at times by his example and at times independently of it, other contemporary spirituals and spiritual movements were likewise finding the leper indispensable to their own self-realization.

Already in the late twelfth century, Yvette of Huy betook herself to her local leprosarium. According to her biographer, Hugh of Floreffe, at twenty-three years of age—that is, in 1185—she gave up her worldly goods and moved to the derelict chapel in which they were housed, "leaving all that she had in order to make herself more vile in the eyes of man and more beautiful in the eyes of God."[24] Anticipating a theme common to subsequent female spiritual biography, she ministers to the lepers, not only in order to humble herself by overcoming aversion, but charitably, for the love of Christ within them: "She laid the lepers in bed and helped them to rise and gave the most faithful service to all with all care and reverence for she believed that Christ is in all things and was seen to revere Christ in each of them." So did the Beguines of the early-thirteenth-century Lowlands seize upon occasions for involvement with lepers and lazar houses in order to establish for themselves a new spiritual demarcation. Jacques de Vitry tells, for example, of Mary of Oignies (1176–1213), whose first steps toward a spiritual vocation included resolving upon a caste marriage and her and (initially) her husband's decision to take up residence in the leper house of Willambroux[25]—a residence she ultimately left only when the crush of friends and the curious who came to visit her there became overgreat.[26]

Linkages, and mutual curiosities, can be established between the Franciscans and the Beguines.[27] Yet the turn toward the leper may also be seen as an expression of early-thirteenth-century spirituality more broadly conceived; and in this regard the importance of devout women and mystics must be broadly acknowledged. Consider, in this regard, the example of Elisabeth of Hungary, Francis's younger contemporary and an avid early sponsor of Franciscanism within her husband's domain. As told by her earliest biographer, Caesarius of Heisterbach, and her spiritual director, Conrad of Marburg, Elisabeth was constantly involved with lepers, acted as a kind of magnet for them, and insisted even in the face of opposition from her family and her spiritual director upon affording them sustenance, shelter, consolation, and familiar love. We read in Caesarius, for example, that she took occasion of a feast day to gather lepers in her lodging, washing their hands and feet, and earnestly kissing ulcerous and scarred places on their bodies ("In quadam cena domini plurimos leprosos hospicio collegit, pedes eorum et manus lavans, et ipsa loca magis ulcerosa et horrenda deosculabatur") — avid in seeking them out ("Ubicunque enim leprosos reperit"), all for the love of Christ, whose sufferings they exemplify ("Nec mirum; Christum in illis aspexit et fovit").[28]

Even the draconian Conrad, who shared with Elisabeth's family a distaste for the idea of lepers in the home, offers us evidence of her penchant for smuggling them in. In her dossier for sanctification, Conrad complains that, one object of her charity having died, she then without his knowledge hid within her house a leprous virgin, accepting the burden of every office of humanity, not only feeding and covering her and washing her, but even taking off her shoes, supplicating her family that they not be offended by these things ("ne super hiis offenderetur").[29] Conrad's typically extreme reaction to learning of this conduct was to exact corporeal punishment: "Having realized this — God forbid — because I was concerned that she had not confessed it, I beat her most gravely" ("quia verebar eam inde infici, gravissime castigavi"). Nevertheless, Conrad soon rid himself of the leper ("Tandem leprosa per me reiecta"). No sooner did Conrad absent himself, though, than Elisabeth was at it again, taking on a poor, scabby boy, without a hair on his head, and attempting a cure by bathing and medicating him.

Elisabeth's proclivity was so apparent, and so central, that it promoted subsequent inventions. In midcentury, Dietrich von Apolda wrote more popularly of Elisabeth's activities, including an episode set in Nuremberg Castle, when she took advantage of her husband's absence to bathe a leper and settle him in her lord's bed.[30] Her scandalized father-in-law led his son to the bed, saying, "Do you notice how Elisabeth is accustomed to infect your bedclothes?" Yet God intervened, revealing to the devout prince, via a vision or inner sight, the image of Christ crucified there in his bed ("Tunc aperuit deus devoti principis interiores oculos viditque in thoro suo positum crucifixum"). Assuaged, the pious prince encouraged his holy wife to summon lepers to his bed on a regular basis ("Qua contemplacione consolatus pius princeps rogavit sacram coniugem suam in stratu suo leprosos frequenter collocaret"). As indicated by these Christological associations — more fully developed as we progress in Dietrich's account—we encounter a different vector here, one that more fully realizes the potentialities of the leper, not just as occasion of personal ascesis, but as a basis for associating Christian love with invigorated social critique.

THE PAST AS UTOPIAN SURPLUS

Nietzschean genealogy famously proposes that, when we go looking for an origin, we never find a singular or simple one. A further, less recognized but equally important, Nietzschean postulate is that, whether actual or imagined, origins never stand still; that we are never to be surprised when we find an originary idea wandering far from its own starting point: "The cause of the origin of a thing and its eventual utility, its actual employment and place in a system of purposes, lie worlds apart; whatever exists . . . is again and again reinterpreted to new ends, taken over, transformed, and redirected."[31] The quest for an origin reveals, not a "true origin," but what might be styled a "usable past," a past eligible for diversion to new and potentially important purposes. Although Foucault's use of Nietszche is often interpretative rather than literal, he seems rather directly in his predecessor's spirit when he argues that an origin, once disestablished as a source of unchallenged authority, is eligible for new use. He argues that "every origin of morality from the moment it stops being pious . . . has value as a critique."[32] His meaning, if I understand it correctly, is that the genealogist uses his or her tools of analysis to demonstrate the delusional quality of our ideas about origin— including, in this case, the fact that the Franciscan leper was as much a matter of personal ascesis as of charitable enterprise, as well as the evanescent nature of any sustained attention to the leper on any grounds at all. Nevertheless, even when we deal roughly with the matter of origin, we simultaneously discover that the fleeting centrality of the leper to Franciscan origins still possesses an afterlife and potential value: as social critique. Present at the beginning as a "mixed case"—partly as the ground of a personal test and partly as an object of charity—the leper resurfaces within Chaucer in the latter aspect.

The leper's appearance in Chaucer's late-fourteenth-century poem fractures time. He is, of course, the leper of Chaucer's own day, the leper with whom Huberd might have been consorting, instead of taverners and rich people. But more than that he is the leper of fictional Franciscan history, the leper without whom the order could not have been founded or even devised in thought, the leper who sprang so briefly but persuasively into view, only, in a sense, to go "underground" — to haunt mendicant and Christian conscience as an unassimilated demand. For Huberd's leper reinstates a demand, which is that we imagine a different and more diverse Franciscan origin than its devolution into practices like Huberd's would presuppose. Even when largely expunged from the official transcript and subsisting mainly on its later margins, the leper remains latently available as what Bloch terms a moral "surplus" — an unexhausted reservoir of past beliefs and practices upon which the present can draw. This is the sense in which Bloch explains to us that the archaic and the apparently superseded, on the one hand, and the utopian, on the other, finally become one.

Speaking of the "deep glance" that is the recourse to the past, Bloch says:

> A deep glance proves its worth by becoming doubly profound. Not only downwards, which is the easier, more literal way of getting to the bottom of things. But rather there is also a depth upwards and forwards which takes up into itself profound material from below. . . . [The utopian function includes] those archetypes which still arouse consternation and which have possibly been left over from the age of a mythical consciousness as categories of the imagination, consequently with a non-mythical surplus that has not been worked up.[33]

Without denying historical specificity, we might also regard the leper as an archetype that retains the power to arouse consternation and that, not having been "worked out," still possesses an admonitory ethical power. And this is a power to which we would have enjoyed no access, had we been confined to Chaucer's text's own — in this case ethically depleted — present.

A text's *inability* to stay in its own present is foundational to its effectiveness as a vehicle of reform. A text's temporal discontinuities thrust it into a zone of mixed perspective in which beliefs or actions must stand the competition of ideals more commonly attached to the unsuperseded past or the unrealized present. The leper's reemergence within Chaucer's account of Huberd's world tears a veil—sunders a careful containment, opens an unruly possibility. Chaucer's leper stages the kind of flare-up described by Walter Benjamin—who had also read his Nietzsche, and who celebrates the return of the past, not as a link in a consistent narrative chain, but episodically, momentarily, becoming available at a moment of danger.[34] This is the past, not as systematically or routinely available, but waiting to be tripped, provoked, or sprung, as an affront to presentist complacency.

A wrinkle in the text's time opens a door through which we potentially pass to the utopian—a space between what is and what used to be or might be. Teased by our text to desert present time and to enter the wider stream of time in the quest for an origin, we discover an unexhausted, usable "surplus"—a font of critique and socially transformative hope.

6

CHAUCER'S *TROILUS* AS
TEMPORAL ARCHIVE

My reflection begins with the archive, the repository. I am stimulated in this discussion by Derrida's *Archive Fever*,[1] in which he suggests that an archive incorporates two different impulses: one conservative or stasis-seeking, one progressive or institutive. The "fever" in the archive, as Derrida describes it, is the fever for repetition, a bias in favor of nonrenewal that inscribes the death drive at its very heart. Yet, I wish somewhat to separate myself from Derrida, by reflecting upon the more constructive or potentially progressive aspect of the archive. This is the "institutive" sense in which the archive is seen as a repository of meanings that await discovery. In this aspect, the archive does not arrest time, but rather exists as an unstable amalgam of unexhausted past and unaccomplished future. Open toward the future—that is, toward the activities of future interpreters—the archive consists of texts that await meaning, part of whose realization includes what they "will have meant."[2]

What can be said of the archive can also, I believe, be said of its constituent units—those texts which we preserve from the past. Each such text, in my view, serves its own archival function. It "archives" language, motifs, and, inevitably, ideas of time. For, whatever its declared intentions or apparent purposes, a text cannot escape time or avoid temporal implication. Some texts (like *Troilus*) actually talk about time, accept their own status in time as overt subject matter, and have a great deal to say on the subject. Others (especially narrative texts, again like *Troilus*) model or simulate time's passing, enact an idea of time as a concomitant of their own narrative processes—for every narrative is also an implied theory of time, a theory of time in action. And, finally, no text fails to bear within itself a range of alien temporalities, imported into its bounds as unavoidable part and parcel of the words and images of which it is made. No text, that is, can be temporally self-consistent, for the very reason that it does not own its words and cannot specify their prehistories. By virtue of the different prehistories and associations of the words in which it is written, each text *harbors* different notions of time. And this too is very true of *Troilus*.

TROILUS MODELS TIME: THE IMPOSSIBLE PRESENT

Troilus executes writing's most solemn cultural assignment, which is to connect the past with the future. It is always about the burdens of its own prehistory: the abduction of Helen, the narrowed options imposed by the precondition of the Greek siege. And it is no less about its own unhappy future: the end of love, the fall of Troy, Troilus's own death. It is founded in a moment of enlarged temporal vision—the prophet Calchas's recognition of Troy's inevitable doom—a recognition it always tries to forget and never succeeds in forgetting.

One might say, drawing on a more recently popular image: this ship's iceberg was already out there when it set sail; an aspect of destiny rumored, discussed, but never embraced ("taken on board?") as an inevitability. I mention this "schlock icon" in order to suggest that our culture has its own fascination with the concept of a present held hostage to the past and future. A present that, however banal, gains a certain luminosity from our retrospective knowledge of its ephemerality. Just as I was writing this essay I encountered a story in the *New York Times* about the very high auction price of a boarding card for the *Titanic*. The boarding card (framed, auctioned by Sotheby's, reverenced) is the icon, or mark, of a wound in time, a moment when time is fractured or divided within itself, a major part of its meaning reliant upon retrospective illumination.

Arrested between past and future, what it did mean and what it will mean, *Troilus* finds itself unable to define its *own* moment, to capture its fleeting Now. Always divided between an unsuperseded past and an unachieved future, its narrative offers at best the evanescent present described by Augustine in his great meditation on time (*Confessions,* bk.

11): a present sliding ceaselessly into the past or unremittingly devoured by the future. It offers us an "impossible present," a moment that cannot be fully grasped or satisfactorily enjoyed. This is not to say that *Troilus* is not "present-seeking." It wishes constantly (and it contains a character *who* wishes constantly) for closure, repetition, and stasis. But it also constantly acknowledges the impossibility of standing still—the impossibility of fixity or self-closure to time.[3]

Symptomatically, nobody in this poem ever knows what time it is. Our narrator protests that he didn't know how long Troilus courted Criseyde, or how long their period of happiness lasted, or how long it took for Diomede to seduce her, or how long Troilus waited before he gave up. The narrator's temporal uncertainty is only a pretense (for the poem is undergirded by an iron and inexorable chronology of events), but it sorts well with the characters' experience, which is to be constantly befuddled about their own, and each other's, temporality. For the characters of this poem inhabit what Ernst Bloch, in an admittedly unwieldy but analytically irreplaceable term, calls "nonsynchronous temporalities."[4] Which is to say that (although they inhabit the same space and even, in the case of Troilus and Criseyde, the same romance) they are noncontemporary with each other.

Troilus (the character) is for slow time: swoons and langours, bedridden bouts of depression and stasis so complete as to approximate death in life. Whereas his friend Pandarus is so sped-up and goal-centered as to seem a product of another kind of society altogether. Even their discursive modes bespeak incompatible temporal ideals, with Troilus wedded to the repetitive atemporalities of "complaint time" and Pandarus choosing the forward-moving and timebound velocities of pure narrative. Criseyde introduces yet another temporal perspective, reliant upon moment-to-moment calculation of advantage, equally estranged from Troilus's unproductive dilations and Pandarus's extended intrigues and overintricate causal sequences.[5]

What the characters know is that the Now is inherently frail, that it resolves back into what it never stopped being or what it has not yet become. Meaning, in this state of affairs, is inevitably postponed or thought to lie elsewhere. For all Pandarus's daily bustle and for all Criseyde's intelligent calculation, neither inhabits his or her moment. Each, as in the case of Pandarus's nagging worries about his own neglected love affair, exhibits what may be called "nostalgia for the present"—a sense that the present is a place they cannot go, that they can hardly even visit. Their thoughts turn most often to the future, and to how their actions will appear to readers of a subsequent time. (As well they might, considering what Henryson will do to Criseyde and Shakespeare to the entire cast of characters!) Pandarus uneasily (and correctly) predicts that, were his operations as "meene," or go-between, widely known, "al the world upon it wolde crie" (III.277). And Criseyde ominously (and correctly) predicts that she will not fare well in the marketplace of reputation:

> Allas, of me, unto the worldes ende,
> Shal neyther ben ywriten nor ysonge
> No good word, for thise bokes wol me shende.
> O, rolled shal I ben on many a tonge!
>
> (V.1058–61)

Like Criseyde, the poem as a whole waits to receive its meaning; observes different temporalities but "archives" them against a later discovery of what they "will have meant."

These uneasy attitudes toward past actions and future renown are replicated in the author's own representation of himself as torn between a respectful wish to join the ancients and an edgy concern for the ultimate reception of his literary efforts. I refer, of course, to the leave-taking in which he declares his book on the one hand "subgit...to alle poesye" (V.1790) and to revere the steps of Virgil, Ovid, Homer, Lucan, and Statius, and on the other hand to risk an uncertain reception as a manuscript circulating beyond authorial control:

> So prey I God that...
> ...red wherso thow be, or elles songe,
> That thow be understonde...
>
> (V.1795, 1797–98)

To his characters and his authorial persona Chaucer attributes the anxiety-producing knowledge that meaning awaits them and will be retrospectively conferred, and that they have no reason to be sanguine about this process.

TROILUS'S TEMPORAL UNCONSCIOUS

The precariousness of this poem's surface is, in turn, restated at a different level of meaning. For this poem also possesses something very like a temporal unconscious, constituted by the hodgepodge of different prehistories and temporal assumptions borne by its many acknowledged and unacknowledged sources.[6] This hidden temporal heterogeneity is signaled or overtly acknowledged at the text's own surface—but falsely or misleadingly so. Thus, the narrator pays bogus homage to Lollius, Dares, Dictys, Homer, and other unconsulted authorities, even as it conceals its own major debt to Boccaccio's *Filostrato*. But, scholarship and the text's own incidental admissions allow us to disaggregate its relatively consistent surface into a plethora of segments with radically different experiences of, and assumptions about, time. These segments include not only Chaucer's many borrowings from Boccaccio's *Filostrato* (itself an amalgam of various historically derived sources), but also innumerable lyrics, letters, songs, complaints, Boethian utterances, saws and proverbs, scraps of sincere and bogus history, traditional invocations, and the like— each with an implied temporality of its own.

As ordinary readers, we do not usually perform such radical acts of disaggregation. But source study, and the disaggregation of texts, is an operation we scholars learn how to perform. The knowledge it conveys, the knowledge of the "expert practitioner," is gained at a price: the price of certain, more immediate enjoyments, in favor of other, more spare or specialized ones. (I might here mention one of the special themes of my ultimate predecessor, J. R. R. Tolkien. I take him often in his fictions to write about the price of "wising up"—the substitution of special knowledge for uncomplicated enjoyment and the price of that substitution.) Whatever its cost to spontaneity, the specialist knowledge of the literary scholar—who can disassemble a text into disparate sources and influences—offers its own distinctive enjoyments. And it also offers insights not to be achieved by other means, one of which I want to pursue here.

Allow me to illustrate *Troilus*'s myriad textual prehistories with a single example. You will recall that Troilus, having glimpsed Criseyde at the temple, returns to his chamber to sigh, groan, and mirror her in his mind, and to think about how "to arten" her to love, and the composition of a song turns out to be his first recourse. As composed by Troilus, and as ostensibly reported word for word by Lollius, and as clearly demarked in the text (and by scribes who accept Chaucer's cue and title it "Canticus Troili"), it consists of three verse stanzas, the first of which I will quote here:

> If no love is, O God, what fele I so?
> And if love is, what thing and which is he?
> If love be good, from whennes cometh my woo?
> If it be wikke, a wonder thynketh me,
> When every torment and adversite
> That cometh of hym may to me savory thinke,
> For ay thurst I, the more that ich it drynke.
>
> (I.400–406)

As a few initiates within Chaucer's audience may have known, and as has certainly been known since 1582, when Thomas Watson composed a headnote comparing his translation to Chaucer's own, these stanzas are a rather direct translation of Petrarch's sonnet 132, written and circulated before, and then included within, the 1359 version of his *Canzoniere*—the only undoubted translation of a Petrarch sonnet known in English before Wyatt.[7]

And here we have what is, in at least a mild way, a "scandal" for traditional literary history. This fact, of Petrarch-in-Chaucer, is well enough known and has been a staple of editorial annotation in all modern editions of Chaucer (at least since Robert Bell's edition in 1854)—with each editor, of course, introducing it in such a way as urbanely to imply that it is a routine issue from his own stock of general knowledge. But the unresolved problem resides in a scantly acknowledged contradiction between one thing popularly known—Petrarch as Chaucer's predecessor and as 'available' to Chaucer—and another thing popularly known—Petrarch as a harbinger of the Renaissance, an incarnation of the early modern, with Chaucer resting docile in his own period, the later medieval. Here within the ostensibly ordered surface of the *Troilus* we encounter a kind of fold or wrinkle in time—or time at least as literary history normally portrays it. For the temporality of the Petrarch sonnet is, at least in terms of what it *will* mean or will have meant—"nonsynchronous" with its surroundings. Contrasted with the aube or the complaint or any of the other lyric forms inhabiting Chaucer's poem,[8] it contains a predictive kernel, an intimation of the "not-yet," that thing which has not yet happened being the remarkable expansion of Petrarchan influence in the fifteenth and, especially, sixteenth centuries.

IMPRESSIONIST CÉZANNE?

A decade ago I attended an exhibition at the National Gallery in Washington, D.C. It was a re-creation of the first impressionist exhibition, held at the Boulevard des Capucines in Paris in 1874.

Although, like any exhibit or show, this one consisted of disparate pictures, it possessed that synchrony or simultaneity which results from their display at a single time and place. This simultaneity was, in fact, twofold, in that the National Gallery show was a repetition and reaffirmation of the common endeavor that resulted in the 1874 convergence at the Boulevard des Capucines. That first show additionally possessed a core of artists whose work underscored its unity through a sharing out of traits: Degas, Monet, Morisot, Pissarro, Renoir. All may be said in one way or another to exemplify qualities identified by Mallarmé in his strikingly prescient 1876 essay, "The Impressionists and Edouard Manet":[9] affinity to the open air, simple color, palpitating movement, natural (and hence surprising) perspective, the arbitrarity of the frame, and so on. Mallarmé himself observes the remarkable affinity of Monet, Sisley, and Pissarro.

Nevertheless, no sooner was the affinity of these re-collected works noted than one began to notice difference — such as the stylistic difference between the more painterly colorists Monet and Morisot and the more linear and draftsmanly Degas. But also, with the advantage of hindsight, one could notice another kind of difference, proceeding from differing relations to history and tradition. Certain residual tendencies were, for example, exemplified by the rather backward-looking work of Stanislas Lépine, working under the influence of Corot and other earlier painters. Nor could one, from the vantage point of the late twentieth century, help but notice a contrary and emergent tendency, as exemplified by those canvases which seemed somehow oddly lodged in relation to the future, somehow predictive of the "not-yet."[10] And this brings me to what was, for me, the surprise — or perhaps I should even say "jolt" — of the exhibition. For, viewable upon entrance to the first impressionist show — and perhaps through curatorial mischief viewable immediately upon entrance—was a painting, *Paysage à Auvers,* by that noted "postim-pressionist," Cézanne.

Cézanne was an active and consenting member of the group that planned and staged the 1874 impressionist exhibition. In fact, he not only belonged in that show, but was already an old-timer when he appeared there. With the exquisite condescension endemic to the reviewer's art, Zola observed in his notice on the 1874 exhibition that "Paul Cézanne, who has been struggling for a long time, unquestionably has the temperament of a great painter."[11] Nevertheless, something in Cézanne's appearance in that show remains anomalous. Seeking to understand the anomaly better, I went on a subsequent day to see a closely related work hung elsewhere in the National Gallery under the title *House of Père Lacroix.* This second canvas shares a room with Sisley, Morisot, and others, and my research into these matters was furthered by the appearance of a typically verbose and emphatic tour guide, whose bearing suggested a general affinity with the "false guide" known to us through medieval dream visions. This guide announced, "Cézanne is a *post*impressionist and shouldn't be in this room. They've got him cataloged wrong." And, in a good protoacademic move, the guide cited various postimpressionist tendencies—including Cézanne's precocious cubism and his anticipation of van Gogh's heavy (and undisguised) brush stroke—in support of his position.

We confront a paradox. As we have seen from the 1874 exhibition, and as confirmed by Cézanne's own associations and self-identifications of the 1870s, he had every right to be there in the room with Sisley and Morisot, and was not miscataloged at all—five hundred art history textbooks notwithstanding. No less true is the presence of such stylistic tendencies as his two-dimensional canvas and his near-cubist division of space, which have enabled subsequent generations of artists and viewers to form a retrospective relation to his work differing in kind from their relation to Pissarro or Monet or Degas. And so the authors of standard art history books are not entirely wrong to discern something in Cézanne's work that associates him with subsequent developments—something that marks him as subsequent to those contemporaries among whom he appeared in 1874.

On the one hand, *Paysage* was fully entitled to its position there on the wall at the Boulevard des Capucines in 1874. On the other hand, it might have rattled a bit there on the wall, containing as it did an imperceptible (or at most barely perceptible) tremor of the new—a tremor that, coupled with a knowledge of subsequent cultural developments, built for the observer of 1988 into a full-scale "shock." This same shock rests—latent and *in potentia*—at the heart of every historical moment. Often, as in this case, its revelation is a function of retrospectivity—a by-product and consolation of the viewer's own belatedness. It is available to the viewer who glimpses, from the standpoint of retrospectivity, those discontinuities which may be read off as harbingers of eventual outcomes. This viewer may be said, in a certain sense, to know more about historical actors than they knew about themselves. Yet, in another sense, we may say that a viewer's special knowledge enables recovery of what should have been known all along: a temporal multiplicity or uncertainty at the heart of each historical event.

"RENAISSANCE" CHAUCER?

"Renaissance" Petrarch within "medieval" Chaucer is like "postimpressionist" Cézanne in the "impressionist" show—an apparent contradiction. I say "apparent contradiction" because we must always remember that any scandal here is a consequence of our own categories and terminologies, explanatory superimpositions upon a situation that may have caused Cézanne or Chaucer no distress at all.

The impressionists, for one thing, did not at first know they were impressionists. The organizers of that first show called themselves "the anonymous society of painters, sculptors, engravers, etc." They *became* impressionists only after the fact, beginning with the introduction of the term later in the same year, and then by a skeptic rather than a partisan.[12] Nor, by the same token, did Chaucer know himself "medieval" and certainly did not know Petrarch as "Renaissance," let alone "early modern"! They presumably thought they were just fine, living in their moment, without benefit of terminology—except when medieval people occasionally for rhetorical purposes of their own called themselves "men of today," *moderni*. To ask them to live in any other way would overattach them to time, to an unnuanced time that nobody actually lives. Or, worse still, to award them that most dubious distinction available to the more traditional sort of art historian, who, if not seeing an artist as unambigu-

ously representative of a monolithic period, consigns him or her to the
dreaded noncategory of The Transitional.

We must not let terms like "medieval" and "Renaissance" get the
better of us, by allowing them to oversimplify situations or to override
the complexity of historical actors' self-understanding. A revisitation of
Chaucer's text enables us to register the special qualities of his medieval/
Renaissance moment, its inherently mixed and unresolved character. Presenting itself neither as wholly unexceptional or as wholly exceptional,
this moment is actually, as we might expect, both at once.

First, on the side of the *nonexceptionality* of Petrarch's appearance:
Written some thirty years before Chaucer's poem, Petrarch's sonnet is
its perfectly plausible stylistic near-contemporary. Its paradoxes (or, as
Thomas Watson would describe them in 1582, its "contrarieties")[13] were
already established in European poetry well before Petrarch, bolstered
both by the imagistic precedent of Provençal love poetry and by the an-
titheses encouraged within scholastic discourse. Jean de Meun, drawing
on Alain de Lille, already in the thirteenth century thought the figure
ripe for playful elaboration;[14] Reason in the translation of the *Romaunt*
tells the Lover that

> Love, it is an hateful pees,
> A free acquitaunce, withoute relees,
> A trouthe, fret full of falsheede,
> A sikerness all set in drede.
> In herte is a dispeiryng hope,
> And full of hope, it is wanhope;
> Wise woodnesse, and wod resoun;
> A swete perell in to droun;
> An hevy birthen, lyght to bere.
>
> (Lines 4703–11)

Petrarch's sonnet is richly arrayed in a diction that Chaucer's contemporaries would have had every reason to regard as well established within
their own literary horizon. Thus, it is no surprise within the translation
itself that Chaucer shows himself capable of augmenting Petrarch's poetic statements, showing himself master of a kind of rudimentary Petrarchan *langue* within which he creates such *paroles* as "for ay thurst I

the more that ich it drynke" (line 406) and "vn-wery... I feynte" (line 410).[15]

Nevertheless, we do find within (and beyond) Chaucer marks of the *exceptionality* and strangeness of this sonnet he has chosen for translation. Chaucer treats it with a kind of provisionality, not about this or that conceit, but about the entire translation exercise. I find this provisionality, for example, in the fourth line of Chaucer's lyric, when he pauses and, as it were, steps out of the Petrarchan frame to declare the whole business a bewilderment: "a wonder thynketh me." Or in the eleventh line of the lyric, when he brackets "swete harm" to declare it "so queynte." Or when, in a characteristically histrionic and self-dramatizing turn that has a little to do with Petrarch and a lot to do with Troilus, Chaucer concludes his translation with the add-on, "I dye."

In attributing a certain wariness to Chaucer's treatment of the sonnet, I do not, by the way, mean to associate myself with the recent contention of early modernists that the "subjectivity" afforded medieval characters like Troilus must necessarily differ in kind from that afforded within the early modern period. To be sure, Petrarch and Watson do include a line about the narrator's uncertainty ("I waue in doubt what helpe I shall require") reworked by Chaucer into a more general question that points out and away rather than in toward the speaker ("Allas, what is this wondre maladie?"). Yet at other points Chaucer deliberately redirects the sonnet's issues in a way that implies the presence of a speaker with as much interiority as we could wish. Watson's "what is it then?" becomes Troilus's "what fele I so?" And Watson's rather nonspecific "how chance I waile?" becomes in Chaucer a specific question about Troilus's interior state: "ffrom whennes cometh my waillynge and my pleynte?" Of course, the subjectivity that Joel Fineman, for example, claims for the Shakespearean sonnet is not a more "authentic" or psychologically deeper inwardness anyway, but a language effect, a consequence of the thwarting of a language of praise by partially acknowledged impedances and deficiencies in the object of adoration.[16] Nor is Troilus's language to be exempt from these pressures within the course of Chaucer's poem; the preliminary tumult of this embedded lyric will give way to many more and deeper-seeming consternations before this narrative is through with him.

Even setting aside this pseudo- or nonissue of Renaissance interiority, however, Chaucer nevertheless seems to find other grounds on which to hold Petrarch's sonnet at a certain distance. He entertains it as a stance, worthy of interrogation, but ultimately to be rejected. Elizabethan sonneteers might seem to hold Petrarch at a similar distance, but they do not, really. Yes, they groan constantly about the necessity of laboring under the burden of belated Petrarchanism. Thus, Mercutio's jibe at Romeo: "Now is he for the numbers that Petrarch flow'd in" (2.4.39–40). And thus Sidney at the very origin of the Elizabethan sonnet sequence pretends to dismiss the master with a crack in number 15 about those who "poore *Petrarch's* long deceased woes, / With new-borne sighes and denisend wit do sing." (Or, in one textual variant, dismissing him even more decisively with "old Petrarchs.") But there is a difference here. For all their bemusement, and for all the changes they work on the tradition, the sonneteers are content to a far greater extent than Chaucer to remain within its bounds, to rework it for new meaning. Whereas Chaucer is willing to call it quits, to go so far with this tradition, but no farther; in the case of Troilus, to expose its deficiencies and then to pull away.

Nevertheless, the Petrarchan tradition in English will not allow itself to be declared exhausted. Its tenacity began to assert itself in the fifteenth century, when the Petrarchan translation turned out to be one of Chaucer's more anthologized pieces. Chaucer's own rendering received separate fifteenth-century attention in such manuscripts as Bodleian 1123 and Jesus College 39 and Cambridge University Library Gg. 4. 12. Further, Chaucer's rendering was copied out in the sixteenth century, within the Bannatyne collection, amidst "luvaris ballattis," in a form that shows it to have been extracted directly from a manuscript of *Troilus*,[17] and (as previously noted) Chaucer's poem was well known to Thomas Watson in 1582. In other words, Chaucer's experiment in Petrarchan paradox enjoyed a form of uptake or adoption that suggests that it may have been appreciated in posterity for reasons surplus to, or at least other than, those for which he included it in the first place. In this sense, it enjoys an expansive subsequent history rather different from the limited history imagined for it within the bounds of Chaucer's poem.

Petrarch is thus found on both sides of Chaucer: chronologically "pre" and, with respect to certain kinds of adoption and exploitation, stylistically "post." His sonnet within the bounds of Chaucer's narrative constitutes a fold or wrinkle in time, a doubling back or superimposition: a nonsynchronous intimation of past and future at the heart of the present.

Such "wrinkles" have interested postmodern theorists; although, just because they have described them doesn't mean they get to claim them as their own, or as a special property of the postmodern. The issue posed by the embedding of the post- in the pre- has been most prepossessingly addressed (and indeed, at least tacitly claimed for the postmodern) by Lyotard, in *The Postmodern Condition* and in *The Postmodern Explained to Children*. Drawing his examples from nineteenth- and twentieth-century art, he declares that "a work can become modern only if it is first postmodern. A Postmodernism thus understood is not modernism at its end but in the nascent state, and this state is constant."[18] This is a very promising idea so far, but one discovers upon reading further that the presence of postmodernism at the naissance of modernism is presumptive rather than literal, a matter of implication or presupposition. Thus, as he puts it, "What space does Cézanne challenge? The Impressionists'. What object do Picasso and Braque attack? Cézanne's." In other words, Lyotard contents himself with (for him) the rather unambitious point that predecessors initiate a dialectic, that they set the terms of their own succession. Thus, the impressionists somehow conjure a postimpressionist who is not there yet, but will be. Here Lyotard relies on a commonplace of literary history—in fact, on one of literary history's founding (and ultimately debilitating) assumptions. For his is the "apophatic" method in which that which succeeds a moment in time shows its difference by being something other than that moment, a departure from it.[19] Thus, the impressionist Monet is, in Lyotard's account, succeeded by the nonimpressionist Cézanne ... as is the medieval Chaucer by the nonmedieval Petrarch.

What, though, if this relatively curtailed notion of the aesthetic successor state already implied at the birth of an artistic tendency were replaced by a more energetic conception? What if impressionism's successor movement were, at the moment of its founding, not simply implied, but quite literally *already there*?[20]

THE PRACTICE OF LITERARY HISTORY

The literal presence of Petrarch in Chaucer and Cézanne among the impressionists mounts a strong challenge to literary history—at least, to the understanding of literary history as that orderly succession of periodizations which plays so large a part in the composition of our academic subject. For the text of mixed temporal indebtedness resists periodization, asks what we mean by "period" and how periods need to be studied.

Certainly, *Troilus* is a medieval poem, and I am enough of an "old historicist" to believe that nothing in it can be foreign from, or impossible to, its moment of composition. It was written in 1385–86, and everything in it must in one way or another pertain to, or be realized within, various possibilities at large in that moment. Among such lateral or synchronous relations are these: The poem's generic identity understood within an array of contemporaneous texts. Or its language, understood, as the narrator himself understands it, in relation to the instability of the vernacular, and the continuing competition of vernaculars. Or its relations to contemporary politics, and the precarious vision of London in the 1380s as a "New Troy."[21]

Yet, even as we regard *Troilus* as a poem utterly of its moment (and this is certainly the kind of work I have most done), we must also regard its moment as inherently divided. Its moment is always marked by traces or residues of an unexhausted past, and equally by intimations of an uncompleted or unrealized future. Even when we try to stop time, to freeze a moment for synchronous investigation as part of a literary cross-section, that moment nevertheless turns out to bear within itself intimations of past and future that amount to a form of implicit diachrony. I do not mean the reassuring diachrony of a securely periodized literary history, but an unruly diachrony, referring in the most surprising and unpredictable ways to what has been and what is not yet, to the residual and the emergent.

So what then does a term like *medieval* mean in application to a work so backward- and forward-looking? Or, for that matter, what does or should it mean to those of us who practice under its aegis? Certainly, it is a term and concept that we need, upon which we rely. First of all, it offers a curricular boundary or limit that enables a concentration of skill and knowledge upon problems of interpretation. Its very existence enables us to work in a way that would otherwise be unavailable to us— as a collectivity, agreed among ourselves to focus upon commonly identified problems. Period terminologies like *medieval* and *Renaissance* also serve as a vital reminder to view textual problems as historical problems, itself an important gesture today when the past is vulgarized or despised.

Further, with respect to the kinds of temporal problems I am discussing today, terms like *medieval* and *Renaissance* act as a baseline, enabling us to define and identify moments of exceptionality—those very "wrinkles in time" that have captured my attention in this essay.

But here, now, a caution asserts itself, for we must always remember the arbitrariry of the period marker, the necessity that it remain open to challenge and traversal. Even as we employ terms like *medieval* and *Renaissance* to identify issues and problems, we must equally remember the incapacity of these terms to resolve the very problems they have enabled us to define. The problem, for example, of Petrarch within Chaucer can be stated but cannot be resolved within the terms of the Renaissance/ medieval dichotomy, because *it is precisely this dichotomy that Petrarch's appearance challenges and ultimately subverts.* Its subversion is to display these terms as overly rigid designators, unable to deal with the layered and contradictory nature of time as actually experienced.

Thus, when C. S. Lewis argued that what Chaucer did with *Filostrato* was to "medievalize" a Renaissance poem,[22] he was being characteristically insightful, but not in a strictly necessary cause. For Chaucer presumably never thought to consider Boccaccio and Petrarch as anything *but* perfectly plausible near-contemporaries, sharing diversely, like himself, in various aspects of fourteenth-century literary culture. Lewis did a brilliant job of saving the terms *medieval* and *Renaissance* by clearing up an impossibility (the impossibility of Renaissance elements in a medieval poem). But, had we not reified such terms in the first place and insisted on the impossibility of their interpenetration, this possible category confusion would not have been a problem to be solved.

Here emerges a problem for literary history—in its confrontation with those paradigm-threatening exceptions that Kuhn used to talk about, or that we used to use Kuhn to talk about.[23] This is the fact that, having discovered a moment like Petrarch in Chaucer (or Renaissance in medieval), literary history is then obliged to save appearances by solving the problem it has created—in this case, via Chaucer's "remedievalization" of his source. Yet, rushing to the rescue of our own practices, we risk an abuse of the very analytical power that belatedness confers. This is the risk of overriding, rather than simply acknowledging and appreciating, each historical moment's internal self-difference. We need concepts like *medieval* and *Renaissance,* in part to identify and appreciate the exceptional excitement of moments like Petrarch-in-Chaucer... but they "work" for us only to the extent that they help us to index temporal complexity; never when they are allowed to regiment time into an orderly march or succession with one period or school trimly following another in succession.

Here I wish to invoke the urbane attitude of my predecessor, Douglas Gray, toward periodization in literary study. Virtually inventing a field of study, lying at the intersection of Middle English and Early Modern English language and literature, Professor Gray published among his many works the provocative and perhaps even mischievous *Oxford Book of Late Medieval Verse and Prose.*[24] This work is marked by what one of our associates aptly calls "liberal boundaries."[25] But I want to observe that Gray goes farther even than that, not only liberalizing boundaries but positively dismantling them. Noting that "one or two of my authors — notably Skelton and More — are often labeled 'Renaissance,'" he goes on to observe that this apparent contradiction "does not worry me overmuch." He then incidentally but devastatingly — I hope he won't mind my using this term — "deconstructs" the imagined boundary of the medieval and Renaissance periods. His argument is antievolutionary (opposing the literary applicability of the "pseudo-Darwinian view" that the earlier is supplanted by the later). He argues instead for the kinds of coexistences, or wrinkles in time, of which I speak here: Henry VII viewing a "medieval" mystery cycle; Henry VII interred in an English Perpendicular chantry, even as his and his wife's effigies are done in the newer Florentine style; Castiglione bringing a Raphael to London in 1506.

Literary works must be read and appreciated as expressions of their moment, but their purchase on their moment must also be read as inherently unstable — as ever ready to dive into period-defying elements and attitudes toward time. It is hard (or impossible) to remain in a period. Pursuit of any past indebtedness reminds us of our period's reliance upon anterior utterances and events. Pursuit of any future meaning reminds us that texts are valued not only for what they were but also for what they have become. So much of any text is thus divided — between what it was and will be — and thus inevitably we are again and again thrust from our period and into our larger subject. (I liken our situation to that of certain small countries that have trouble training their air forces because their airplanes no sooner achieve full speed than they discover that they have crossed a boundary and penetrated somebody else's air zone. Of course we always hope that, in the academic context, such border crossings will not necessarily cause us to be shot down!) My recommendation in this state of affairs is an obvious one: at once to regard ourselves as medievalists *and* to recall our inevitable and welcome state of interdependency with our subject at large.

This, for me, is the lesson of *Troilus* as an elegantly constituted temporal archive. For an archive through its organization has something to say about how it will be studied, how it will be used. *Troilus* is about the past in the present, about anachronism, about the inevitability of linguistic and aesthetic change, about the ephemerality of the Now and the ceaseless slide of written work into what it was or will have been. Such a poem demands of us a certain attitude: a certain receptivity to contradiction, to a work as both "settled" in its own time and perpetually "unsettled" in relation to all time. This attitude, in turn, positions us as particular practitioners in a chronologically delineated field *and* as participants in a chronologically more expansive configuration, which is our subject— English language and literature (or perhaps I should just say "language and literature") in its largest and most generous description.

PART III

READING THE HISTORICAL TEXT

7

PROHIBITING HISTORY

CAPGRAVE AND THE DEATH OF RICHARD II

Michel de Certeau observes that certain descriptive discourses have the effect of supplanting what they describe; of installing themselves in its place, thus preempting or even prohibiting its expression.[1] So does history writing stand in relation to the events of the past. However humble its professions, it effectively occupies and colonizes the place of recollection, deciding for itself the past's undecidabilities. Yet the repressed past has its own resources and devices of repropagation. Which is to say that the past continually eludes the prohibitions of history writing, stages a continual "return" within the historical text—within, as de Certeau says, "the discourse that prohibits it" (250). The challenge, then, is to identify the circumstances and means of the past's return. Even more particularly, the challenge is to identify the marks of this return, to know how and when it has occurred and the forms under which it might be recognized.

Much textual analysis has proceeded on the assumption that certain "fault lines" in a text—variously identified as inconsistencies, contradictions, slips, or fissures—can provide privileged glimpses into that text's own prehistory or to the materials that have been suppressed in the process of its construction. To the extent that the words and other components of a text enjoy differential, and partially recoverable, prehistories, this approach enjoys a certain validity, and I have employed it often enough myself. The possibility persists, though, that the matter glimpsed through the textual "aperture" is actually an epiphenomenon of the text's own inventive process, a further stage of the text's own self-imagining, rather than a source of new historical information. Ruth Morse observes, in an essay close in spirit to this one, that "we cannot expect, even equipped with the most sophisticated rhetorical sensitivities, to be able—with those sensitivities alone—to peel away excrescences to reveal a substratum of decodable facts."[2] Granting this proposition, I turn to an alternative source of historical information: freshly perceived or newly imported data resting at the text's surface. Like stones churned or tossed to the top of a cultivated field by each year's winter freeze, new bits and augmentations seem somehow to work their way to an old text's, or a venerable textual tradition's, surfaces.

My proposal in this essay is that, whatever fissures a text might naturally possess, a close interior or intrinsic analysis of those fissures is unlikely to tell us all we want to know about that text's relation to history. I am less interested in naturally occurring fissures than in those bends, buckles, or surface distortions resulting from the additional pressures brought to bear on a text by extrinsic circumstances. I might provisionally say that those pressures result in something very like "stress fractures": points at which a rupture occurs and is awkwardly re-mended. At these moments an external event or new circumstance creates a previously nonexistent textual gap that needs to be filled with new information, or opens a circumstance in which neglected material gains new relevance, or allows that which was previously hidden to stage a return. My working assumption, in any case, is that texts and textual traditions are likely to be shaken or surprised into some of their most valuable resignifications as a result of subsequent events, of perturbations beyond their own bounds.

My illustrative example involves a cluster of seemingly opaque or impenetrable texts dealing with the mysterious death of Richard II during Lancastrian imprisonment. I will first reflect, pessimistically, on a line of approach to these texts favored both by medieval commentators and modern historians: that approach which would seek historical information or resolution by a technique of "averaging" or compromise among extant (and highly divergent) accounts. On the far side of this impasse, I will pursue the question of history's "return" to a textual tradition, canvassing the external conditions conducive to such return and some signs of its reemergence. My case in point will be taken from a belated and lightly regarded text, a text certainly accorded little value as a witness to the events of Richard's deposition and death: Capgrave's mid-fifteenth-century *Chronicle of England*.

SPLITTING THE DIFFERENCE:
HISTORICAL TRUTH AS A MEAN OR AVERAGE

The most spurious of the historian's claims involves the imagined gains
of detachment: the interpretative advantage to be gained within the zone
of neutrality, the secure middle space between extreme and conflicting
claims. In his *Book of the Illustrious Henries,* for example, Capgrave dis-
closes such an ambition for his recital of the events surrounding Richard
II's supplantation by Henry of Lancaster: "Having," he says, "investigated both sides of the question, I set myself diligently to elucidate the
truth alone."[3] Yet the problem is that the truth cannot be achieved simply
by (as Capgrave implies) balancing one set of claims against another.[4]
Moreover, this problem presents itself with particular starkness in the
case of Richard II's death, when the two available near-contemporary
explanations were such polar opposites as practically to exclude the possibility of a sensible middle.

One account of Richard's death, which may reasonably be considered
"Lancastrian" both for its relation to the interests of the new dynasty and
the means of its encouragement and promulgation, had an admittedly
imprisoned, but also sorrowing, Richard starving himself to death without the intervention of his jailers. The classic expression of this view, as
embodied in the *Annales Henrici Quarti* and ultimately in Walsingham's
Historia Anglicana, delineates this position and—incidentally—seeks
authority for itself by providing a wealth of physiological and other detail:

> It is said that, immersed in so great sorrow, he wished to destroy
> himself by starvation ["semetipsum inedia voluit peremisse"].
> He is said to have abstained to such an extent that, the orifice
> of his stomach having closed, when, by the counsel of friends,
> he decided to satisfy nature by eating, his appetite having been
> completely suppressed, he was unable to eat. It thus happened
> that, through natural debility ["debilitata natura"], he failed, and
> ended his last day ["diem supremum clauderet"] on St. Valen-
> tine's day.[5]

The artfulness of this passage rests in its apparent surplus of detail, all
of which is directed to Richard's bodily functions, and none to the sus-
picious circumstances of his imprisonment. For all we know from this

account, only Richard's *amici* have been visiting him, whereas every aspect of his captivity and fate suggest that he was subject to far more ominous visitation. This passage is additionally successful in emphasizing the naturalness of the process of his death — Richard's wish ultimately to satisfy nature and the failure of his natural processes. Yet, for all its art, this passage does not quite succeed in resting easy. Evidence of a guilty conscience rests in a certain disavowal of responsibility: all is known by report ("ut fertur"; "dicitur"), all "happened" or "turned out" ("ut factum est") and nothing was actually *done* to anyone.

At the other extreme is the French account, as embodied in *Chronicque de la Träison et Mort.*[6] In this account, and without any apparent historical authorization beyond French dynastic and political reasons for favoring the Ricardian cause, the infamous Pierre Dexton is conjured as an embodiment of Lancastrian malice, arriving on the scene accompanied by seven assassins. Seizing an ax from one of them, a valiant Richard gives as good as he gets, slaying four of them in combat before he is felled by a dastardly stroke. The French chronicles were, of course, the principal repository of surviving anti-Lancastrian opinion, and it is no wonder that accounts of the remasculinized Richard of the *Träison* were frequently recopied there.[7]

Presented with the extremes of Richard's entirely self-inflicted death on the one hand and Lancastrian savagery on the other, subsequent chroniclers naturally enough edged as best they were able toward some kind of middle ground. Representative here might be the Evesham Chronicler, who in *Historia Vitae et Regni Ricardi Secundi* repeats the Lancastrian story and then adds a view of his own:

> [H]e declined into such great sorrow, languor, and weakness . . .
> that he took to his bed, not wishing to be strengthened by any
> food, drink, or anything else. Thus on Saint Valentine's day . . .
> he ended his last day in prison ["in carcere diem suum clausit
> extremum"]. Nevertheless, to the contrary, it is said, and more
> truly, that he perished miserably by starvation ["Aliter tamen dicitur et uerius, quod ibidem fame miserabiliter interiit"].[8]

This chronicler thus exercises that faculty expected of all ancient and medieval historians — and implicitly claimed by most modern ones —

that of prudent reconciliation of extreme accounts, based on the historian's life experience and sober good sense. Each view is cited, and then, following a durable canon of historiographical propriety, the chronicler adds his own. For, although *interire* (in the sense of "to perish" or "to die" rather than "to be killed") signals Richard's destruction without literally asserting his murder, the implication of Lancastrian hugger-mugger is sufficiently clear.[9]

Certainly, the Evesham Chronicler's judgment about the locus of truth must strike any observer with the weight of its common sense. Yet one must still observe that the chronicler's method, which involves an effective averaging of two extreme possibilities (that is, suicide or murder), seems unlikely to produce a *new* truth or a truth with any footing outside the ambit of the original circle of conjectures or inventions.

We will, of course, never know what happened in that room at Pontefract Castle. In this regard, the truest commentator is, for once, Froissart, with his emphatic statement that "the cause of his death, nor its means, I do not know at all" ("point je ne le scavoie").[10] Yet we would wish to know more; would we not? The remainder of this essay concerns an attempt to learn more, by reconsideration of an apparently unpromising and exhausted textual tradition.

CAPGRAVE AND THE RETURN OF THE YORKIST REPRESSED

For the year 1400, Capgrave's *Chronicle of England* reports the failed rebellion of the Ricardian earls, and then adds: "This cam to Kyng Richardis ere in the castel of Pounfreit, and, as sum men sey, he peyned himself, and deyed for hungir. Summe othir seide that he was kept fro mete and drink whil a knyte rode to London and cam ageyn."[11] The first sentence effectively reiterates the standard "Lancastrian" account. Its authority is bolstered by its form, which asserts a causal connection between the generally acknowledged fact of failed rebellion and Richard's decision to "peyne" himself or take his own life through self-deprivation. Further enhancing this explanation's authority is Capgrave's insistence that, a half century later, this is what people are still saying: what "sum men *sey.*" Yet, in his second sentence, Capgrave indulges what might be considered a "Yorkist" memory, a memory of what men used to say or "seide": that food was withheld from Richard, that he starved while a knight rode to London and back again.

A determination between these two sentences requires a decision about relative weight and prestige of what men are saying versus what men said. My own first assumption was that the utterance still in currency, the Lancastrian explanation, must be given pride of place. Until, that is, I showed my first draft to Karen Winstead, who replied in this vein:

> It seems to me that "men sey" is an ambiguous, even suspicious, formulation, because it lacks the authority of history. "Summe othir seide" seems stronger to me—especially coming from Capgrave, who, throughout his writing, is obsessed with authenticating his accounts through the testimony of ancient authorities or contemporary witnesses to the events he is reporting.

After weighing Karen Winstead's remark, I find the subordinated, or Yorkist, explanation on the brink of overtaking the dominant, or Lancastrian, account.

Whence does this Yorkist memory—of what men said—come? How and why do memories enter a text? Partially, perhaps, from the past, from the first decade of the fifteenth century, a time of unresolved pro-Ricardian nostalgia, tumult, and protest.[12] But, more urgently, they come from the future—from a new alignment of circumstances that brings new possibilities into view, or enables the articulation of what was previously regarded as unsayable. If Capgrave's *Book of the Illustrious Henries,* written in the 1440s, was at least nominally Lancastrian,[13] then his *Chronicle,* written in the troubled last years of Henry VI's reign and abruptly concluded shortly before Capgrave's death with a dedication to the new Yorkist monarch Edward IV, inhabits a space considerably more conducive to retrospect and reconsideration. (In the new textual environment of the *Chronicle,* for example, Henry IV is said to have died as a foul leper, his body shrunk to "a cubite of length," hectored by his own confessor over "wrong titil of the crowne" [291, 302–3], and in Capgrave's new dedication Henry IV is said to have become king "be intrusion," whereas Edward IV "entered by Goddis provision" [4].) In this case, an alteration of extratextual circumstances — the imminence and advent of a new dynasty — appears to be closely linked with a textual "return of the repressed."

Thus, an extratextual event (involving a new Yorkist ascendancy) permits something new to be said within the text, enables something to be newly seen. In other words, the precondition for learning something new from and about this text is not just its careful analysis, or even its "deconstruction," but rather a recognition of the changes the text has undergone in a process of recontextualization, its "iteration" in a new set of external circumstances. Here, even though I depart from Derrida and deconstruction in one sense, I return to him in another. For I agree with his point that through recontextualization a text enters the world of politics, attaches itself, or is attached, to the political.[14] At times, verbatim repetition of a text within a new set of circumstances is already a political act; imagine, in this regard, the recopying of a once orthodox and now heretical religious treatise. But this is an occasion on which something additional has occurred: a space has been made, within which a previously suppressed utterance — what "summe seide" — now regains its voice, can be resaid in a new political context. A judgment must still, of course, be made as to whether we are dealing with previously repressed information or craven and newly minted political propaganda. But the salient point is that new circumstances have encouraged the promulgation or production of fresh material, a fresh object of consideration and analysis.

TELLING SOME OF THE TRUTH
AS PART OF THE LIE

Good medieval building practice involved use of materials from a demolished edifice to augment a new structure. So with the textual fabrication of a lie from the shattered materials of a former truth; the mortar is sometimes found to contain an inadvertent accuracy. Even a residual fragment that seems, as de Certeau says, to keep "nothing of its own" retains a latent power as the point of a suppressed explanation's possible reentry. Capgrave's use of the fate of the rebellious earls as the pivot of the Lancastrian explanation for Richard's death provides a case in point. For the conjunction of the 1400 rising (January) and Richard's death (February) does in fact suggest a relation between the two events, even if not the one that Capgrave first proposes.

The Lancastrian explanation, in the Evesham Chronicle and else-where, imagines that Richard died as a result of disappointment and lost hope upon learning of the failure of the rebellion of the earls and the death of John Holland. But the mention of the earls' rebellion suggests an unintended alternative account, according to which the failed rebellion enabled Henry's advisers to assess the threat posed by the living Richard and to act upon that assessment. In February 1400, the month after the abortive rising, Henry's ministers directed to the royal Council an inquiry rather obviously shaped by the earls' claims that Richard was free and available to lead a rebellion, wondering whether Richard was still alive, as some supposed he was.[15] The response of the Council was that, in case Richard were still alive, he should be held in appropriate security, and that, if he had died, he should be shown openly to the people so that they might know of it.[16] The Council then evidently acted upon its own thinly veiled suggestion. Although the circumstances of Richard's death remained in doubt, contemporary commentators generally agreed with Walsingham that he died on 14 February, the day of the feast of Saint Valentine. Expenses were recorded on 17 February for transport of his body to London, and his body was, consistent with the Council's suggestion, widely displayed to the populace.[17] Here to be glimpsed is a causal chain, beginning with the earls' rebellion and ending, not in Richard's self-mortification, but in his political murder.

Borrowing the death of the earls to fabricate its maudlin and obfuscatory lie, the text thus accidentally admits a bit of what might be the truth—or at least narrates events in a temporal order and proximity that permits an alternative truth to be seen: that, as a result of the rebellion of the earls, Richard's continued survival (and continued availability as a rallying point for anti-Lancastrian opposition) was understood by the Lancastrians to be strategically unwise.

SWYNFORD'S VALET: A "MATERIAL" WITNESS

I turn now to the strange suggestion that Richard might have been starved, "whil a knyte rode to London and cam ageyn." Once again, information from outside the text permits its explanatory recontextualization. For a second text does exist, within the Issue Rolls of the Exchequer, that places Capgrave's rather free-sounding speculation on a new and different evidential footing. Rolls dated 20 March 1400 (but recording expenditures that might have been authorized a month or more earlier) contain a cluster of interrelated items.[18] First, payment is recorded for clerks, including trusted servant William Loveney, to journey from London to Pontefract on secret business of the king. Then, this telling item:

> To a certain *valletus* of Thomas Swynford, knight, coming from Pontefract Castle to London, in order to certify to the Council of the King with respect to certain matters concerning the advantage of the lord King ["ad certificand*um* consilio Regis de *certis* materiis com*modum* dom*ini* Regis concer*nentibus*"] — in money for his wages and expenses and for the hire of a horse for the expediting of said journey — 26s. 8d.[19]

Finally, closely following items provide for custody of Richard's body and its transport to London.

Crucial here is the journey of the unnamed *valletus* — not the *knyte* of Capgrave's account, but the servant *of* a knight — coming down (as in Capgrave's narration) from Pontefract to London and then returning, on business advantageous to the king.[20] That the *valletus*'s name is withheld suggests something of the urgency and secrecy of the business at hand, since issues are almost invariably attached to some kind of name. But, knowing that his master was arch-Lancastrian Thomas Swynford, we can be sure that this business was supervised by one of the most trusted servants of the king.[21]

Moreover, the name of Swynford comes to us from yet another source. Adam Usk's chronicle account appears to be another of those "balancing acts," but with the addition of a significant detail. As Usk has it: "[H]e pined away even unto death, which came to him in the most wretched of circumstances in Pontefract castle... tormented, bound with chains, and starved of food by N. Swynford ['catenis ligato et uictualium penuria, domino N. Swynford ipsum tormentante, sibi... miserabiliter contingentem']."[22] Given-Wilson points out a certain slipperiness in this passage ("What is Usk saying: that Richard starved himself or that he was starved?"; lxxxiii). Its evasions multiply upon examination. Although Swynford obviously made Richard's life less happy, it is effectively the ablative construction — rather than Swynford or any particular person —

that binds him in chains and deprives him of food. Resolving less than it seems to resolve, this passage nevertheless introduces a name, presumably—despite the "N."—that of Thomas Swynford, and his placement at the scene seems yet an additional confirmation of the information provided by the issue rolls.

Even allowing for the extreme uncertainty of the dates of the events to which they refer, the issue rolls allow the construction of an implied narrative in their own right: Loveney and his men to Pontefract to spell out the wishes of the king, a *valletus* of trusted Lancastrian Swynford to London to report that the king's wishes were being carried out, another *valletus* back to Pontefract to guard the body until it could be carried to London for display. I would not go so far as to say that this narrative, which still depends upon certain imagined extensions and a dash of the *post hoc ergo propter hoc* for the imposition of meaning, is "more true" than that of Capgrave. But I do suggest that, since it rests on Exchequer issues, it possesses a different kind of truth, exists within what Paul Veyne would call a different "program of truth" (21–22).

Let me put it this way: it is not that we have just moved from a duplicitous text to the superior authority of a nonduplicitous one. As I view them, *all* texts are suspect, up to and including the phone book and the A to Zed. Despite the apparent solidity of the disbursements in question, mysteries remain at the heart of these Exchequer issues that cannot easily be resolved. The name of the valet, his particular business, the date of the event, the nature of the Council's interest—all these aspects, and more, remain as matters for conjecture, or at best as occasions for interpretation, rather than "evidence" in any very solid or satisfactory sense of the term. Andrew Prescott insistently reminds us that—despite the odd deference in which all researchers, and especially those literary researchers new to the archive, hold these supposed "documents"—they are finally only "texts" in the end, and as texts must be regarded with no more or less suspicion than other kinds of writing.[23] The importance of the issue roll is not necessarily that it is "more true" than the chronicle account, but rather that it comes from a different explanatory register or documentary range than the fifteenth-century chronicle. It possesses a different location in time (closer to the event), involves different kinds of testimony (bureaucrats and politicians rather than a mid-fifteenth-century ideologue), possesses a specific materiality (disbursement of funds)— all of which may be relatively impartial with respect to truth claims, but which nevertheless establish it on a different footing than the chronicle, possessed of its own decorums and motives and paths of persuasion.

The point is not that the issue roll necessarily provides a better or more reliable kind of testimony, but rather that its different and independent purpose and provenance enhance its value for purposes of corroboration. On this matter of corroboration, I and many other Americans received a crash course last year while listening to televised legal commentary on the Bill Clinton–Monica Lewinsky hearings. Still scrawled on a scrap of paper in my wallet is one commentator's pronouncement on the matter: "A corroboration is an independent fact that shows something actually occurred." Let me set aside the metaphysical difficulties surrounding "actual occurrence," in favor of the more important phrase: that an "independent fact" is required. Upon reconsideration, let me jettison the concept of the "fact" as well, and rely simply upon the criterion of independence. The important principle for purposes of corroboration seems indeed to be that of two differential or unrelated sources, existing independently of each other and without possibility of prior collusion. Thus, the same lawyer argued that the despised Linda Tripp's testimony about Monica having told her something during the affair with Clinton was not corroboration. His point was that Monica was still the source, and that the standard of independence had not been met. By contrast, the relatively distinct origins of the anecdotal or hearsay evidence offered by Capgrave and the purpose-based information of the issue rolls do lend each other a degree of independent corroboration, inviting more credence in Capgrave's belated and seemingly fanciful story of a knight riding to and from London than it would otherwise possess.

THE USES OF THEORY

And so what are we learning here? I do not want to make the mistake described by Veyne, in which each myth is presumed to possess a nugget or kernel of truth at its inception and has only to be "purified" of dross or admixture for that kernel to be regained.[24] For one may easily enough imagine a text that, although marked by history, contains no literal historical truth at all—that is, no truth bearing on external or material or "eventual" history. No matter how much imagination and speculation and interpretative ingenuity we pour into the event of Richard's death (into what Lyotard calls the "bidon vide," or "empty barrel," of the event),[25] we cannot fill it; it retains aspects unknowable to us, unsusceptible to our complete knowledge. But, without imagining that we can fill the empty space of this event, we can at least "pour" some of our specula- tions into it. To put it differently: obviously, an event cannot be fully known, but more things can be known *about it*. Only a radical skeptic would conclude that, the entire truth of an event necessarily eluding us, we have no obligation to pursue the various partial truths that an incom- plete and treacherously deceptive textual record affords.

Our inability to achieve complete understanding of an event through its textual residues seems sometimes — in my discipline at any rate — to be celebrated in the form of an oddly triumphalist skepticism. The triumphalism rests in a celebration of the impossibility of knowledge, a curiously smug satisfaction in knowing the worst, which is that we can- not, finally, Know. One aspect of this satisfaction is that the inaccessibil- ity of empirical knowledge is then seen to foster another kind of knowl- edge, a nonknowledge-for-its-own-sake, which is (inappropriately, in my view) sometimes called "theory." Speaking of Freud, Ned Lukacher ob- serves that "the impossibility of satisfying [the] desire to understand the mystery... becomes a kind of satisfaction that one calls theory."[26] Cele- brated is, in other words, the advent and enjoyment of textual theory it- self, with frustrated desire embraced as the essential condition for theory's emergence. I agree with Lukacher that impossibility attends the birth of theory, and I also agree about theory's provisional satisfactions. Yet I think that the most promising linkage of theory with historical investi- gation is not its promotion of skepticism but its ultimate promise to win back disputed epistemological ground. Having gained acceptance of its proposition that complete or secure knowledge is unattainable, theory must then consider its job undone. Its further task is to act as our practiced and wily ally in the effort to recapture such partial knowledges as a flawed and duplicitous textual record affords us.

Theory's value rests in the restricted but real promise of its assis- tance in reclaiming provisional knowledge in the face of impossibility. I must therefore disagree with those advocates who seek to secure and extend theory's claims by elaborating or even exaggerating the unattain- ability of historical knowledge. In my alternative view, theory has both an important short-term use and an accompanying long-term responsi- bility. In short-term or provisional use, it may indeed demonstrate the undecidability of certain matters related to a textualized event. This is how people in my discipline of literary and textual studies, owing to their heightened awareness of textual duplicities and evasions, usually employ what we call theory: to shatter complacencies, to show that a matter is more complex and its meaning less accessible than we had thought. But the long-term responsibility of theory lies elsewhere: in its potential for enlistment in the task of multiplying things that can be known and ways of knowing them. Thus, the potential of theory for history may *first* rest in its disclosure of a chasm between past events and historical reconstructions, but *second* and finally it rests in theory's potential assistance in re-bridging the very chasm it has disclosed.

Something happened to Richard in his captivity, and I would like to know as much about it as I can. I would, that is, rather be energized than paralyzed by what I lack. I join those who find a *jouissance* in theory, although I situate it not in theory itself, but in theory mobilized against what I do not know or understand.

8

TRADE, TREASON, AND THE
MURDER OF JANUS IMPERIAL

The written record begins with the discovery of a body and the supposition of an unsolved crime. "It happened," in the laconic words of the coroner's inquest, "that a certain Janus Imperial of Genoa lay slain."[1] The murder had occurred the night before, on 26 August 1379, in St. Nicholas Acton Lane, before Imperial's London residence. Arriving to view the body, the coroner and sheriffs gathered a jury from among men of Langbourne and adjacent wards and set about to determine how and in what way this foreign merchant met his death.

The jury's inquest was only the first step in an inquiry that would ultimately involve the mayor of London, the Court of the King's Bench, a second jury, the king and his Council, and Parliament itself. So, too, did questions of motive and interest spool out from this seemingly random act to embrace the ambitions of London's mercantile elite, vicissitudes of royal finance, and the future and locus of the international wool trade. Starting with an apparent insufficiency of evidence, this investigation eventually found itself knee-deep in pertinent information, plausible motives, and likely suspects. Although it finally stumbled to a sort of stopping point, it never really achieved a satisfactory end.

The original investigation offers suggestive analogies to the task of historical reconstruction. The would-be historian is, like the crime's contemporaries, challenged to arrange known details into a coherent narration—and, as new elements emerge, into revised renarrations. The historian's location outside the crime's own participatory pattern is one of weakness and strength. Working from an inherently incomplete and evasive written record, the retrospective analyst knows less than the least of the crime's participants. Yet a location outside the event's network of involvements and interests also confers significant and offsetting analytical advantages. In the end, both the original investigation and the task of historical reconstruction must confront a common problem. Whether medieval or modern, the explanatory attempt is shadowed by inscrutabilities and irrationalities, elements of the case that refuse accommodation to calculations of motive, interest, or rational purpose.

THE "COVER-UP"

Considering that Janus Imperial was slain on a public street in front of his own dwelling, and that his murderers made no attempt to flee London, and that the jury for the inquest was composed of persons drawn from the immediate neighborhood, the initial inquest was remarkably unsuccessful. When they met the next morning to view the corpse, the jurors agreed that Janus had been wickedly and feloniously slain "by certain malefactors and disturbers of the present king's peace," but, pleading the fact that the murder occurred at night, they declared themselves "at the moment utterly ignorant of their names and how and in what way it happened." Confronted with these professions of ignorance, the coroner and sheriffs granted the jury an additional two days to inquire into the truth of the matter. Yet, on that following Monday, the jurors still had nothing to add, asserting that they were not able "in any way" ("aliquiter") to learn more about the death.

Now granted a month, the jury reconvened on 27 September and finally had something to say—though a bit anticlimactically, since on 10 September two key suspects had been arrested by the civil authorities on the order of Mayor John Philipot and were being held in Newgate pending the outcome of a trial. The jurors acknowledged that the murder was indeed committed by one John Kirkby, mercer, with the additional involvement of John Algor, grocer, but its members adamantly insisted on viewing the matter as an innocent, or at least randomly occurring, scuffle. As they now told the story, Janus Imperial was sitting on a bench in front of his place of residence, while four of his servants stood conversing before him, when Kirkby and Algor crossed between them and Kirkby "suddenly and by no wish of his own trod unwittingly on Janus Imperial's feet" ("subito se non volente super pedes ipsius Iohannis Imperialis ignoranter peditabat"). Incensed by the verbal retorts of Imperial's servants, Algor drew his knife and engaged them, even as Kirkby, considering himself affronted by Imperial's demands for peace, drew his sword and attacked the merchant.

Kirkby and Algor had probably supposed that they had little to fear from a London jury. Fourteenth-century juries were characteristically reluctant to convict in similar felony cases.[2] Certainly, these fellow Londoners showed every sign of willingness to interpret the evidence in the two murderers' favor. The jury's vindicatory tone was established in its insistence on the coincidental and unmotivated nature of the encounter. Most of the aggression in the encounter was, from the jury's point of view, attributable to Imperial's "clamor" for peace and his angry behavior; his feet trodden upon, they say, he "clearly began to lose his temper" ("irassi incepit manifeste"). Although the coroner and sheriffs repeatedly pressed questions about other persons procuring or assisting in the crime, the jurors persisted in their denials. In fact, they did not "hold any one else suspect in any way in any particular." Finally, as the jury also took care to point out in Kirkby's and Algor's behalf, they had lingered in London after the crime, making no attempt to conceal themselves or to flee.

The surprise is that the jury indicted Algor and Kirkby for felony at all. However reluctant the jury's indictment, the two accused felons now found themselves in a more difficult predicament. Instead of walking free, they were returned to the king's prison of Newgate, where they were subject not to London jurisdiction but to that of the King's Bench. And, from Newgate, they were subsequently transferred to the more secure confines of the Tower.[3]

Despite this slightly ominous shift in their circumstances, they continued to act as if they entertained hopes of either acquittal or pardon. They pleaded not guilty before the king at Westminster on 3 March. Their trial was set for the Octave of Trinity, but had to be postponed, evidently for delay or difficulty in composing the jury.[4] When the trial finally went forward, on 1 June 1380, at Saint Martin-le-Grand, London, the jury did indeed refuse to convict. Chief Justice Cavendish delivered the verdict, taken in a hearing so marked by stubborn evasions that its official summary merits quotation in full:

> The jury came. And chosen, tried, and sworn for this purpose, they say on their oath that John Kirkby slew the aforesaid Janus Imperial in self-defense. And when the said jurors are asked how this was in self-defense, they say that they are completely igno-

rant And when the said jurors are repeatedly asked by the justices if the said John Kirkby found his movements so restricted . . .
that he could not escape in any other way, they say, as before,
that they are completely ignorant about it. The said jurors are
further asked whether or not they wish to say anything else as
their verdict . . . and they absolutely ["precise"] say that they are
neither able nor willing to say anything else as their verdict.

This hearing occurred not only before Cavendish, but also in attendance
were Robert Belknap, chief justice of the common bench; Robert Tresilian, pleader before the king and later chief justice; and Justices Skipworth,
Fulthorpe, and Percy of the common bench — in other words, a most
formidable array of the chief legal minds of the realm. As the summary
emphasizes, their questioning of the jury was both persistent and shrewd.
The jury was, in fact, able to uphold its absurd finding of self-defense
only by extreme denials ("completely ignorant") and by tenacious refusal
to amplify or to modify their claims.

Despite the jury's determination to acquit, Algor and Kirkby were
not to walk free. The justices expressed their skepticism by availing themselves of the established but somewhat unusual expedient of returning
them to custody of unspecified duration in the Tower ("Et interim pre-
dicti Iohannes et Iohannes committuntur prisone Turris London' ad saluo
custodiendum, etc.").[5] Several clues lodged in the record thus far suggest
a pressure of larger motives and interests that might have stiffened the
justices' resolve. On their part, in committing an open crime and then
lingering in the city until their arrest, Kirkby and Algor behaved with
an insouciance that suggests that they enjoyed the protection of powerful allies. The evasive behavior of the juries would also suggest that this
was so. But the counterpressure of a second group — connected in some
way with the interest of the king's Council — is also tacitly suggested by
the arrest of Algor and Kirkby before the first inquest was even concluded,
the transfer of the felons from Newgate to the Tower (and the change of
legal venue), and now the determination of the justices that the case not
be closed.

A BREAK IN THE CASE

After six more months of extended and varied imprisonment,[6] John Algor
finally gave in. He turned approver, availing himself of the established

mechanism whereby a confessed felon could prolong his own life by turning against his former confederates and accusing them, in a circumstantially detailed appeal of their crimes ("deuenit probator et fecit appellum").[7] On 3–5 December 1380, appearing in the remote venue of Northampton before an illustrious group that included the coroner of the King's Bench and the cream of the royal Council and household, Algor confessed his and Kirkby's crime. Equivalent to a "break" in the case in a modern detective novel, Algor's *appellum* amounts to a major narrative rupture, in which a flood of new and informative disclosures permits the reconfiguration of events in a new and more satisfactory sequence.

Given its dramatic consequences, a break such as this is likely to appear "lucky," as fortuitous or otherwise unmotivated. But, as in analogy with good detective work, such apparent breaks most often result from unobtrusive but thorough groundwork by persons dedicated to the crime's solution. Algor's confession was, in fact, compelled by a series of pressures, and especially those exerted by an influential coalition of justices of the King's Bench and members of the king's Council.[8] This coalition's first significant move had occurred in the winter of 1379–80, while Kirkby and Algor as indicted felons still rested in prison, awaiting their appearance before the king at Westminster in March. Its ingenious point of entry was a hitherto unused provision of the 1352 Statute on Treason, to the effect that instances of supposed treason not covered by the statute were to be referred to Parliament, which was to decide whether they were treasonous, and thus to be handled with the full formality of the King's Bench and opened to the sanctions appropriate to that crime.[9] The Councillors of the king accordingly took advantage of the Parliament of January–February 1380, meeting in Westminster, to press for a parliamentary declaration endorsing a specific claim: that the murder of Imperial amounted to a treasonous act, and specifically a "crime du roiale Magestee blemye," or crime of lèse-majesté,[10] based on the fact that Imperial had entered the country under letters patent assuring him of the king's own "safe-conduct, protection, and special defense."

This safe-conduct, granted 6 March 1378 and possessing a duration of two years, was in force at the time of the murder. It reveals Janus Imperial as a vastly more important person than his portrayal in the first London inquest as a hapless Genoese merchant rather pathetically caught in a routine street scuffle would suggest. According to its text — preserved in the form of its submission by the king to his justices in March 1380

but presumably available to Parliament in January/February as well —
Janus Imperial, master of the tarit called *la Seinte Marie de Ianua,* is authorized to bring his ship to any port in England and to load it with wool
and other merchandise and to ship it to his own country, first paying to
the king and others the customs and subsidies that would otherwise have
been owed at Calais ("soluendo nobis et aliis... custumas et subsidias
et alia denaria inde debita que apud Calesium vel alibi solui deberent";
Sayles, 18). I will have more to say about the Calais staple before the end
of this inquiry. But, upon learning that Imperial's cargoes represented a
revenue source that bypassed payment of duties at Calais and flowed directly to the always impoverished Crown, we already know enough to
appreciate the importance of this Genoese merchant to the king. A tarit
was a large seagoing vessel, oared and sailed, the immediate predecessor of the huge carracks that would sail between Venice and Genoa and
England in the fifteenth century. Like their successors, the masters of tarits tended to mistrust the Thames and to prefer deep-water ports like Bris-
tol and, especially, Southampton.[11] Loaded with several thousand pounds'
worth of wool and other merchandise, a single tarit could represent a
substantial source of custom revenue. But other indications in the word-
ing of the parliamentary declaration suggest that Imperial's importance
far surpassed his captaincy of the *Holy Mary.*

Trusting in his safe-conduct, Imperial had come to London — not
just as captain of the *Holy Mary* and not just for trade (which he would
ordinarily have conducted in Southampton in any event), but as a representative of the duke and commonalty of Genoa to negotiate a treaty of
alliance ("une trete d'alliance") with the king of England. This treaty had
already been discussed by king and Council, and had been recorded in
Parliament and found likely to be "honorable and profitable to the king
and the realm." The treaty in question would presumably have supplemented the parliamentary act of October/November 1378, which opened
Southampton not just to a single tarit but to a massive volume of Italian
shipping, on conditions similar to those offered to Imperial in his safe-
conduct.[12] This is certainly the supposition of Thomas Walsingham, whose
denunciation of the murder includes an outline of the program that Imperial was seeking to elaborate at the time of his death. His intention,
according to the chronicler, was no less than to turn Southampton into
the preeminent port of western Europe ("eo provexisse portum Hamp-
toniae, quod nullus portus in hiis Occiduis Europae partibus aequiparari

potuisset eidem").[13] All that was required, as Walsingham tells it, was for the Crown to have made over a newly constructed castle for use as a warehouse for Genoese goods, and Southampton would have become a nonmonopolistic port of entry for all the goods of the East—a plan replete with advantages for the king, which Imperial would have made good had his life not been cut short.

The murder of Imperial—now revealed as an ambassador of the Genoese state engaged in business of the greatest importance and potential profit to the Crown—was found in Parliament to be treasonous in nature. Thus, the initial plea of Kirkby and Algor before the king at Westminster in March 1380 was altered from the charge of felony on which they were originally indicted to a charge of *seditio,* or treason. As indicted felons, they would presumably have been tried in the King's Bench anyway; but now there was no escaping this austere venue. Their transfer to the Tower probably occurred soon after the January/February parliamentary declaration.

So great was the determination of some members of the royal party to obtain a conviction that, when the London jury of Saint Martin le Grand persisted in finding Kirkby and Algor innocent of any charge, whether felony or treason, they invoked yet another stratagem, involving not only the return to custody but a delay of sentencing and a further change of venue. In November/December 1380, the king and his Council had relocated to Northampton, along with the entire session of Parliament, despite many objections about difficulties of access and provisioning.

Knowing that this parliament resulted in the poll tax that sparked the Rising of 1381, a modern analyst might casually assume that the removal to Northampton was arranged to gain approval for an unpopular levy in a setting remote from the public eye. In 1380, however, the king's councillors had no idea how unpopular the new tax would be, and Walsingham proposes an astounding alternative theory: that the removal to Northampton was arranged in order to sentence Kirkby and Algor without interference from their London partisans. Observing the harshness of the Northampton winter, the shortages of fuel and housing, and the protests of magnates and Londoners alike, he announces:

> The true cause whence the councillors arranged this Parliament was the desire for punishment which they pa; 'ed ["anhela(ve)- runt"] to lay upon John Kirkby. . . . In truth, they considered the

animosity of the Londoners, and they reflected that, should Parliament be held in London, by no means would the Londoners permit the same Kirkby to suffer death for the killing of the Genoan. Rather, if they attempted such things in London, they would place themselves in danger. Consequently, with this plan already in place, they arranged for Parliament to be held at Northampton. (Walsingham, 449)

Whether or not he was a cause of the relocation, Algor in Northampton was ready to sing like a bird. He did so on three occasions, including a hearing before the king's justices on 4 December. In the actions that built pressure for this appeal, a proroyal coalition, including the leaders of the king's Council (John of Gaunt and Thomas Beauchamp) and his chief justices (Cavendish, Belknap, and Tresilian), had shown its hand. As a renarration of the crime pivoting around new motivational coordinates, Algor's confession now permits fuller construction of the countervailing coalition upon which he and Kirkby had pinned their hope; new characters are introduced, and the presence of other, less visible actors is implied as well.

The writ for Algor's and Kirkby's transfer to Nottingham Castle had revealed the former to be a grocer, the latter a mercer.[14] But we are almost certainly dealing with apprentices rather than full-fledged masters, for the king's writ instructing the coroner and sheriffs of London to send all documents to chancery identifies Algor as the servant *(serviens)* of Richard Preston and Kirkby as the servant of John More. Preston and More were both already big fish in the City, though issues already emergent would soon place them on different sides of a factional divide. Preston was not only a prominent grocer, but a burgher of Calais (by virtue of substantial trading interests) and a four-term alderman, in 1378–79 and repeatedly during the Brembre heyday of 1384–87.[15] John More was somewhat less eminent and prosperous than Preston, and achieved most of his civic posts through his factional involvement with John Northampton. But he did stand on the brink of election as alderman in the Northampton surge of 1381, and would be advanced by Northampton to the position of sheriff in 1383.[16]

Preston and More, and especially the former, provide a significant link between our murderers and leading citizens of London. This link is, in turn, affirmed and enhanced in Algor's confession, in which he "names names" galore, though with only a partial understanding of their interest in the crime:

> John Algor said to the aforesaid John Kirkby that he wished Janus Imperial could be killed on this account, because he was suing before the king's council to obtain the release of a certain ship that the servants of Richard Preston, his master, and the servants of John Philipot of London had captured in war upon the sea and from which they would have had a hundred pounds in profit . . . and also because he frequently heard from rumor and gossip in the households of Nicholas Brembre, William Walworth, and the aforesaid Richard Preston and John Philipot in London among their servants that Janus Imperial would destroy and ruin all the wool merchants ["mercatores lanarum"] in London and elsewhere in the realm of England in the event that he could bring to a conclusion what he had in mind. ("Appeal," 40–41)

The "certain ship" would appear to be the *Godesknyght*, under the captaincy of fellow Genoese Lewis Cattaneo; the Close Rolls on 2 April 1379 (just under three months before Imperial's death) record a suit in which he served as ambassador, together with other Genoese merchants, for its recovery.[17] But this suit would have gone on with or without Imperial's involvement, and its mention here would appear to be something of a red herring, in relation to the perceived threat posed by Imperial's plans to the English wool trade. The households in which Algor says he heard dire predictions about Imperial's plans were, in fact, those of the leading merchant capitalists of London. Algor's master Preston is here associated with the three men who were to be the very mainstays of the Ricardian party in London in the years between 1381 and 1387: Nicholas Brembre, grocer, was a four-term mayor and twelve-term alderman, served as collector of customs from 1379 to 1386, was named mayor of the Westminster staple in 1385, and was knighted by Richard for his actions during the Rising of 1381; William Walworth, fishmonger, was a two-term mayor and fourteen-term alderman, longtime mayor of the Westminster staple,[18] named by Parliament as collector of the wool subsidy in 1378, and also knighted in 1381; and John Philipot, grocer, was a mayor and nine-time alderman, served in 1377 as mayor of the Calais staple, was named by Parliament as collector of the wool subsidy in 1378, and was also knighted in 1381.

Their capsule biographies suggest these magnates' interest in the wool trade. The extent of their interest is apparent in the following list of leading London wool exporters, which shows sacks of wool exported from the port of London in 1365–66, early in the respective careers of all concerned:[19]

Exporter	Sacks
Nicholas Brembre, grocer	1432
John Curteys, fishmonger	677
John Lovekin, fishmonger	544
William Baret, grocer	540
Adam Francis, mercer	538
Edmund Oliver, fishmonger	470
Fulk Horwode, grocer	375
John Philipot, grocer	353
Richard Preston, grocer	312
William Vine (?)	300

One point of immediate interest involves the total absence of alien shippers from the chart, and the absence even of provincial English shippers from its upper reaches. Another is that grocers, rather than woolmongers, dominated the trade; in fact, in 1365–66 the largest shipper among the woolmongers sent only 187 sacks of wool. This group of capitalist victuallers includes all the magnates in whose homes Algor heard gossip about Janus Imperial's threat to the wool trade, excepting only William Walworth. Yet we need not worry about Walworth: T. H. Lloyd observes that, "although not exporting in his own name," Walworth was deeply involved in the trade, as suggested by his imminent advancement to the mayoralty of the Westminster staple (251). In 1380–81, the next year for which figures exist, Walworth does join Brembre and Philipot as a shipper, albeit on a small scale (PRO, E122/71/4); in 1384–85, Brembre remains highly active, joined by Preston, the latter on a lesser scale (PRO, E122/71/9).

In short, that group of victuallers to which Algor's master Preston belonged had a virtual hammerlock on London wool exports. In round figures, the 16,000 sacks of wool shipped from London in 1365–66 slightly exceeded the amount shipped from all other English ports combined, and almost three-quarters of that total was sent by London, as opposed to provincial or alien, shippers.[20] The share of wool shipping showed every sign of growing with the institution of the Calais staple in 1376, a regularization avidly supported by our very group of London capitalists. Lloyd, observing that the London merchant capitalists were consistently "the main proponents of the Calais staple" (252), points out that in the summer of 1377 they marked the institution of the new monopoly and their own domination of the flow of exports by advancing the Crown a loan of ten thousand pounds, to be repaid out of wool duties (226).

In nearly complete control of the port of London (recall Brembre's incumbency as collector of customs) and the policy-making apparatus of the Westminster staple (recall Walworth's long incumbency), and well represented in the governance of the new Calais staple, the London merchant capitalists would seem to have had little to fear from the Genoese initiative championed by Janus Imperial. But we must remind ourselves, among other things, how very fragile the Calais staple would have seemed. Its ups and downs in the period between its institution in 1376 and its vindication as a permanent home for the staple at the end of the century have been documented by Power and Lloyd.[21] The point of most relevance for us is that the staple had no sooner been established in 1376 than it was breached in the autumn of 1378 by the very legislation of which Janus Imperial had been a proponent, allowing Italian merchants to export wool to the Mediterranean without paying duties at Calais.[22] Here are a few relevant dates, in what might have been seen as a quickening tempo of challenge to the newly established London-Calais axis:[23]

April 1376	Good Parliament removes staple to Calais
Summer 1377	£10,000 loan by London wool merchants to Crown
March 1378	Letters patent granted to Janus Imperial, master of the *Holy Mary*
Autumn 1378	Parliament confirms broad Italian exemption
April 1379	Suit by "ambassador" Imperial to recover cargo of Genoese ship *Godesknyght*
August 1379	Janus Imperial in London, seeking added concessions; the murder

Two ships, even capacious Genoese tarits, do not necessarily constitute a major trading onslaught. But alien wool exports from the port of Southampton suggest that significant developments were under way. According to Carus-Wilson and Coleman, total alien exports for 1378–79, the first year in which the Italian exemption might have taken effect, were zero. (They might have been something more than that, depending on the destination of the *Godesknyght*.) But alien exports for 1379–80 rose to a robust 1,804 sacks, and for 1380–81 to 2,416 sacks. These figures become a good deal more significant when linked to a related trade in finished wool cloths, in which London was substantially uninvolved. Alien exports of cloths in 1378–79 were a minimal 235, and in 1379–80 a still minimal 247. But in 1381–82 the figure rises to a very respectable 3,812, and it rises again the year after.[24]

Knowing some of the concealed players and the game that was actually being played, we are considerably better positioned to hear Algor's confession. It amounts, as I have said, to a renarration of the event, now stripped of its adventitious overlay and reconfigured in terms of cold intent. Acknowledging his and Kirkby's collusion, he says that they met on Cheap street after sunset and proceeded to Lombard Street and then to St. Nicholas Acton Lane, for the purpose of seeking out ("explorando") Janus Imperial. He continues:

> When they had arrived there and saw him sitting on a bench outside his door, with his servants standing around him, John Algor said to John Kirkby that he wished Janus Imperial could be killed ["quod vellet quod idem Iohannes Imperiall' foret interfectus"]. . . . And John Algor immediately went past the aforesaid Janus Imperial and came back three different times, each time stumbling over Janus Imperial's feet, in order to provoke a quarrel between them ["causa mouendi contumeliam inter ipsos"]. And one of Janus's servants, noticing this, went up to John Algor with a drawn knife in his hand, asking why he had done this to his master. And the said John at once drew his knife and struck the servant on the head and wounded him. And forthwith John Kirkby drew his sword and feloniously struck Janus Imperial on the head, dealing him several fatal blows from which he died at once.

A good many things in the 27 September jury account had never added up, including such questions as what Kirkby and Algor were doing on St. Nicholas Acton Lane in the first place, how the quarrel flared so quickly, and (a line of questioning pursued by the justices at the 9 June hearing) how Kirkby found his movements so restricted that he could not escape without killing Janus Imperial. Now, with Algor's and Kirkby's purpose specified, these issues are resolved in the renarration: they conspired together to kill the Genoese merchant, they met and went to his house for that purpose, Algor created a distraction and engaged his servants, and Kirkby did the deed.

The paradox of accusation by approvership is that the successful approver saves his life by establishing his guilt—along with that of his confederate. Algor is a good approver, to the extent that his account is both detailed and persuasive. Satisfied by Algor's account, the justices meeting on 4 December 1380 sentenced Kirkby to be drawn and hanged for the murder. Algor, confessing his own instigation and abetment of the crime, was spared but returned to prison.[25]

Many of the traditional objectives of investigation and detection would appear to be satisfied by Algor's renarration. Occasion, intent, and motive have all been established, as have the means and motives of the prosecution. But certain explanatory requirements remain unmet even by Algor's more satisfactory retelling. His confession is marked by major suppressions or exclusions that become retrospectively evident in relation to the final disposition of the case. Since Algor was ultimately to receive a royal pardon (Sayles, 41), the only person actually to suffer for this crime was an exceedingly minor player: mercer's apprentice, or servant, Kirkby. Surely, a considerable disproportion exists between the prosecutory zeal of king and Council, who went so far as to obtain a parliamentary declaration of treason and an extraordinary venue change for Kirkby's sentencing, and this impoverished result! Ample evidence enables the reasonably conscientious investigator—even from a distance of five hundred years—to settle on an identifiable cluster of London wool magnates as the procurers and abettors of the crime, yet in the final determination they remained untouched. Their exemption from a prosecution initially geared at a level of formality suitable to the indictment of the most powerful persons in the land must be considered an anticlimax, at the very least, and an ultimate challenge even to the new and more complete narration of the case.

"NOUS SOMMES TOUS DES ASSASSINS"

The convictions of Algor and Kirkby may be said to result from an investigative procedure common to detective work (and not unknown to historical work) in which the investigator winnows through a field of suspects to identify a single locus of guilt while absolving others from responsibility for the crime. Such procedures possess an undeniable strength that may, however, become a methodological shortcoming in its own right. An investigation artificially narrowed to the motives and deeds of a single suspect—or even group of suspects—risks neglect of the sense in which participation in a crime, and enjoyment of its consequences, might be diffusely held among and across a larger community of suspects.[26]

Principal responsibility for the murder must indeed rest with an inner circle of wool merchants. But civic support for the crime seems to have extended well beyond the members of this small circle. After all, the record shows that no fewer than thirty-seven different citizens of London, proven and sworn for jury duty, stood firmly behind the claim that Kirkby and Algor acted on their own, without malice aforethought, and in self-defense—even in the face of persistent questioning, first by their own sheriffs and then by justices of the highest court in the land.

A small but revealing indication of the breadth of civic involvement is the surprising association of mercer John More, master of John Kirkby, with the events of the crime. I do not want to overstate More's importance to the conspiracy, since his man Kirkby was probably functioning in this case as a hireling rather than as More's servant, and More was not necessarily an abettor of the crime. But More's involvement in *any* capacity whatever might surprise anyone acquainted with the factional politics of subsequent years. For 1381–88 would be years of evident cleavage between Brembre, Walworth, Philipot, and Preston and other leaders of the proroyal circle of merchant capitalists on the one hand and Northampton, More, and their party of drapers, mercers, and lesser guildsmen on the other. More was to be highly visible in these years, first with his election to alderman in the Northampton surge of 1381–82, and then with his advancement to sheriff during Northampton's mayoralty in 1383. He would be repeatedly named as a Northampton partisan in the indictments of 1384, including Thomas Usk's "Appeal," and he would subsequently be expelled from London along with his leader.[27] But, in

1379–80, Londoners of radically different views and affiliations could still pull together on issues they perceived as affecting the entire city; whatever stresses would ultimately divide the patriciate, this threat to the wool trade appears to be an issue on which they could unite.[28]

Suppose, though, that participation of Londoners in the crime and its cover-up involved many more people than the handful of wool merchants. The crime would still seem to have been abhorred outside the city: in the royal Council, which pressed for the declaration of treason that brought Kirkby and Algor before the King's Bench, and in Parliament itself, where the declaration of treason was approved and where Kirkby's conviction was evidently countenanced (Walsingham, 1:449). The interest of the Council and the Parliament in seeing this crime punished would appear to be self-evident. It was king and Council that had invited Janus Imperial to bring his tarit to Southampton in the first place, in return for direct payment of taxes and dues, and such concessions remained tempting to the Council as a way of alleviating its chronic shortages of cash (Lloyd, 228–29). Furthermore, the national constituency of wool growers (including the dukes of Lancaster and Gloucester with their great estates) was well represented in Parliament, and the wool-growing interest would seem best served by competitive trade and a multiplication of markets.[29] Aligned, too, against the wool staplers and their protectionist policies would seem to be the growing English cloth industry, which stood only to benefit from Italian trade, and the burgesses who were profiting from the cloth industry did not lack parliamentary influence of their own.

Yet, somewhat paradoxically, each of these parties also had at least as much to gain from the maintenance of the Calais staple. Whatever short-term exigencies drove king and Council to make concessions to the Italian merchants, they had found their longer-term interest to be served by the staple system, with its provision for assured revenues over longer time periods; so, too, did the exceptional enrichment of a handful of merchant capitalists provide the groundwork of loans upon which the Crown came increasingly to depend.[30] Although Parliament was willing to juggle competing claims of alien and denizen merchants, the fact remains that it, too, was heavily invested in the concept of the Calais staple.[31] And even the domestic wool growers and the nascent English cloth industry stood to gain in a wholly unintended way through the monopolistic activities of the staple; for, as the staplers raised taxes in order to meet their obligations to the Crown, they created a favorable discrepancy between high prices abroad and low prices at home.[32] This extreme and potentially immobilizing mixture of motivational cross-currents may help to explain the ease with which the Council's and Parliament's thirst for justice was so easily slaked, with the sacrifice of a single, symbolic criminal, coupled with a prevailing inclination to let the real instigators go free. Indeed, so feeble and so quickly exhausted was the justice-seeking impulse of these bodies that they might virtually be considered unindicted coconspirators in the concealment of the crime.

We here find ourselves in a shifting field of claims and counterclaims, ostensible and actual interests, determination that guilt will be assigned and convenient circumscription of its actual extent. Confronted with such complexities, an investigative procedure leading to assignment of singular guilt may be criticized for its inattention to what Slavoj Žižek has called the "intersubjective dimension" of a crime — inattention to the sense in which a crime binds together an expanded group of suspects, all of whom share in motive, opportunity, libidinal possibility, and unconscious desire.[33] In this respect, the investigative or judicial procedure that succeeds precisely by localizing and assigning singular guilt may fail adequately to acknowledge the actual extent of shared complicity in a crime, paradoxically permitting the larger community to evade responsibility for its desires. The assignment of sole guilt to Kirkby would seem to facilitate such an evasion. This is a guilt in which larger elements of the community must share — not just Kirkby, and not just the wool merchants, but Parliament and courts and Council as well.[34]

ANTAGONISM AND
THE LIMITS OF EXPLANATION

Thus far I have sought to explain guilt in terms of a rational calculation of interests, and to defend my assignments of guilt by expanding and diversifying membership in the circle of those whose interests this death served. But certain elements of the trial records suggest the presence of a form of guilt less connected with any rational calculation at all. Through certain rents and apertures in the trial record blows the idiot wind of the inexplicable — or that which at best is explicable only in terms of an irrational fear of otherness, a xenophobia implicated in, but exceeding, any computation of profit and loss.

The rents and apertures of which I speak may be considered as inevitable symbolic inadequacies, resulting not from a thinness or unavailability in material available for symbolization, but from its very excess. These are the moments identified by Laclau and Mouffe as "antagonisms," in their subversion of language and symbolic structure, issuing in the impossibility of their inclusion in a coherent social narration.[35] At such moments of antagonism, the process of symbolization itself fails in its function of collecting and reconciling materials from outside the symbolic system to the demands of that system. Such points of failure may be signaled by the presence of a representational surplus, a virtual overflow of materials with highly diverse and contradictory ramification and unaccommodated threat to established arrangements.

As a fellow merchant *and* foreign competitor, as a source of possible economic advantage *and* a threat of possible ruination, as a credentialed diplomat *and* freewheeling interloper, Janus Imperial inevitably overwhelms later fourteenth-century English society's capacity for orderly symbolization, for representing its own norms and procedures and reconciling itself to persons and interests "other" than itself. Symptomatic of symbolic overflow in the case of Janus Imperial is failure of trial records and chronicle accounts to achieve even a minimally consistent representational strategy.

The letters patent and records of parliamentary action prior to the murder emphasize the economic benefits to arise from dealings with the Genoan, including emphasis on the customs and subsidies and other monies to be paid directly to the royal treasury, and the profitable nature of the agreements to be drawn between the king and his city (*RP*, 3:75). For these reasons, Janus Imperial was taken under special protection and was to be spared the varied mistreatments to which foreign merchants were frequently subjected: "injury, loss, molestation, arrest, violence, hindrance, or other wrong." Reasonably enough, considering the nature of these documents, emphasis falls on the single possibility, that profit might arise.[36]

The trial records, on the other hand, treat this merchant somewhat more circumstantially, less as a wealthy shipper and representative of a sovereign state than as a foreign visitor to the city. Testimony, pointed

toward the exoneration of the Londoners, portrays him in a vaguely clown-
ish way, as a figure given to rages and threats but lacking in the power
to back them up. In the legal Latin of the jury report, actions that might
otherwise seem reasonable and pacificatory are given an odd and aggressive tilt. When Kirkby treads on his feet ("through no wish of his own,"
in the first version), Imperial is said to have become angrily stirred ("se
mouit et irassi incepit manifeste"), and his evident puzzlement over a
seemingly unmotivated provocation and attack is treated as further evidence that he is consumed with anger ("irassiter interrogando . . . qua de
causa ipsi predictos seruientes suos sic percusserunt et verberauerunt").
In accepting the main thrust of the Algor-Kirkby account, the jury seems
ready to believe that foreigners even of the highest station are predis-
posed to rage out of control, to demand adjudicatory authority where
none exists.

A more sympathetic, though not necessarily more realistic, response
is to be found in chronicler Walsingham, who treats Imperial not only
as the proposer of an advantageous mercantile arrangement, but also as
an offended innocent, slain by a malicious and avaricious London throng.
Walsingham, in short, partially assimilates this Genoese merchant to the
model of the crucifixion itself, portraying him as a *vir innocens et moliens*,
a man suspecting no evil intent, and portraying his slayers as consumed
by detestable malice, avarice, and perfidy. The whole event, he suggests,
will stand as a "sign" ("nota") of human infidelity and a source of anger
to God.[37]

These representational cross-currents are, of course, related to the
generic properties of the respective texts — letters patent, indictments,
chronicle entries — within which they are conceived. But they also suggest a prevailing inability to adopt a steady policy or even a stance toward
an increasingly complicated economic situation, in which merchants as-
pire to a monopolistic staple but accommodate themselves to the Crown's
need for short-term capital, in which a domestic cloth-making industry
is on the rise but relies upon foreign shipments of alum and woad, in
which an affluent urban patriciate would guard the London franchise
but cannot resist imported luxury items like gold cloth and cheap pepper.
In this sense, the foreigner is not simply "other" to the system but is already halfway inside, useful but despised, partially incorporated but always liable to expulsion. The foreigner resides in a charged practical/
symbolic space with the potential of attracting to itself a range of larger

tendencies, including the late-fourteenth- and early-fifteenth-century en-
croachments of self-serving nationalism into the more diverse field of
rivalries characteristic of the earlier Middle Ages. The politicization of
this symbolic instability may be gauged in the extreme variability of alien
fates in England in these decades — alternate acceptance, and even encouragement, and rejection, often in convulsively violent ways.[38]

Symbolizing strategies cannot exhaust every aspect of an event, or
foreclose every blur or blind spot, or fail to leave an unsymbolized residue
in their wake. Antagonisms are inherent in textuality itself, and texts
are never adequate to the infinite recesses of the Real. Analysts do, however, retain some choice of which aspects of a situation to illuminate
and which to cede or leave blind. Suppose that, in concluding homage
to Janus Imperial, we were to shift representational ground to treat him
not just as antagonistic other but with more deference to his claims and
possible motives. The shift might be figured by imagining a portrayal of
this Genoese merchant not from the atavistic-xenophobic but from the
pan-European point of view. He might, in such a case, be seen as a typically individualistic Genoese merchant adventurer. As such, he was in-
comparably more daring than the conservative London wool monopo-
lists; equipped, to be sure, with letters from his duke and commonality
(*RP*, 3:75), but also very much master of his own ships and enterprise,
on the Genoese rather than Venetian or state-capitalist model.[39] He might
be seen as a victim of larger economic circumstances, including the severe downturn that afflicted the Genoese precisely in the 1370s.[40] Driven
to seek new wool and woolen cloth markets, but blocked by the 1379 re-
volts of the Flemish weavers,[41] he was forced into what any fourteenth-
century Genoese would have considered a secondary market to make
his cargo. Burdened by English piracy and empoundments,[42] he had no
choice but to sojourn in a hostile city in order to argue for trading concessions from the quarreling Council of an English boy king.

Without pretending to invade his subjectivity, to which the records
give no access at all, I cannot help but impute to him a certain fatalism
as he went about his difficult and dangerous task. Fatalism, rather than
Babbitry and mindless optimism, is what my own favorite contemporary writer, Geoffrey Chaucer, imputes to the French merchant of his
"Shipman's Tale."[43] Doubting that his "curious bisynesse" can easily be
explained to nonparticipants, Chaucer's merchant muses in this vein:

For of us chapmen...
Scarsly amonges twelve tweye shul thryve
Continuelly, lastyng unto oure age.
We may wel make chiere and good visage,
And dryve forth the world as it may be,
And kepen oure estaat in pryvetee,
Til we be deed...

(VII.228–33)

I offer these lines as an epitaph for Janus Imperial, slain in a remote and, in this case, inhospitable land. And also in frustrated acknowledgment of the limits of textual access to his (or other participants') ultimate and inevitable *pryvetee*.

9

SHAKESPEARE'S OLDCASTLE

ANOTHER ILL-FRAMED KNIGHT

Many more things were imagined about and for John Oldcastle than he could ever have performed. But, even granting his exceptional stimulus to the creative and narrative imagination, how are we ever to reconstruct an itinerary linking the empirical Oldcastle to the arrant swaggerer and extravagant clown to whom Shakespeare, in *Henry IV,* parts 1 and 2, originally assigned that name? And to whom, in the recent Oxford Shakespeare and other editions in the making, that name has now been restored?[1]

Ruptures, orchestrated forgettings, and new departures separate the historical Oldcastle from Shakespeare's extravagant creation. So many, in fact, that no orderly genealogy can connect the historical original, or even his early representations, with his lavish counterpart. Different textual traditions—including the customary view of Oldcastle as seditious traitor and the revisionist view of Oldcastle as proto-Protestant martyr—abounded in the sixteenth century, but Shakespeare seems not formally to have consulted them. The one work he appears to have consulted ignores most of the textual riches at its disposal, portraying Oldcastle in an extremely attenuated and idiosyncratic way. This is *The Famous Victories of Henry V,* in which Oldcastle appears rather sketchily as one Jockey, a boon companion of the prince. In other words, Oldcastle entered late-sixteenth-century English drama largely stripped of historical complexity, his appearance in the *Famous Victories* requiring only two suppositions. The first is that Oldcastle was an intimate of the prince. The second is more complex, in the sense of involving a main proposition and several derivatives. The main proposition is that the prince experienced a reformation—a night-to-day transformation—upon assumption of the throne. The derivatives are that his youthful companions must have been his abettors in vice and folly, and that his unregenerate companions must have been set aside when he became king.

These suppositions are venerable. They are even quasi-historical, if we use that term to describe actions "believed by many," or actions "conceived within a skein of historically situated beliefs and purposes." But they are founded upon no empirical authority and, in that sense, are historically untrue. I would describe their status as that of historically saturated inventions. My purpose here is to revisit the scene of their textual invention, which I situate not in the Elizabethan period (the period of their elaboration) but in another culturally dynamic period: the early fifteenth century. For in that century were accomplished the preliminaries to the act of "imagining Oldcastle."

Both suppositions — Oldcastle's friendship and Henry's reformation — originated within the circuit of a characteristic fifteenth-century representational endeavor. I would describe this endeavor as the rehearsal of turmoil and dissent within structures ultimately vindicatory of civil order. Divided political loyalties (resulting from Lancastrian usurpation) and divided religious sympathies (resulting from Lollard critique) supplied a never-ending challenge to Lancastrian loyalty. The ideological mandate of loyalist writers was to conceive potential scandals within imaginative structures that neutralized their disruptive potential. Resituating apparent threats within providential or Lancastrian design, these writers discovered a way to use potential destabilizations to enhance, rather than derogate, the beholder's sense of Lancastrian authority. By this route, apparent subversions could become vital representational assets for regimes that needed all the legitimacy they could command. Consequently, I would identify the potentially destabilizing events of John Oldcastle's career as a major challenge to Lancastrian historiography, and the extension of Lancastrian dominion to those events as one of the new regime's major imaginative accomplishments.

FAILED FRIENDSHIP

The notion that Oldcastle and the prince were acquainted does possess some scattered and inferential foundation in the historical record. Oldcastle was, for example, active against the Welsh rebels in the period between 1403 and 1408 when the prince served as lieutenant of the Marches of Wales, and could have been known to him there.[2] In 1411 he took part in a pro-Burgundian sally against the French at Saint-Cloud, in an expedition sponsored by the prince (and opposed by the king).[3] In 1413 Oldcastle was among a group of persons advancing the new king money to purchase a jeweled belt buckle.[4] Oldcastle may have been involved, with Sir William Bourchier, in arranging an entertainment for the new king in August 1413.[5] Most centrally, Henry V as new king is depicted as having personally endeavored to persuade Oldcastle from his heterodox course. But the time has come for a close look at the passages, from Archbishop Arundel's own account, upon which ideas of Henry's personal involvements are founded.

Arundel's account of the matter describes a clerical deputation to the new king, then at his manor of Kennington, for the purpose of detailing the spiritual defects of John Oldcastle. He says that the matter was accorded this degree of formality, "out of respect for our lord King, of whose household lord John was a member at that time ('cujus adtunc idem dominus Johannes familiaris extiterat'), and no less because of the honor owed to his military rank."[6] He adds that, the presentation having been made:

> At the request of the same lord King, desiring to lead said Lord John back to the unity of the church without further unseemliness ["sine dedecore"], we delayed prosecution of the previous charges for a considerable time. But at last, since our lord King failed to make progress in his rehabilitation, even after great labors, he accordingly deigned, both orally and in writing, to refer the matter [to us].

The notion of Oldcastle as "familiaris" (as a member of the new king's household or following, or, alternatively, as a person simply in the king's military service) is introduced to explain Henry's interest in the case. The fifteenth-century term does not, however, suggest that Oldcastle was Henry's "familiar" or "friend." What is established here is not intimacy, but something equally important to the fifteenth century: an "interest," a tie between the two men based on loyal service within the "familia." This service would presumably have fallen short of "retention," and implies something just short of it, service by temporary indenture, either in the extended household of the prince, or (more likely, given what is known of Oldcastle's career) in trusted capacities within military endeavors important to the prince. We are, in other words, speaking not of "friendship" but of "loyalty" and "obligation."

These hints at a closer-than-routine relation were subject to development by other early writers on the subject, with loyalty, rather than friendship, still as their central theme. The author of the *Gesta Henrici Quinti*, writing after the fact (but with Oldcastle still at large) in 1416, expands Oldcastle's service and its impact, describing him as "one of the most valued and most substantial members of his household": "unum de precarissimis et magis domesticis suis."[7] I have attempted a measured translation of these words, but they raise the stakes in several new ways. "Precarissimus" might be rendered "the dearest" as well as "the most valued," and even the qualifier "one of" does not temper its superlative qualities, and its hint of a certain affectivity that transcends simple "good service." At the same time, the simple "familiaris" in the sense of "follower" has now become "domesticus," staking a more definite claim for Oldcastle's location in the immediate household, and, with "magis," as one of the most important of his household servants.

The *effect* of such elaborations is to exacerbate the gravity of Oldcastle's crime. For treason always involves a violation of trust, an offense against one to whom loyalty is owed — one, in the language of the 1352 Statute, "a qi il doit foi & obedience."[8] Once an act of treason is alleged — as it was alleged against Oldcastle after the events at Saint Giles's fields — then much is to be gained by the additional discovery that a relation of special trust had been violated. The relation of subject to king was already one of presumptive trust. But if that relationship were augmented by other bonds (of class solidarity, military or familial service, or even of friendship), then the treason would be much aggravated. This was, for example, urged in the case of Scrope two years later. The *Gesta* described this treasonous lord, with somewhat more evidence, as one of the greatest in the king's household and one of the most intimate with the king's secrets (18). Subsequent accounts would urge that Henry and Scrope had often shared the same chamber, or bed.[9]

Aggravated treason, high treason, and diabolical treason are fueled by a surplus of oppositional energy that would seem to threaten the king, but which, if brought under control, may be converted into a heightened affirmation of the true king's value. The author of the *Gesta* achieves this control (and ultimate affirmation) by installing opposition in the larger framework of God's probation or "approval" of his elect. Oldcastle has in fact, according to the *Gesta* author, been raised up *by* God for this very probationary purpose: "God himself, Who is the searcher of hearts ... in order that ... His elect be proved ('probaretur') in the furnace of tribulation, allowed an adversary to rise up against him" (2–3). In short, no worry: the *issue* of this contest is never in doubt (and it proceeds under the most serene sponsorship). Proven, the king will be found unalloyed, just as Oldcastle will be found counterfeit, a bad penny. But this passage of proof will redound all the more to Henry's credit, the gravity of his false friend's treachery having been established.

To prevail in the face of such high treachery is to be God's elect indeed. And so treachery, interpreted as violation of ties of special trust, is underscored in every facet of the fifteenth-century invention. It is to be seen, for example, in such details as Adam of Usk's suggestion that Oldcastle was invested with the spurs of knighthood by the prince and his brother Clarence, and his bitter observation that, "afterward, nevertheless, he was such an ingrate that he was not ashamed to turn against them" ("post tamen in ipsos tamquam ingratus recalcitrari non eribuit").[10] The point of Adam's elaboration is, of course, that royal favor renders the rebel guilty, not only of his rebellion, but also of additional transgressions of personal loyalty and gratitude.

Also foundational to the prince's and Oldcastle's invented friendship is the assertion, first traceable to Archbishop Arundel, that the prince invested considerable personal time in conversation aimed at Oldcastle's successful reintroduction to the path of truth. Arundel's register describes several face-to-face interviews, the latter conducted at Windsor in August 1413, at which Henry finally set aside his lenience and chided Oldcastle for his obstinacy, and Oldcastle, "plenus diabolo," withdrew without permission to his castle at Cowling (353).

Why, given the king's willingness to petition for postponement, his personal concern, and his involvement in face-to-face interviews, do I remain dubious about this matter of personal friendship? In part because Henry's conversation with Oldcastle reenacts a preexisting model, one that has nothing to do with friendship at all. This model is exhibited in an instance at which Henry set out to reform a heretic, and in which household ties (or at least a royal pension) were at issue, but with no pretense of friendship at all: the prince's intervention at the burning of condemned heretic John Badby in 1410. Chroniclers represent the prince as personally intervening at the scene of Badby's Smithfield burning — first with persuasion prior to the lighting of the fire, then ordering the flames withdrawn in order to promise Badby a royal pension (and, in effect, entry to his *familia*) should he recant, and, after Badby's final refusal, ordering the flames rekindled.[11] This scene has been far more fully analyzed by Peter McNiven than I can possibly undertake here.[12] But I do want to consider one of its aspects: its theatricality, as well as the impetus behind its theatricality.

The burning itself, and Henry's role in it, is a form of "loyalty theater," that sort of state theater described by Michel de Certeau in which an ostensibly religious drama is deployed without its own consent in the name of another, tacitly political and secular, function. In such theater, the political and secular arm, pretending compliance with religious institutions, actually bends those institutions toward its own purposes. "What is new," says de Certeau, "is not so much religious *ideology* (power imposing a return to Catholic orthodoxy) as the *practice* that, from now on, makes religion serve a politics of order. . . . On this level the weakened Christian 'system' is transformed into a sacred theater of the system that will take its place."[13] The point about Henry's intervention is not its outcome; the point, rather, lies in the intervention itself. For Henry, in the case of Badby *and* the case of Oldcastle, positions himself to win either way. If the heretic recants, the prince demonstrates his powers of persuasion, his powers of recruitment. If the heretic refuses, the prince demonstrates his ultimate deference to the wishes of the church; demonstrates, even, the sense in which he is the church's necessary upholder.

Stray evidence suggests that Henry's interventions were not invariably welcome to the religious establishment. The Badby exploit went unmentioned in Arundel's register. The alternative account of the Oldcastle interview in Arundel's register says that clerics "murmured" ("non absque murmure cleri . . . quieverunt"; 352) over the time required, and Walsingham comments stingingly that Henry was employed with Oldcastle for a long time, emptily ("Dominus Rex circa reductionem ejus longum tempus trivisset inaniter"; 291–92). Nevertheless, we cannot doubt that Henry's assiduous self-representation of himself as the Church's effective "Protector" would have been generally pleasing to the religious establishment of the day — just as we cannot fail also to see, in the light of sixteenth-century history, how ominous and potentially *un*protective this royal role (virtually invented by Henry) would turn out to be.[14]

And so loyalty, rather than friendship, is at issue thus far. Nevertheless, a *structure* is in place: that structure which starts as a claim for a more limited or motivated attachment, but is then available for colonization and elaboration around and along the lines of friendship. The first actual employment of this structure in the service of friendship is Oldcastle's placement among the prince's boon companions in the *Famous Victories,* seconding Hal with lines like "We shall never have a merry world till the old King be dead."[15] Interestingly, once in place, the friendship claim is not only adopted by Shakespeare, but by many other constituencies as well. Among its most ardent advocates are the late-nineteenth- and early-twentieth-century historians who have most urgently advocated documentary scrupulosity. Solly-Flood sets the modern tone by returning to Arundel's description of Oldcastle as a member of Henry's household or *familiaris,* translating the term as "familiar friend" (135), and Wylie interprets it as "one of Henry's intimate friends" (1:245), and Waugh expands the notion even a bit farther, by imagining that Henry had staked with Arundel a claim based on personal friendship, "reminding Arundel of the close friendship existing between Oldcastle and himself" (448). In a similar vein, the usually restrained Taylor and Roskell render "unum de ... magis domesticis suis" as "one of the more intimate members of his household" (3), a surprising enhancement of an already enhanced claim.

HAL'S REFORMATION

And so one precondition of Oldcastle/Falstaff—proximity to or intimacy with the young prince—was established early on. But what about Oldcastle as Hal's *raffish* intimate, his intimate-in-folly? This elaboration depends upon another freshly made fifteenth-century conjunction, in which the idea of transformation, of the Pauline "new man," is adduced to explain Hal's reformation upon acceptance of the crown.[16] If Hal as prince is to be regarded as gross or imperfect matter, perfected upon assumption of the throne, then each of these states has implications for the caliber of his associations: "fallen" companions before, "perfected" ones after, with a necessary rejection of those youthful companions who remained unregenerate.

An early, and comparatively modest, imposition of this pattern is already present in the near-contemporary account of the *Historia Anglicana*. Noting that Henry V's April coronation was visited by snow, Walsingham ventures a symbolic interpretation, in which winter is to be followed by spring. He then adds that, as soon as the new king was invested with the regalia, he immediately changed into another man ("in virum alterum"), a man of honesty, modesty, and *gravitas*, seeking that no virtue should be omitted that he desired to exercise (2:290). This idea of a drastic reformation was widely elaborated in the later fifteenth and sixteenth centuries.

Titus Livius repeats the idea that "he was sodenlie changed into a newe man."[17] The necessary augmentation of this idea, that he then rejected his old riotous friends, is added by his English translator in the sixteenth century: "And to all them that woulde perseuer in their former light conuersacion he gaue expresse commaundement vppon paine of theire heads neuer after that daye to come to his presence" (19). Fabyan further develops the notion of a riotous entourage, saying that before his father's death Hal "drewe vnto hym all ryottours & wylde dysposed persones," but that after, "nat to be reduced therunto by the famyliaryties of his olde nyse company, he therfore, after rewardes to them gyuen, charged theym vpn payne of theyre lyues, that none of theym were so hardy to come wythin x. myle of suche place as he were lodgyd."[18] Subsequent accounts, in which the prince disports himself in robbery and other lawbreaking with fictitious low companions, were elaborated in the sixteenth century (especially by the translator of Titus Livius), as was Thomas Elyot's wholesale fabrication of another imagined confrontation between the prince and the law, in this case his quarrel with the chief justice of the realm and subsequent imprisonment.[19]

The historian's temptation, as Paul Veyne suggests in the case of any myth, is to suppose that mythic patterns like that of Hal's reformation must contain some "kernel" of truth, that the myth itself can be purified by hermeneutic suspicion and reduced to the factual substratum that gave it birth.[20] But what if there *is* no substratum, no irreducible kernel of truth? The historical record (of Hal's distinguished military and administrative service in Wales, and on the royal council, and his own regal ambitions) suggest *no* rout of low companions, and in fact contain *no* imputation of self-misrule. He was, according to the record, *always* a person of self-imposed restraint. As demonstrated in the nineteenth century by Solly-Flood, in the early years of this century by Kingsford, and more recently by Christopher Allmand,[21] Henry as Prince had spent his time in the most blameless ways. He acquitted himself assiduously in military campaigns in Wales (1403–7), as a member of the king's Council (1407–9), as virtual regent and artful fabricator of a pro-Burgundian strategy (1410–11), and as somewhat impatient and self-publicizing but dead serious heir-in-waiting (1411–12).

Hal's passage from profligate enjoyment to sober self-regulation is a product, not of history, but of imagination: a recasting of his conduct in a convenient and well-established frame. This is, as David Carr and others suggest, the move to narrative, to a pattern that organizes actions in the interest of intelligibility according to a preunderstood scheme: beginning/end, was/is now, conversion from/to.[22] Whether our term be "pattern" or "structure" or "myth," the point is that historicity does not undergird it or lurk within it. At the same time, this notion of the prince's passage from sobriety to maturity *does* possess an undeniable historicity. This historicity rests, not in a "kernel" or core, but in its "hull" or outer surface. What is "historical," in other words, is the pattern itself, and more particularly the decision to exalt and edify Henry's kingship by reconceiving it in the terms of a known, affirmative pattern. We do learn something about history from Titus Livius and the others, but our learning is not through a process of distillation; rather, it occurs from trying to understand the fact of recourse to this preexistent pattern at this particular time, together with the historically specific motives underlying the choice and its consequences.

Even in the fifteenth century, and even in relation to Hal, this pattern is adaptable to different historically inflected objectives. The myth of sudden conversion supports late medieval kingship in its sacramental aspect. Coronation is thereby viewed as transforming and renewing, with unction internally altering its recipient. Thus one late medieval chronicle argues that "in his youthe he had bene wylde recheles and spared nothyng of his lustes ne desires . . . but as sonne as he was crouned enoynted and sacred anone sodenly he was chaunged in to a new man."[23] Benefiting from this transformation is not just Henry himself, but Lancastrian legitimacy as well. (Shakespeare, in a new political-ecclesiastical environment, edifies kingship along more secular lines, portraying Hal's transformation as a consequence of policy and wise statecraft: "By so much shall I falsify men's hopes..."; *1 Henry IV*, 1.2.208.) Later in the fifteenth century, Titus Livius deploys Hal's conversion differently, as an illustration of the sacrament of penance: "After [Henry IV's] death the prince...called to him a vertuous Monke of hholie conursacion, to whome he confessed himselfe of all his offences, trespasses and insolencies of times past. And in all things at that time he reformed and amended his life and his manners" (17). Finally, in addition to serving (or defining) short-term objectives, the myth of Hal's regeneration functions in its own right to bolster the position of the king. I have already mentioned the prestige of its implicitly Pauline origin, with the old, "fallen" man replaced by the new, "regenerate" one. And it may likewise be seen, in an alternative theology with its own transcendental aspirations, to track the Freudian pattern of *Totem and Taboo*, whereby the father of obscene enjoyment is supplanted by the father of restraint and respect for the law.[24] This conversion, from the father who enjoins delight to the father who conserves delight, sustaining his subjects' enjoyments by stationing them at a proper distance from the fulfillment of their desires, is a virtual recipe of good rule, a structural apologue for Lancastrian self-legitimation and right to rule.

A pattern this powerful and productive dies hard, and even modern historians, who know better, have trouble letting it go. Thus, we find as respected a commentator as K. B. McFarlane following on from Thomas Elyot and others in abetting this fictionalizing process: "That with some wild friends he had lain in wait and robbed his own receivers, that he attracted to himself low and riotous company...and that William Gascoigne, the Chief Justice, had then so far offended him as to be dismissed at the beginning of his reign, can now hardly be doubted."[25] Let's face it: none of us can resist a good story. And Oldcastle is one of those now recruited to make a good story better.

HAL'S WILDEST FRIEND

The conversion pattern's power may also be measured in its potential for self-augmentation and propagation, not only encouraging related stories (Hal as highwayman, Hal and the chief justice), but extending its own cast of characters, adding fictive members of the prince's unruly train. Concomitant with this impulse toward fictionalization is its close cousin, the act of stripping historical characters of their other attributes and fitting themselves out to play contributory roles in the drama of conversion — as wastrels, profligates, or what you will.

A certain logic here unfolds: if (1) Hal's early familiars were lowlifes, and if (2) Oldcastle was Hal's early familiar, then (3) low-living Oldcastle seems an almost unavoidable point of imaginative destination. This imaginative conjunction is further abetted by Arundel's account of Oldcastle's impetuous withdrawal ("recessit") to Couling.[26] For this account to become usable, the energy of the voluntary withdrawal needed to be transmuted into an expulsion, and Oldcastle's insurgent or oppositional religious views needed to be reworked as corporeal unruliness. But even in our *post*structural age these seem thinkable, even plausible, transformations. The wonder is not that these available structures and perspectives ever converged, but that they were so long kept apart!

Their delayed conjunction occurs in *Famous Victories,* where boisterous Oldcastle shares Hal's highwayman fantasies, is encouraged to imagine himself Hal's annuitant, and experiences the new king's rejection:

> *Henry V.* Thous say'st I am changed; so I am indeed, and so
> must thou be, and that quickly, or else I must cause thee to
> be changed.
> *Oldcastle.* God's wounds! How like you this? 'Zounds, 'tis not
> so sweet as music.
>
> (Scene 9, lines 39–43)

Lurking in this conjunction may be found a few dimly historical preconditions and trace elements: some "tie" (though probably short of friendship) between the prince and Oldcastle; the possibility of an estrangement (though probably initiated by Oldcastle, rather than the other way around); a notion of Henry's reformation (though developed more as a riposte to Lancastrian legitimacy problems than as any properly historical evidence). But this conjunction was primarily an imaginative feat, and the ground for it was prepared, not by Elizabethan dramatists, but by an overlooked and underestimated cluster of fifteenth-century ecclesiastics, chroniclers, and early biographers (including, evidently, the antiaesthete, Arundel).

Nor have we exhausted the senses in which these same writers prethought, or otherwise cleared ground for, the complex valences of Shakespeare's Oldcastle/Falstaff. I list here some of these optionally available imaginative preconditions, potentially or tacitly linking the early fifteenth and the later sixteenth centuries.

Forward/backward looking. The stigmatized Oldcastle, like heresy itself, is ever old and new, with his obsolescences and his novelties: "cum sua vetustate et novitate," according to the *Gesta* (8). Oddly old and young, Falstaff/Oldcastle's white hairs witness his age (*1 Henry IV*, 2.4.468), even as he claims the licenses of youth (*1 Henry IV*, 2.2.82).

Solitary but accompanied. Walsingham describes Oldcastle as a solitary, isolated from the church by his beliefs ("more solito"; 307). But he also moves in a band of followers and *pertinaces* and *sequaces* (297), accompanied by his special attendants ("de suis specialibus asseclis"; 326), conspiring with his confederates in their haunts and holes (*Gesta*, 6–7). Hoccleve sees him "twynned" from Christ's faith (line 8), but also as presiding over a "broken meynee" (line 391). So does Falstaff/Oldcastle crisscross the stage, alternately soliloquizing and carnivalizing with his ragtag band.

Hypocrite. Like all heretics, Oldcastle cloaks himself in sanctity, operating "sub velamine sanctitatis" (*Gesta*, 10), and so is Falstaff/Oldcastle constantly "not what thou seem'st" (*1 Henry IV*, 5.4.136) — constantly duplicitous, miming positions other than his own.

Traitor. Not just heretical but seditious, Oldcastle is a very raven of treachery, even as Falstaff/Oldcastle jokingly but ambiguously flirts with traitorousness and betrayal (1.2.144).

Counterfeit. Himself a false coin that once "shoon ful cleer,"[27] Oldcastle is committed by his Lollardy to an imagery of false alloy, and (as in the accusation of William Carsewell) imagined — with his fellow Lollards — to traffic in adulterated coin.[28] Shakespeare's Henry, in contrast, hopes to shine "like bright metal on sullen ground" (1.2.209f.). Falstaff/Oldcastle himself sees Henry as "a true piece of gold" and "no counterfeit" (2.5.497–98; 5.4.112f.). So is Falstaff/Oldcastle drawn constantly into association with images of the counterfeit. He constantly asserts his own materiality and vitality, but with equal consistency slips back into subterfuge and counterfeit, as with his own mock death, when "'twas time to counterfeit" (5.4.110f.). As Hal says upon discovery of his deceit, he is not what he seems.

Gross materialist. The Lollard has doubts about transformation, about the possibility of severing "seeming" from "being," and hence the libel directed at the Lollard concerns his affinity to the material or gross remainder, the scandal of untransformed substance. Lollard "materiality," in the eyes of the orthodox, seems metonymically predictive of Falstaff/ Oldcastle's gross corpulence, his existence as a bag of "fat guts" (2.2.31), a "huge hill of flesh" (2.5.247). His own very fleshly materiality may be viewed as a kind of obscene *contrapasso* or requital for his inability to think away the material residue of bread in the transformative miracle of the orthodox Eucharist.[29]

These dispositions travel no discursive high road from the fifteenth century to the pen of Shakespeare. Although halfhearted attempts have been made to argue that Falstaff/Oldcastle is a "lampoon" of the historical Oldcastle,[30] these tantalizing linkages are not really solid enough to argue that this is the case. With Holinshed (and, via Holinshed, Hall and other chroniclers) at his disposal, and with Foxe within reach, Shakespeare could have been thorough in establishing an irrefutable linkage with the historical Oldcastle—had he wished. But many of the similarities I have mentioned remain tacit in nature, owing more to the common discursive common ground shared by these two outcasts than to historical specifics. Each figure struggles under the opprobrious baggage customarily heaped upon those found threatening to the regulatory economy of good rule. Each represents some form of illicit indulgence, a refusal to be restrained by a monarch suddenly intent on binding and regulating subjects' desires. Each is therefore imagined to suffer a necessary rebuke, the sharp chiding and expulsion from intimacy required to discipline the obdurate.

ANTI-PURITAN OLDCASTLE

As first extensively argued by eighteenth-century editor Theobald, Shakespeare's reference to "my old lad of the castle" and other textual ephemera conclusively establish "Oldcastle" as the name borne by the character since known as Falstaff upon his first appearance in *1 Henry IV.* The explanation most often given for Shakespeare's change—first offered circa 1625—indeed does refer to a contemporary situation: that influential Cobhams (including the former Lord Chamberlain) demanded that a less embarrassing name be found.[31] But this argument seems to me both overparticular and underexplanatory. Only one of many objections is that the Elizabethan Cobhams were not actually Oldcastle's descendants but merely the bearers of his title, and thus — since the name "Cobham" is not mentioned in the play — less likely to be riled. Preferable, in my view, are explanations couched more broadly in terms affectively important to contemporaneous society at large. Here I find Shakespeare bent on a very timely affront, directed against devout Protestants (and especially those of the "Puritan" persuasion) of his own day.[32]

To be sure, Shakespeare's creation does entail certain of the broad historical indebtednesses I have described, including the notions of friendship with the prince and the necessity of his ultimate rejection. But Oldcastle would seem mainly to be valuable for the resonance of his name — that of a prominent proto-Protestant martyr — in 1597, and its capacity via misassignment and near-blasphemous misuse to offer present-day offense. The offense in question is to those Protestant proponents of moralizing and antitheatrical views, with whom Shakespeare's position in his "productive field" guaranteed inevitable animosity.

Ample evidence exists of a continuing quarrel between theatrical and antitheatrical parties in the second half of the sixteenth century, complicated by such variants as "crossover" participants and middle-ground reformers who found possible virtue in a virtuous or morally rearmed stage.[33] Even the milder attacks, like those of John Northbrooke, assailed the stage for "fleshlye" displays, for teaching "mischiefe, deceytes, and filthinesse, etc. . . . Howe to . . . obtayne one's loue, howe to rauishe, howe to beguyle, howe to betraye, to flatter, lye, sweare, forsweare, how to allure to whoredome . . . howe to . . . bee ydle, to blaspheme, to sing filthie songs of loue, to speake filthily, to be prowde, howe to mocke, scotte, and deryde . . ."[34] Sound like any Shakespeare character we know? My suggestion is simply that Shakespeare's Oldcastle is a walking, talking, sweating rejoinder to Puritan antitheatrical critique. In this sense the form of Shakespeare's rejoinder is akin to that of Chaucer's Wife of Bath: to discomfort an opposing party by airing a character who embodies that party's most disturbing dream. The affront is given by this character's abuse of a revered name. And, lest the point be missed, it is furthered by the character's indulgence, not in historical retrospective, but in very pointed present-day parody of Puritan and moralistic speech ("Well, God give thee the spirit of persuasion and him the ears of profiting, that what thou speakest may move and what he hears may be believed"; 1 Henry IV, 1.2.150–52).

Even Shakespeare's disclaimer, attached to 2 *Henry IV,* to the effect that "Oldcastle died a martyr, and this is not the man," is less an apology for an accidental error than a parting shot. That his affront hit home is confirmed in a rejoinder mounted in 1600 on the stage itself—by a moral (but, given their chosen medium, not an antitheatrical) party within the theater. This virtuous rejoinder, *Sir John Oldcastle,* part 1, is launched with the announcement that

> It is no pampered glutton we present,
> Nor aged counsellor to youthful sins;
> But one whose virtues shone above the rest,
> A valiant martyr and a virtuous peer. . . .[35]

The shape of a coalition may be glimpsed in the fact that Anthony Munday, early opponent of theatrical excess (as well as Protestant pamphleteer and Grub Street hack), was one of this play's authors. Their production's blatant sanctimoniousness suggests something of the tempting target that Shakespeare found ready to hand.

I wish to stop short of arguing for a complete evacuation of history in the case of Shakespeare's Oldcastle. Shakespeare knew a lot about the Lancastrians, and his analysis of Hal's and Oldcastle's relations replays important fifteenth-century themes (though with Elizabethan coloration). As I commented earlier, Hal's regeneration, normally portrayed as sacramental in the fifteenth century, becomes a policy matter in Shakespeare (1 *Henry V,* 1.2.191f.). And so does Shakespeare also find other thematic resonances that link the early fifteenth and late sixteenth centuries, including Hal's invariable control of situations, his devices of othering and exaggeration, and his cynical manipulation of ostensible camaraderie. From whatever angle we approach him, though, Shakespeare's Oldcastle remains more of his sixteenth-century present than his fifteenth-century past, more about settling present-day scores than bearing a historical grudge.

OLDCASTLE'S "LOST ORIGINAL"

Thus Shakespeare's Oldcastle—imagining himself a counterfeiter— joins a host of counterfeit Oldcastles. No more than any other is he "the man." Neither is the seditious traitor of Walsingham, the martyr of Bale and Foxe, nor the high-minded and rather befuddled protagonist of Drayton and Munday's play. This rout of Oldcastles is, of course, to be cherished, as a testament to the alternative imagination and its capacity to renew the present by radically reimagining the past. No matter that none is "the man," or could possibly be. Rather than regarding the inventions as "bad copies," we are better off regarding them hardly as copies at all, but as inventions in their own right, fully responsive to and integrated within their own contemporaneity. Why, then, the nagging continuance of an impractical and methodologically untenable interest in the lost and irretrievable "original"?

The irretrievable original, in the person of the historical Oldcastle, exerts an absent but inescapable pressure, a form of unfulfilled and unfulfillable demand. This demand is that a difference at least be recognized: the difference between one who once lived and one who never lived at all, between the unknowable Oldcastle who once lived and the various representations who did not live. The conceptual space of this difference is hard to establish and hard to maintain, since our attempts at representation are inevitably simplifying, vulgarizing, appropriative. The best hope for maintaining this difference would seem to rest in our understanding that its nature is ultimately less epistemological than ethical. Here I cite Derrida, when he speaks in *Specters of Marx* of the recurrence of the past in the present, and its capacity secretly to unhinge the present, with the claims of those who can no longer speak in their own behalf. To them, he says, we bear a responsibility: "Without this responsibility, and this respect for justice concerning those who are not there, of those who are no longer... living, what sense would there be to ask the question 'where?' 'where tomorrow?' 'whither?' "[36] I interpret the responsibility in question as a demand for ethical treatment of the dead, for what might be called "historical fair use." Fair use, in my view, includes the excitement of discovery, the provocation of difference, the inspiration of an image that (as Benjamin formulates it) "flares up briefly" at a moment of need or danger.[37] But it excludes certain forms of forced ventriloquization, the temptation to dragoon figures of the past as unconsenting totems or exemplars, the unproblematic yoking or harnessing of the past to the form of our present desires.

An extreme and puritanical interpretation of what I am saying might argue against *any* sort of historical re-presentation of those who once lived, and of course I mean no such thing. Cherish the rout of representations. But, separate from any of these representations, may — must — be posited an Oldcastle who once lived, a figure of passionate conviction. Little enough can be known of this figure, and still less found embedded in Shakespeare's Falstaff/Oldcastle: some service in the extended "familia" of the prince, the possibility of an angry interview, an imputation of disloyalty. Nevertheless, even in their slightest and most vestigial form, hints of the historical Oldcastle suffice to pose the past's demand on the present, the demand for rememorative reconstruction. Such acts of reconstruction can be concurrent with other kinds of celebratory invention, of which Shakespeare's figure is so radiant an example. But our enjoyment of Oldcastle/Falstaff need not preclude awareness of a divergence from what is known or might be supposed of the historical figure. With the historian or with no one at all rests the responsibility to maintain a difference between rememorative reconstruction and other forms of invention. I associate the maintenance of this difference with the historical impulse itself, with its ethical imperative, with what the historical endeavor means to us now.

10

POSTMODERNISM AND HISTORY

A CONFERENCE AND ITS PARADIGM

This essay began as an invited commentary on a highly stimulating conference on medieval "cultural frictions," held at Georgetown University in 1995.[1] The conference title itself seemed to me valuably indicative of a somewhat awkward amalgam under which many of our current theoretical efforts proceed. The full title was "Cultural Frictions: Medieval Cultural Studies in a Postmodern Context." Even casually scanned, it is seen to contain a number of somewhat discrepant emphases and choices, all of which indicate a current eclipse of history, either proposing substitutes or limiting its relevance.

Culture over history. First to be noted in the umbrella term "Cultural Frictions" is the preference for culture over history, akin to the current triumph of anthropology over history as the preferred disciplinary companion of literary studies. One element of this triumph is the seemingly more generous or inclusive scope promised by anthropology to objects of consideration, although practitioners like Robert Darton and Carlo Ginzberg have long since shown that history need not be any more restrictive than anthropology in its choice of subject matter. The more pertinent support for anthropology's claims appears to rest in its promised escape from historical depth or the burden of the past, the possibility of easing that burden in favor of a synchronous consideration of the text and its concurrent affiliations.

New Historicism. Suppressed in favor of culture, "history" is nevertheless allowed a radically subordinated form of return. I refer to our title's punning reference to "frictions" — invoking Stephen Greenblatt's landmark essay, "Fiction and Friction." A classical articulation of New Historicist procedure, this essay brilliantly amplifies the premise that we may historicize a text by "restoring it to its relation of negotiation and exchange with other social discourses."[2] History is thus admitted to consideration at a price, which is acceptance of its effectively discursive nature. Certainly, a "discourse" may embrace historical participants and entail material consequences, but in New Historicist practice the "discursivization" of history seems to refer to its textualization, and the practice of history as a textual and interpretative, rather than material and explanatory, activity. That the past is mainly, or even in some senses exclusively, textually available cannot reasonably be denied. The point of difference between historicisms old and new would appear to rest in matters of intention or aspiration: whether the text is seen to register the pressures of external events and material consequences, or is permitted to rest easy within a contemporaneous sign system. This debate is, in turn, often transferred to the adjacent sphere of cultural studies.

Cultural studies. Our title now returns to "culture," albeit revised into an interest in cultural studies. "Cultural studies" is, of course, North America's reconceptualization of its more rigorously defined British precursor, "cultural materialism." The difference rests in the abandonment of cultural materialism's defining encounter, between the text and the obstinate material realities of textual circumstance. Abandoning its predecessor's insistence upon materiality and the material consequences of the text, cultural studies gains a certain fluidity in its consideration of the play of text or relations of text to text — although a familiar price is once again paid, here expressed as the loss of those terms of sponsorship and appropriation in which the material foundations and consequences of textual relations might be defined. In exchange for the relative freedom gained by separating itself from the materialist premise of its precursor movement, North American cultural studies has dealt away its principal means of maintaining itself as a practice separate from the larger range of available poststructural theories and rationales against which it seeks to define itself.

Postmodernity. This preference for the cultural over the historical and the textual over the material issues in the additionally emancipatory promise of the postmodern. Here I allude to the popular perception of postmodernism's promised "end of history" — or at least, as in architecture, a flattening of historical difference that opens items of the past to arbitrary and playful citation. But did we not constitute a sorry spectacle, gathering upon the shared ground of our medievalism, even while imagining that we could somehow place ourselves beyond history's reach? So contradictory and impossible is this aspiration that I cannot imagine we were seriously entertaining it; if "escape from history" seemed to be the game we were playing, I would suggest that we were not really playing it to win.

Between history and postmodernism lies no quarrel but only a mock quarrel, a pretended antagonism concealing an ultimate reassurance. The reassurance rests in the fact that, even as it struggles to emancipate itself from history, postmodernism repeatedly and insistently announces the utter inescapability of historical contingency and awareness. At the most rudimentary level, its incomplete emancipation is announced in its name ("post-"), with the implicit acknowledgment of its own tacit reliance on ideas of period and progression. But I want to pursue the question of postmodernism's involvement with history in several additional and more important (though often un- or underarticulated) ways.

POSTMODERNIST HISTORIOGRAPHY

My heading may seem an oxymoron, but it is only apparently so. For, to state an obvious but frequently neglected point: neither in theory nor in practice does postmodernism neglect history. Preoccupied with history and ceaselessly concerned with the nature of the claims the past exerts upon us, postmodernism might almost be defined as "a way of having an attitude toward history." Postmodernism, as Diane Elam has remarked, far from uncaring about history, "is concerned with practically nothing but the problem of trying to think historically," always with the understanding that this is an unending project, that "we can never fully come to terms with the past, we can never justly represent it."[3] Seen in this way, the reluctance of postmodernism to discover a singular or final meaning in an era or an event is less a refusal of history itself than something very close to the opposite: a refusal to *decide* about history and put it away; hence, a refusal to leave history alone.

In addition to "worrying" about history, postmodern theory develops its own theory of the historical event. Having toyed with, and abandoned, the idea of staking a temporal and territorial claim — as the period that follows the modern—postmodern theory then chooses a more mobile and less fixed role for itself. Discarding the mantle of modernism's successor, postmodernism declares that it awaited nothing but was "there all along." This is Lyotard's paradoxical insertion of the postmodern at the moment of modernism's founding: "A work can only become modern if it is FIRST postmodern. Postmodernism thus understood is not modernism at its end but in the nascent state, and this state is constant."[4] Postmodernism thus becomes an endless rewriting of modernism, authorized by the fact that its visitation is really a revisitation, a rediscovery of its own presence in the founding moment of its supposed historical precedent and cause. Lyotard here offers a model for thinking about causes and effects, and finally a way of thinking about history itself: that events have multiple causes, some of which may even be discovered among their supposed consequences or outcomes.[5]

Generalized, this perception undergirds a powerful point of analytical procedure, which is insistently to restate those complexities the rejection of which was essential to any event's or movement's founding as an integral and self-coherent period. Postmodernism, as a movement or attitude, thus pits itself against those simplifications which attend the creation of a pure "moment," a singular causal sequence, a self-consistent movement or party or period. As the declared enemy of bogus stabilizations, postmodernism is always seeking and finding jettisoned materials: multiplicities, alternative discourses, and all that resists binarization or monological narration. The attitude of the postmodern entails a return to "prenatal" complexity and a (necessarily incomplete) act of redress to what was once there but has since been silenced or lost.

I discover one of the crucial operations of postmodernism in confrontation with either present or past in Carolyn Dinshaw's aside during her conference presentation on Margery Kempe: "[W]hen we call [her life] saintly *imitatio,* what do we leave out?" That is, when we categorize, when we call it "x," or when we set category "x" against category "y," what fringe of possibility, or what possibilities of intermediary diversity, do we exclude? The attempt to contain Margery Kempe's inherent excessiveness within the categories of the saint, the good woman of religion, the heteronormal—or any other—does intrinsic violence to the special properties of her existence, to the commotion and sheer trouble she constantly sets out to cause by cross-category confusion, as when this mother of many children dons virginal white to exemplify the state of inner grace she has achieved. To recontain or recategorize her is, of course, to associate ourselves with those confessors, fellow travelers, and church officials who are attempting exactly the same thing. In this sense, Dinshaw's "touch of the queer,"[6] with its revelation of disjunction within categories presented as inevitable and natural, contains its own "touch of the postmodern," its own return to multiplicity and irresolvable contradiction.

And so I am claiming for the postmodern an attempt in which any good medievalist would describe himself or herself as engaged: the attempt to restore complexity to our understanding of the past. But what distinctive form of retrospect does postmodernism offer upon the past, and what are its claims to validity? A trait of the postmodern — Jameson calls it postmodernism's "supreme formal feature" — is its seemingly ahistorical erasure of depth in favor of surface, its refusal of temporal or hierarchical subordinations.[7] This refusal of the "depth" model issues in a refusal of any "latent" meanings at all, a refusal to acquiesce in the notion that the non-normal is latent or repressed in the normal, or that the extracategorical is latent or vestigial in the dominant category. The postmodern habit of mind rejects the claims of a *repressed* alternative (to be reclaimed through depth psychology) in favor of the claims of an *excluded* or *jettisoned* alternative, a broader printout of possibilities denied in a founding moment of representation. This is Kristeva's "exorbitant outside," ejected beyond the scope of the possible, the place of the jettisoned object: "What does not respect borders, positions, rules. The in-between, the ambiguous, the composite."[8] The postmodernist refusal of repression and depth in favor of exclusion is not necessarily antihistorical. But it does assign historiography a particular goal: one in which muffled or swaddled possibilities are not just glimpsed during brief forays into the depths (as when Cousteau's crew put their lights on elusive neon sea creatures) but are, in effect, raised to the surface. They are instated *alongside* the privileged categorizations to which they were originally sacrificed. The effect of postmodernist historiography is not, then, finally, to probe the (exotic) depths but to restore the variegation, the fully contradictory variety, of the historical surface.

Different procedures of historical recovery have different prospects for success, and the practice of postmodernist historiography must still be analyzed in terms of its promises and its capacity to deliver on them.

HETEROGENEITY—WHERE AND
HOW TO FIND IT

Perceiving that the establishment of the medieval "body political" proceeded by excluding and jettisoning unwanted parts and components in order to create a shapely whole, the postmodernist opts for complexity, disorder, and contrariety. Postmodern analysis aims at the rediscovery and redescription of hidden or marginalized alternatives. Yet here methodological perplexities arise. The creolized or hybrid middle term can certainly be imagined or asserted, but what evidence enables its substantive retrieval?

The first step in looking for something lost in the process of representation is to decide "where it went," and here certain difficulties remain unconfronted by advocates of postmodern theory. A residually modern model imagines the "repression" of the fullest array of mixed or contaminated possibilities, their lodging in what amounts to a textual unconscious. But, as I have just said, the postmodern model imagines the expulsion or abjection of alternatives, where they tarry, not within the text but in some postulated limbo outside its bounds. The issue between these models—one existing prior to the postmodern and the other proper to it—remains unsettled, even by or within postmodernism itself. An indecision between these two models permeated the language of the conference, where "abjected and repressed" realms were frequently cited as equally important objects of attention.

The clash between a text that has repressed something and a text that has abjected or expelled it may seem the narrowest kind of terminological quibble, yet it possesses considerable ramification for the analyst. The former model imagines hidden treasures to lie within textual depth; the latter concentrates on the pleasures and limitations of the textual surface. The former is, of course, implicitly Freudian, and the latter non- or post-Freudian. And so we have two allied ways of talking, one Freudian and the other post- or even anti-Freudian, one fully modern and the other aggressively postmodern, and their interpenetration signals postmodernism's persistent difficulty in theorizing or maintaining itself as a distinctive critical position. For, in my view, postmodernism continues to harbor an unacknowledged procedural reliance upon the modernist and Freudian view of repression and the textual unconscious.

This reliance is intelligible, since so much is to be gained by prefer-ring the model of a text that *will not* tell something it latently knows, over one that *cannot* tell something it never knew in the first place. After all, an obstinate text, which contains knowledge "under wraps," can still be pressured to speak... whereas the unknowing text, which is not only suffering from amnesia but never knew, has nothing else to tell. The advantage of the modernist/Freudian model is that, unlike the less completely articulated claims of the postmodern, it takes responsi-bility for specifying the conditions under which a text may be persuaded to tell all that it knows. Its resource in this act of persuasion is the text's own unwitting eloquence, as embodied in the concept of the symptom. The symptom is, in Freud's terms, a consequence of repression's in-ability to sustain itself, with the symptom remaining our best hope of breaching those defenses which conceal the content that has been re-pressed.

Perhaps I may briefly illustrate the phenomenon of the textual symp-tom, and its analytical uses, from my own past work.[9] Several years ago, I noticed that Thomas Hoccleve devotes a disproportionate amount of attention — and, to be sure, emotion — to and around the subject of coun-terfeiting. I then noticed additionally that, in legal indictments and else-where, accusations of coin clipping and counterfeiting repeatedly attached themselves to Lollards and Lollard activities. As it happens, the very terms in which Hoccleve denounces counterfeiters — as members of a "secte," and so on — are the terms of frequent anti-Lollard invective. My conclu-sion was that the counterfeiter enters Hoccleve's text not only *in propria persona* (for, certainly, coin clipping did occur in the fifteenth century) but also as a symptom of a more general agitation, in this case about the continuing irritant of Lollardy and the yet more disturbing ambit of social blasphemies for which the Lollard was a stand-in and sign. A post-modern analysis might take the counterfeiter as a metonymic replace-ment of the Lollard in a lateral signifying chain, and thus deny greater depth and resonance to the Lollard signified; my own modernist and symptomatic analysis finds in the Lollard a deeper and more comprehen-sive explanation for the counterfeiter-as-irritant in Hoccleve's text — one that helps me to document and understand the urgency that Lollards possessed for later medieval English society, even when their actual nu-merical presence was small.

Like all symptoms, Hoccleve's counterfeiters "irrupt" within a poem that has nothing whatever to do with Lollards per se, announcing by disproportionate attention and emotion the presence of an unacknowledged provocation or irritant. In this way, the symptom offers a displaced or disguised avenue back to the nature of the materials, and the historical antagonism, which it supplants/represents.[10] Paradoxically, "modernist" analysis of the symptom thus serves a "postmodernist" goal, which is to show that our texts are a good deal more crowded than we thought they were, and are often crowded exactly with the materials they seemed to expel.

An opposite worry — less that the text conceals or ejects the monstrous, than that *only* the monstrous will be seen through the postmodern lens — surfaces in a subsequent commentary on the "Cultural Frictions" conference. In a recent essay, "Medievalisms Old and New," historians Paul Freedman and Gabrielle Spiegel discover in the papers of that conference, and in related work, a focus "not only on the marginal but on the grotesque."[11] Because it constantly seesaws back and forth between describing and deploring the attributes of the postmodern, the particular vectors of this essay are somewhat hard to trace. Its tacit contention, however, seems to be that the abandonment of a modernist account of continuity and progress is equivalent to the loss of history itself. They observe, apparently in sorrow, that "what has changed in the postmodern understanding of medieval alterity... is the simultaneity of our desire for history and the recognition of its irreparable loss, a loss we no longer can, or care to, mask beneath the modernist guise of continuity and progress." Unless I am misreading it, "progress" here refers less to "progressive politics" (an absurdity, as a characterization of medieval aspirations) than to a "progressive narration," a coherent account of change over time that locates the Middle Ages within a historical narrative connecting late antiquity to the early modern and thence to our own time. Their fear, apparently, is a pathologizing of the Middle Ages resulting from our own feelings of inadequacy and lack, including a disruption of progressive narrative about the Middle Ages conditioned by our own inability to sustain wholesome narratives about ourselves. Having, that is, lost hold of our own myth of progress, we cease to discover its origins in the Middle Ages, replacing it with an atomized and sensationalized interest in the fragmentary and worse. Now encouraged is "the discovery of the suppressed, the odd, the fragmentary, and the marginal"

(693); morbid Foucauldian emphasis on the Middle Ages as witness to a persecuting society has encouraged new interest "in heretical groups, in Jews and Jewish-Christian relations, in crime, in children, in popular culture, in gays and other marginalized groups. Subjects once marginalized are now reintroduced as centers of concern: incest . . . , masochism, rape, transvestism, even postcolonialism" (699).

Certainly, a purely desultory or sensationalistic pursuit of such topics would raise questions about the historical acumen of its practitioners. Yet nothing in the elaboration of these topics, even in detachment from a grand narrative of progress, is inherently unhistorical or antithetical to an interest in history. The test, I should think, is the effectiveness with which the group or tendency previously "hidden from history" is deployed as an element of historical understanding, both of the excluded group and of the processes of exclusion. If the exceptional and abnormal are related to the normal, and turn out to be inextricably involved in the creation and stabilization of the normal, then their careful study can hardly be thought injurious to study of medieval society writ large. In this respect, I return to Greenblatt, whose "Fiction and Friction" admirably sustains the contention that "the palace of the normal is constructed on the shifting sands of the aberrant" (86). If the aberrant or the exceptional is defined by codes and processes that are also discoverable within the most affirmative models of social emulation, then their careful consideration can hardly be considered a matter of morbidity, or even of redress, but simply as history writing in one of its most admirable functions.

TOTALITY

Until now, I have been talking (with a few cautionary notes) about the enrichment of our discussions by postmodern theory. But postmodern theory also enriches itself by—one might even say battens upon—the past. Our interest in postmodern theory is, if anything, exceeded by its interest in, or its need for, *us*. Of course, "interest" in the sense of "curiosity" always runs the risk of transformation into programmatic or manipulative "interestedness," and postmodernism often displays such narrow or selfish interest in the past. Realizing that postmodernism needs the past more than the past needs postmodernism, we have the right to an opinion about what we might consider the past's "fair use," and the right to set some terms and limits upon its usefulness.

Postmodern theory has always needed us, but for a variety of ends, some of which are less admirable than others. Least to be desired are those postmodern-inspired analyses which seek to justify the study of subsequent periods by simplifying our period's actual complexity. This gesture occurs at its most simple when modernists and others bracket the Middle Ages so they won't have to learn anything about it.[12] More complex, but no less cynical, are the varied uses of our period as a necessary foil to an argument for emergent modernity. Robert Stein commented at our conference that "the contradictory coherence of the medieval . . . is what structures the narrative of modernity." And, I would add, postmodernity, too. For most postmodernist practitioners indulge a furtive and dishonest relation to the medieval past. This relation consists in a shifty double move, according to which the Middle Ages are debunked as static, hieratic, and unchanging, even while these same accusations are called repeatedly into service in order secretly to nourish the illicit relation between most postmodern cultural analysis and the idea of the social "totality" or whole.

The postmodern attack on the idea of the social whole has, of course, been unstinting. I might, for example, just mention Foucault, who, describing history in fully postmodernist terms as "dispersion," dismisses the idea of social totality with the comment that "To speak of the 'whole of society' is to transform our past into a dream."[13] But this dream dies hard, even among the advocates of the postmodern. The dishonesty of postmodernism is to keep the dream alive, illicitly, by techniques of displacement and disavowal. The "displacement" in question is, of course, a displacement onto a dreamworld where a self-coherent totality is — in contradistinction to every postmodernist tenet — supposed to exist and in fact to thrive. Consider, in this regard, Baudrillard's monolithic and cynical deployment of the "feudal" Middle Ages to underwrite the exceptionality of the "Renaissance":

> The counterfeit (and, simultaneously, fashion) is born with the Renaissance, with the destructuration of the feudal order by the bourgeois order and the emergence of overt competition at the level of signs of distinction. There is no fashion in a caste society, nor in a society based on rank, since assignation is absolute

and there is no class mobility. Signs are protected by a prohibition that ensures their total clarity and confers an unequivocal status on each.... In feudal or archaic caste societies ... signs are limited in number and their circulation is restricted. Each retains its full value as a prohibition, and each carries with it a reciprocal obligation between castes, clans or persons, so signs are not arbitrary.[14]

Having been summoned up within an exclusion zone or no-place construct called "the middle ages," totality is then ostensibly dismissed. It leads a continuing shadow existence, as it were, under a sign of negation, as a covert and often unacknowledged staging ground for supposedly antitotalizing readings. This is because antitotality — refusal to allow that "society" exists — cannot flourish without its shadowed opposite — the view that it "once did." At a purely procedural level, the postmodernist microhistorian needs an idea of totality to serve as the field of larger resonance within which his or her telling and discrete anecdotes assume full meaning. The ether within which the New Historicist "anecdote" seeks and enjoys its tacit affinities with other culturally contingent creations is to be experienced only in such artificial environments as the totalized landscape of the imaginary medieval world. Most New Historicists thus find themselves in a contradictory position: the totality itself is regarded as an impossibility, yet only within, or in reliance upon, such defunct landscapes as the totalized medieval world can the New Historicist's dizzying similitudes and juxtapositions be sustained.[15]

Totality is thus sent packing, but told to remain on call, with the Middle Ages as its forwarding address, in case anybody needs to get in touch. But can "the structured whole" survive only as a discarded or quietly abandoned idea, by negation, or as a kind of inferred existence, negated but still implied by the kinds of critical operations we perform? Our obligation to the postmodernists (and, incidentally, to ourselves) is to give them their honesty back, by refusing to allow them to employ the Middle Ages as a kind of Jurassic Park where they stow an ideal of totality that they disavow for their own periods but still need, as an absent guarantor of the homologizing critical procedures they want to employ. We have been treated like a conquered province, commandeered to farm out an otherwise discredited idea of totality, and to export as much of it to more theoretically developed fields as they think they need.

Our retort must be that our period, no less than any other, is the plagued and proud possessor of motile signs, category confusions, representational swerves and slippages, partial and competing and always irreconcilable narrations. The effect of this retort is to force the hands of the postmodernists, requiring a responsible description of the larger societal and cultural enclosure within which their particular or micro-analyses achieve their resonance. And it forces our own hands too. Assuming a general loss of faith in totalities, we too must confront a demand: either specify a modified version of the social totality within which our analyses of cultural particulars may be presumed to resonate, or else say what we are putting in its place. To restate the issue: how is the investigation of a particular textual or eventual moment to become "thinkable in its specificity?"[16] Totality provided the larger field of reverberation within which the specific became thinkable, and even associable with practice; without totality, what is the general import, and social demand, of the specific?

Margaret Thatcher as Postmodernist

The attack on social totality has been primarily anti-Marxist and socially quiescent. I offer you, for example, Margaret Thatcher's "There is no such thing as society," a crucially symptomatic and vastly influential formulation. Thatcher must be seen as an influential late capitalist spokesperson, at a time when postmodernism itself must be understood as a late capitalist cultural phenomenon. I am, of course, joking when I label Thatcher a "postmodernist," and, to be sure, having dismissed the holistic category "society" (or, elsewhere, "civil society"), Thatcher then besmirches her postmodernist credentials by trying to smuggle the reified and occlusive microcosmos of "the family" back into the evacuated space. But her preference for the particular over the general, the individual over the society or the polity enjoys certain disturbing affinities with the atomization and anomie associated with the conservative, antiutopian, socially quiescent, and hence economically permissive, side of postmodernism itself. Without having the time to belabor the points made in Jameson's *Postmodernism; or, Cultural Logic of Late Capitalism*, I would nevertheless agree that the issue for postmodernism is to detach itself from its status as the cultural aspect of a triumphalist, transnational, market-oriented, late capitalist hegemony. The needed elaboration of the postmodern is to discover within the array of postcapitalist alternatives some provisional standpoint, and some point of attachment, for critique.

The challenge is to accept the view of social experience as what Vance Smith and Michael Uebel called in their original conference introduction "a dynamic, heterogeneous constellation," without ceding our right to an ethical self-positioning in relation to particular developments within this varied and centrifugal field. Surely we need not simply gape at this constellation as we gape at the Milky Way; that is, without an accompanying obligation to define a view or a stance toward it. This self-positioning would freely concede society's inability to finalize or constitute itself as a unified object of study, but would nevertheless insist upon certain "nodal points which partially fix meaning."[17]

My starting point would be Foucault's constant concern with "the hazardous play of dominations,"[18] his proposal that our studies include the multiple forms of subjugation. Much of the work of this conference involved the "violence of representation," according to which drastic binaries institute and enforce a mixed pattern of domination/subordination (along lines of race, class, gender, geography, and differential resources). But this multiple and shifting pattern is one toward which we need not remain bored, serene, or indifferent. Although the contents, or the pretexts, of domination and subordination are constantly shifting, we need not remain aloof toward the fact of oppression.

Postmodernism has been devastating in its critique of the authoritative observer, exposing feigned objectivity as a construction founded in privilege and supported by social authority. But its seeming obverse — complete disinvestment — is actually its twin, founded in a similar claim of disinterest and no less privileged (in this case, in its enjoyment of the privilege not to care).[19] I associate unpositionality with privilege because history (past and present) is full of people placed in circumstances that require care, full of people who *can't not care*. Such historical actors can neither be everywhere nor be nowhere; they have no choice but to be *somewhere*. And this is where I suggest we position ourselves: provisionally, precariously, temporarily, maybe sometimes bemusedly — but always *somewhere*. And wherever this somewhere is, that it be an invested place, a place that knows things are at stake.

Here I return to Carolyn Dinshaw's conception of multiple identifications.[20] Let me undertake to say what I think she does not mean, and means. In the Freudian system, identification is a process constitutive of the human subject, and may proceed along lines either regressive or affirmatively enriching. Among regressive identifications, I would include Foucault's description of the pompous, overbearing, and artificially over-stabilized identities that "monumental history" would impose upon us, a process only to be opposed, he argues, with parody, with exposure (as masquerade), with hard work of "unrealization."[21] To these overbearing sponsored identifications, I would oppose constitutive, self-chosen ones. Carolyn Dinshaw observed that Foucault himself broaches an idea of self-chosen identifications, in his "Lives in Documents." And she imagines such identifications as occurring (in Eve Sedgwick's formulation) across genders and sexualities, and also (in her own) across time, and across other barriers of race, class, and nationality.

Always latent in the idea of identification is, of course, the danger of "appropriative" identification, one that imposes one's own desire on another, that demands that the other address or testify for causes or concerns beyond its ken or control. In opposition to self-interested identifications, or those which return to the other only to consolidate "the same," Carolyn Dinshaw insists upon identifications as "crossings" — as encounters with identities radically separate from our own, considered in terms favorable to an enlargement, rather than restatement, of what we have sought there.[22]

Liberatory identification cannot alleviate the predicaments of past historical actors, but can enlarge our own sense of ourselves as historical subjects, multiply our own receptivity to diverse alliance. The politics of medieval situations are our politics, too, in the sense that — as we all know well — our view of the past and past actors is not only conditioned by, but also conditions, the present. This is the level at which the postmodern preference for a crowded and tumultuous past recommends itself: allowed its full scope and most affirmative energies, the "touch of the postmodern" extends our horizon of present possibility.

PART IV

PSYCHOANALYSIS AND
MEDIEVAL STUDIES

11

WHAT CAN WE KNOW ABOUT CHAUCER THAT HE DIDN'T KNOW ABOUT HIMSELF?

A text may state (and therefore discursively "know") things about itself, and it may remain silent on other matters (and therefore not "know" them). In the latter case our interest and our inquiry need not cease, for texts still carry forms of pre- or nondiscursive knowledge within their bounds. I am here presuming the existence of a textual unconscious, effectively constituted by and extensively correlated with that which the text represses.[1] I will eventually suggest that the fullest understanding of a text must include attention to what it represses, to the gaps, traces, and other derivatives of a textual unconscious.

A text with an unconscious will most certainly have a conscious, too, and I have no wish to understate the very considerable range and importance of a text's self-declarations. Such declarations might include its designated precursors (Statius, Petrarch); its ostensible audience (Gower, Strode); its acknowledged exclusions ("I wol nat seyn"); its professed genre (tragedy, story); its conflictual terms (destiny versus free will; tyranny or singularity versus common profit); its meaning or sentence ("swych fyn...."). I mean this list to be a substantial one, and in no way derisory. Most of my own work—certainly, until the latter chapters of *Social Chaucer* and possibly beyond—has relied heavily on things texts choose rather directly and manifestly to announce, on valuable information either proffered or left hidden in plain sight.

But certain matters cannot be pursued in a text's own terms. What about Chaucer's suppression of his debts to Boccaccio? What if the

"Miller's Tale" turns out not to be about jealousy at all? What other willed misdirections or less purposeful misrecognitions displace Chaucerian narratives from their announced emphases and goals? In whichever of the theoretical languages it is ultimately to be made, the crucial point remains: certain textual duplicities, withholdings, omissions, and (especially) repressions can only be identified from a vantage point *outside* the textual system.

My touchstone here is the familiar, and telling, observation that "the field cannot well be seen from within the field." (Incidentally, although bearing some of the marks of the latest poststructural dictum, this observation derives from Ralph Waldo Emerson's "Circles.")[2] Many of us are familiar with Myra Jehlen's related suggestion that feminists need often "to talk about texts in terms that the author did not use, may not have been aware of, and might indeed abhor." She formulates her position in terms of Archimedes' lever, which must be planted on "external ground" if it is to move the earth.[3]

Fine and exciting work has been and will be completed by those who seek to stand on the text's own ground; still, the investigator who refuses the move to an external ground accepts a tacit limitation. Analysis conducted on the text's own ground limits itself to what may be described as knowledgeable reiteration or "respectful doubling" of a text's assumptions.[4] But texts are inherently evasive, and the investigator who wishes to learn more from a text than it cares to avow must sometimes treat its assumptions with a certain strategic *dis*respect. Far from believing that theory should apologize for introducing terms and concepts from outside a textual system, I believe that the refusal of a text's attempt to dictate the terms of its own analysis is precisely theory's province and promise.[5]

This essay catches me (as I hope all the events of my life will catch me) in transition; in this case, between older and newer variants of historicist practice. Without relinquishing an interest in the text's self-declarations, this variant looks to theory for additional contributions to historical understanding. Specifically, I want to solicit theory's support in addressing what a text leaves unsaid — not just what it means to say, but what it cannot know, or especially, what it knows but will not or cannot say.

Such matters are best pursued in terms of examples. My original intention was to cite a number of them. Naturally, the first and most incidental of them has expanded, and expanded, to occupy my full attention today. It involves one of the Pardoner's fluent and unsettling little jokes. This one is his passing jibe at gluttonous bellies and the cooks who labor to fill them, delivered early on in his spiel:

> Thise cookes, how they stampe, and streyne, and grynde,
> And turnen substaunce into accident
> To fulfille al thy likerous talent!

(Lines 538–40)

My original, quite limited, point was that this joke has a Lollard impli-cation that loses its zest owing to events beyond its control, with the burning of William Sautre in 1401. Mulling over this and many more observations about things this text can and cannot and will not say, I happened to see a recent and charming movie called *Thirty-two Short Films about Glenn Gould*. I decided to follow its example with "six short essays on Chaucer's Lollard joke."

A TEXT HAS MORE SOURCES THAN IT CAN NAME[6]

I might seem to have stumbled with my first sally, since Chaucer's joke has a single and authoritative source well known to him and many peers, a source unnamed but effectively acknowledged by a tissue of close ver-bal borrowings.[7] In his 1195 *De miseria humanae conditionis*, Lotario dei Segni (later Innocent III) launched a jibe against gluttons and their cooks, among whom one grinds and strains while another mixes and prepares, and turns substance into accident: "substanciam vertit in accidens."[8] Given such close verbal correspondence, what might it mean to suggest that Chaucer's text cannot know its sources?

If source study as traditionally conceived were our goal, we could declare it accomplished and pretty much close the book on this one. But the straight-line transmission presumed by traditional source study simplifies a more cluttered process, in which words come trailing a riot of incompletely suppressed memory traces. Far from stabilizing a sin-gle meaning for its own terms, Cardinal Lotario's jibe already sits un-stably in a crowded semantic field.

Lotario's joke is founded on what Freud aptly describes as "the re-discovery of the familiar."[9] Already familiar to Lotario and his immediate audience of fellow scholastics and ecclesiasts was the Aristotelian vocabulary of "substance" and "accident."[10] Casting the activities of overingenious cooks in these newly fashionable terms is an instance of the pleasureful condensation common to all jokes, in which words and concepts do "double duty" and the hearer is invited to revel in a form of expressive economy. More specifically, the joke presents its knowing audience with a rapid double entendre, in which the same words are heard first as relatively empty (with an oddly laborious pertinence only to cooks) and then suddenly as very familiar and very full, drawing upon newly fashionable Aristotelian terms to describe food's essence and the external qualities by which it is perceived.[11] This joke may also be "fuller" still, because in the course of the twelfth century these very terms had been employed with more and more frequency in a particular debate, over the nature of the Eucharist.

But, if Lotario's joke is to be understood as eucharistic, his control over its signification already stands in considerable doubt. Within the eucharistic debate, these terms were already being deployed with varying meaning and divergent effect. In works like *De sacro altaris mysterio*,[12] Lotario sided with emergent orthodoxy by divorcing the substance of Christ's body from the accidental properties or external appearance of the consecrated Host. But the terms "subject" and "accident" had long since been introduced into eucharistic discussion, in the first instance by an eleventh-century grammarian named Berengar of Tours. Berengar insisted that an accident and its subject were *in*separable, and that the bread of the Eucharist must therefore remain bread (with a figurative, rather than substantial, relation to the body of Christ).[13] This was an established argument with many participants, including not only Lanfranc but also Guitmund of Aversa and Alger of Liège and more, before it reached Lotario. To the extent that Lotario's joke is incipiently eucharistic, it could actually cut in either of two radically opposed ways. On the one hand, these cooks who provide the butt of the joke by turning substance into accident could be protoheretics, believing not only that substance and accident cannot be divorced, but even committing the flagrant additional error of assuming that substance can be affected or afflicted by manipulation of accidents, rather than varying independent of them. On the other hand, they could be unwittingly orthodox and thus to be commended for their faith in the possible malleability of substance, even if they do not know the right way to go about it. What we seem actually to have here is a state of high and indeterminate play, indulged by a theologian who knows what he thinks about such things, but is willing to take a kind of cognitive holiday from the hard debates surrounding the determination and implementation of orthodox understanding. This sort of play with the fraught elements of consumption, digestion, and transformation, and its uncertainty of outcome, is nicely captured in a comment by Fiona Somerset, in correspondence on this very point:

> If the joke is incipiently transubstantive for Lotario, I think it works like this. The notion that the cooks by grinding and grinding could produce more and more accidental properties to the point where there is no substance left is complete and delightful nonsense.... It makes a sort of nonsensical sense because of our ordinary notion that fancy cooking can remove the wholesomeness of good plain food. But the idea that substance could altogether disappear is just absurd—until we're caught by the awareness that... something like this happens when the host is transubstantiated.[14]

Debates over the fine points of eucharistic theology were by no means settled by Pope Innocent's own preemptive proclamation of transubstantiation as official dogma in his Lateran decree of 1215,[15] or by the Thomistic synthesis later that century.[16] By the end of the fourteenth century, at least three broad categories of thinking about eucharistic transformation may be crudely differentiated: the heretical position in which the accidents of bread persist as a material remainder, joined after consecration by the symbolic presence of the body of Christ; the Thomistic compromise in which accident persists only as quantity after the ceremony of the altar; and the position of Duns and Ockham, in which the material accidents of bread were totally annihilated in the consecration, now to be wholly informed by the new substance of the body of Christ.[17] Lotario's terms were thus borne to Chaucer within a wide and tumultuous discursive stream.[18] His and other reworkings of Lotario's joke had even less chance than the original to withstand divergent interpretation. If the concept of the "authoritative source" is designed in part to control subsequent meanings, then Lotario's jest fails the audition.

A TEXT'S MEANING IS SUBJECT TO
EVENTS BEYOND ITS BOUNDS

From its inception, debate over the Eucharist was inseparable from considerations of political power.[19] In its late-fourteenth-century realization, the church and the secular arm would employ the relation between the substance of Christ's body and the accident of bread as the crucial litmus by which the errant Lollard was to be separated from the orthodox fold. Lotario's joke had been scholastic and only putatively eucharistic. In the heated controversial climate surrounding Chaucer's retelling, this same joke could not *help* but be perceived as eucharistic. Because of the wide use of its terms to discover and harass Lollards, its inherent multiplicity could hardly resist some degree of stabilization within a Lollard frame of reference. Suppose it to be a "Lollard joke," in the general sense of alluding to a controversy in which the Lollards were much embroiled. But what *kind* of Lollard joke, with respect to intensity and with respect even to its ultimate thrust? First, the issue of intensity:

This joke had a fortunate launching, into the kind of invitingly "unsettled" situation in which Freud says that tendentious jokes fare best (122–23). Its likely period of composition and first reception—say, 1388–1395—falls squarely within a mixed climate of opinion about Lollardy instituted in 1382 and ending with a jolt in 1401.[20]

In 1382 Courtenay replaced the murdered Sudbury as archbishop of Canterbury and the serious attack on Wyclif and his immediate followers began.[21] In and around this year, the existence of a *secta* consisting of Oxford theologians, itinerant preachers, and other local malcontents is suddenly advanced as a matter of common conviction. This is the year in which the Latin (though not English) epithet "Lollardi" was first employed.[22] This is the year of the Blackfriars condemnation of Wyclif's views, the concurrent parliamentary attack on itinerant preachers,[23] and the Oxford suppressions. As part of this concentrated anti-Wycliffite campaign, it is the year of mandated church lections and orchestrated demonstrations against Wyclif and in favor of the Blackfriars condemnations.[24] Knighton describes one such demonstration, a procession in which citizens of London walked "nudis pedibus" to hear an antiheretical sermon by a Carmelite doctor, followed by a prearranged miracle in which Wycliffite knight Cornelius Clone (marginally, Clown) saw flesh and blood when the Host was broken at the ceremony of the altar

(163).[25] Even more importantly for its bearing on Chaucer's joke, this is the year in which belief in the consecrated Host as "accidens sine subjecto" was instated as the sine qua non of orthodoxy. A 1381 Oxford inquiry and the 1382 Blackfriars synod took major roles in the process, apparently basing their condemnations of Wyclif's theology on a rather scattered enumeration of his oral and occasional views on the Eucharist entitled "Conclusiones Wycclyff de Sacramento Altaris," and not (as is commonly supposed) on more formal works subsequently composed in his own defense such as *De eucharistia* and *Trialogus*. Ninth on this list of conclusions is a rather scrambled claim that "accidens sit sine subjecto non est fundabile."[26] Yet promoted to first and second among the views condemned at the Blackfriars synod, and promptly broadcast by Courtenay, was the matter of substance and accident: that the substance of material bread and wine remains after the consecration of the Host ("Substantia panis materialis et vini maneat post consecrationem") and that accidents do not remain without a subject ("accidentia non maneant sine subjecto").[27] Henceforth, and throughout the fifteenth century, this rather recondite distinction would be the crucial point of difference upon which heretics were to be identified, and, if they were lapsed (or, later, simply failed to recant), were burned.

Despite such strong moves to consolidate an orthodox position, this remained a fractured field throughout the 1380s and 1390s, and even hostile accounts like Knighton's reveal it not to be single-sided. As he says in exasperation, the sect was multiplying so rapidly that you might hardly see two people in the road without one of them turning out to be a Wycliffite ("Nam secta illa in maximo honore illis diebus habebatur, et in tantum multiplicata fuit, quod vix duos videres in via quin alter eorum discipulus Wyclyffe fuerit"; 191). Furthermore, these Wycliffites were speaking up for themselves. The Michaelmas Parliament of autumn 1382 saw a countermove in which representatives of the Commons protested the previous session's statute against wandering preachers.[28] Under accusation in that same year, the Wycliffite preacher Swynderby thought it was worth his while to seek redress from Lancaster and the king.[29] In the next decade Lollards frequently took the offensive, as in 1395, when they nailed twelve highly assertive conclusions to the doors of Saint Paul's and Westminster Abbey.[30] These conclusions represent a new order of polemic, deriding Saint Thomas and the pope for trying to make a miracle out of the transubstantiation of a chicken from an egg; suggesting that priests in secular office might be named "hermofodrita" or "ambidexter"; satirically suggesting that Judas's lips join the cross as an object of veneration.[31] Although indisputably orthodox, Richard II seems never to have been very interested in burning Lollards; even at the very end of his reign in April 1399, Lollard priest Sautre hopefully (or at least spunkily) petitioned king and Parliament for a hearing on the Eucharist and other points.[32]

Yet an uneven but steady consolidation of the anti-Lollard position had continued throughout Richard's reign. A new note is struck in Roger Dymmok's orthodox rejoinder to the Lollard conclusions of 1395, in which he ominously observed that Joshua destroyed idolatrous priests by burning them on their altars ("Iosias omnium malificiorum genera diluit ac omniphariam ydolorum culturam destruxit infra sui regiminis terminos et sacerdotes ydolorum super aras combussit").[33] This same menacing note is to be heard again in or around 1397, in a virulent petition to Parliament in which, with unprecedented candor, the framers argued that in other realms those convicted of heresy are delivered to the secular arm to be put to death and their goods confiscated ("liuerez a seculer iuggement pour estre mys a mort et leur biens temporales confiskez") and asked that the same penalties be introduced to England (that the king and lords "mettre eide du bras seculer poiur destruire la malece de tieux enemys").[34]

Two years into the reign of Henry IV came the event that translated the words of such tracts and petitions into deeds, constituting a terminus ad quem for any but the most mordant enjoyment of Chaucer's joke. By royal order to the mayor and sheriffs of London (an order that deliberately outpaced and refused to wait a few weeks for parliamentary approval of the statute *De heretico comburendo*)[35] William Sautre was publicly burned. As the *Eulogium* continuator described the event,

> During this parliament the archbishop of Canterbury degraded a certain heretic, who had said that accident cannot exist without a subject in the sacrament of the high altar ("accidents non esse sine subjecto in Sacramento Altaris et panem manere"); who was burned at Smithfield.[36]

Launched and briefly at large within an "unsettled" situation conducive to humor, this Lollard joke's mirth — or at least any possibility of its innocent enjoyment—vanished in the smoke of Sautre's burning in 1401.[37]

A TEXT'S MEANING IS HELD JOINTLY BY ITS AUTHOR AND AUDIENCE

The mixed political situation persisting until the end of Richard's reign would have permitted this joke to evade any of several different censorships, and something similar may be said of the audience situation as well. Freud observes that the most propitious situation for a tendentious joke is one in which "the subject" (here taken as Chaucer and the members of his audience) "has a share" (*Jokes,* 111). As a social phenomenon, the Lollardy of the 1380s and '90s was drastically mixed—when compared, for example, with the first decade of the fifteenth century in which it had found its constituency in the trades and a lord like Oldcastle was a distinct anomaly. So mixed it was that Chaucer's joke could hardly have been uttered before an audience in which *someone* did not have a share.

A generally accepted account would have Lollardy experiencing a straight-line social devolution from the earlier 1380s (when its tenets were expounded at Oxford and it briefly enjoyed "p.c." status) through the later 1380s (when it piqued at least some interest among the knightly classes) to the first decades of the fifteenth century (when converts like Oldcastle and holdouts like Thorpe were decidedly anomalous and when most members were in artisanal vocations). In the brief time available here I want not so much to unseat this account as to re-present it, together with a few words of caution. This account originates less in fresh modern evaluation of the evidence than in contemporary framing by Knighton and others according to hierarchical and "top-down" assumptions about diffusion/dissemination. Knighton traces the promulgation of Lollard views from Wyclif to educated followers like Aston and Purvey to Lollard knights like Clifford and Stury to "pseudopraedictores" who spread their views to a populace forced by Lollard lords to listen to false doctrine even at sword's point (151–98). On the other hand, Knighton's own analysis is contradicted by his own sallies outside his argumentative frame, suggestive of a more diffuse (or, if you will, popular) origin for many Lollard views. He peppers his account with scandalous case histories, like that of "William [the] Smith," who launched his austerities in displaced lust for a young woman and who discovered his own contempt for images by burning a statue of Saint Katherine in order to cook cabbage, or William Swinderby who tried his hand at every kind of hack religiosity (including popular antifeminism—until it backfired when women of his town threatened him with stoning—raillery at the rich, and hermitry) before joining Smith in his cursed chapel beside the local leper house (182–83, 189–93). The social terrain of Lollardy was always less even than contemporary polemics supposed, and fourteenth-century Lollards seem from the beginning to crop up at all points on the social scale.

One possible point is the Ricardian household, and thus—given the overlap between those named by contemporary chroniclers as "Lollard knights" and the group of household retainers whom John Scattergood and others have placed at the center of Chaucer's audience—within Chaucer's own circle.[38] Drastically summarizing a complex debate,[39] I find the phrase "Lollard knights" is unquestionably overspecific and unwarranted, but some aspects of Lollard moral fervor and interest in extrasacramental salvation seem to have found a sympathetic hearing in some court circles.[40] This is a tonality captured by Knighton, when he says that these knights had "zelum dei ... sed non secundum scientiam" (181). It is a tonality since persuasively captured by Anthony Tuck in his description of Richard's courtiers' uneven embrace of various morally fervent spiritual positions, ranging from Lollardy to Carthusianism.

The likely presence of some Lollard sympathies in Chaucer's audience by no means reduces, and may even enhance, a valence in which Lollards are twitted as obtuse and stubborn about accidents. By the same token, though, its audience situation confers a kind of "in-house" quality, one that does not deny a certain volatility to the jest, but suggests that nobody needs to be very discombobulated about it all. For the 1380s and early 1390s were a period when a certain amiable state of not-having-decided-yet about the Lollards was still possible, especially amid the urbane circles in which Chaucer moved. This is, in short, a rather indeterminate audience situation, of some knowledge and undefined interest and partial understanding, an audience situation of which this joke takes delicate but full advantage.

The joke is not, of course, all play; it possesses a possible aggressive dimension, and this dimension will be summoned and fully focused in the years to come. The burning of Sautre will show soon enough where the discursive "othering" of Lollards will end. But our joke's potential aggressivity seems for now to remain latent or unsummoned, suspended in a moment of relative innocence with regard to anti-Lollard intention.

A TEXT'S FORM MAY ALIBI FOR ITS THOUGHT

To muffle or excuse or postpone aggressivity is not to banish it altogether, and beneath its wrappings the shifting center of this joke retains a considerable aggressive charge. In fact, a symptom of potential aggressivity may be found in the very elaborateness with which its "Lollard thought" is screened from view. In the first place (and this is a point that would have been made much sooner in an earlier version of Chaucer criticism), this is not Chaucer's joke at all; it is the Pardoner's joke, ventriloquized, and as a literary character the Pardoner functions as a reservoir of unaccommodated hostility and intellectually superior scorn. A less resolutely historicist reading than mine might simply see this joke as an epiphenomenon of character and bend its properties to augment our sense of its teller.[41] In the second place, it offers us a decoy target or targets — not Lollards at all, but gourmands and bellies and overingenious *cooks*, and, at the next level of interpretation, casuists and intellectuals. In the third place, and here I am quoting from Freud, "the thought seeks to wrap itself in a joke because in that way it recommends itself to our attention ... because this wrapping bribes our powers of criticism and confuses them. We are inclined to give the *thought* the benefit of what has pleased us in the *form* of the joke" (*Jokes*, 132).

The joke, that is, constitutes a witty wrapper that bribes its audience into an unquestioning acceptance of its thought. All of us got here by being, at one time or another in our lives, good readers, and one definition of a "good reader" is that he or she follows the instructions of the text. In this case, the text's implicit instruction is to relax and enjoy this fleeting joke — and then to get on with it. But I want to speak for the occasional importance of resisting a text's instructions — in this case, to push past the joke's screens, to refuse to be distracted by its teller or its immediate topic or its wit from the ramifications of its thought.

NARRATIVE PROCESS CONTRIBUTES TO
A THOUGHT'S EXPOSURE

This joke's aggressive thought is elaborately screened, but it remains subject to exposure. It lies at the boundary between the manifest and the latent, the conscious and the unconscious. Its topographical positioning within the utterance might be likened to that of the Freudian preconscious: consisting of unactivated knowledge and opinion, yet available, when attention is directed toward it, to verbalization.[42] My suggestion here is that the verbalization of this joke — its entry into language and, more specifically, its implication within narrative process — reveals traces of its aggressive charge. The revealing processes that interest me here are the heightened importance of the linguistic, the tendentious employment of comparison, and the unavoidability of temporality.[43]

The *language* of Chaucer's passage is at once backward- and forward-looking. Retrospectively, it associates itself with Lotario, where the belly, for example, emits a horrible efflatus "superius et inferius" — above and below. With this we may compare Chaucer's "at either ende." Such intertextuality might seem a- or antihistorical, acting to defuse contemporary reference. But, at the same time, the language of Chaucer's passage associates itself prospectively with another, and specifically Lollard, verbal environment, parodying the emergent language of bodily self-loathing (in which the "stynkyng cod" of the belly may, for example, be associated with the "stinking carrion" of the Lollard wills).[44] In this "Lollard intertextuality" both the specificity of the joke and its mocking intent are revealed.

A mocking attitude toward the thought is further revealed via *comparison,* the preeminent device, according to Freud, by which the comic deflates earnest abstractions "of an intellectual or moral nature . . . [by] comparison with something commonplace and inferior" (*Jokes,* 210). Here, the Lollard theology of the Eucharist is mocked by comparison with the commonplace and inferior, with ostentatious culinary practice, even as the Lollard Host is ridiculed by subjection to the fate of all nourishing matter.

Still more specifically, the *temporal arrangement* of the passage has the effect of dragging the Lollard theology of material accidents through the most humiliating narrative vicissitudes. Consider this larger segment of Chaucer's text:

O wombe! O bely! O stynkyng cod,
Fulfilled of dong and of corrupcioun!
At either ende of thee foul is the soun.
How greet labour and cost is thee to fynde!
Thise cookes, how they stampe, and streyne, and grynde,
And turnen substaunce into accident
To fulfille al thy likerous talent!

(Lines 534–40)[45]

The temporal effect of this sequence is to place the cooks at the service of the belly's command, which is to fulfill itself at either end, with noisy ingestion and noisy excretion, its proclivity being to turn food to dung. However transformed in appearance, by cooks and by the digestive process, the foodstuffs remain always and excessively material in their nature. The analogy here is with the Wycliffite/Lollard theology of the Eucharist, in which the sacramental bread remains bread in substance (even while it is relationally or by common consent regarded as the body of Christ). These excessively accidental foodstuffs are a material residue, an obstinate and embarrassing remainder of the cooking process, even as the material and literal "breadness" of the Lollard Host is itself an embarrassingly untransformed remainder of a sacramental process. Thus, by metonymic inference, the embarrassing remainder of Lollard theology, the Lollard "conclusion" itself, *is* dung, *is* shit.

THE TEXT'S OVERT ANTAGONISMS PROTECT ITS UNCONSCIOUS CENTER

This is a possible stopping point, and I want to pause for a moment to explain why I am not stopping. I began by mobilizing historical materials to suggest that Chaucer's joke enters a period of social unrest that complements its own restless textual center. Now I have employed certain Freudian formalisms (thus far, of a nature as much tactical as theoretical) to suggest that, despite a permissive historical situation and the bribe of its risible wrapper, its "thought" is hostile to emergent Lollard theology. I want now to introduce a final argumentative turn, with the support of theory but also relying upon some modification of theory.

My observations thus far have been based on the notion that the joke is the wrapping or envelope (or, in Freudian terms, the *Hülle*), and that the Lollard thought is its content (or, in Freudian terms, the *Kern*). But the relation between hull and kernel in Freud's system (or in any system) is notoriously unstable and, in this case, completely reversible.[46] It can be suggested with equal plausibility (or, in fact, given the unruly nature of jokes, with greater plausibility) that the Lollard *thought* here finally functions as the hull or wrapping for the vital center of this passage, and that the kernel or center is precisely the joke itself, endlessly productive and limitlessly anarchic. At a last level of analysis — one that takes into account the joke's own unruly unconscious — the apparent thought shields all participants from an utterly blasphemous possibility.

The unnamable scandal that threatens the center of this joke involves what Miri Rubin discreetly calls the fact of "undignified digestion" (25). I've already suggested that the joke can actually be construed in two ways, and that its alternative brunt — the brunt from which the anti-Lollard reading distracts us — is the orthodox view that the "breadness" of bread, its prior substance, is turned into sheer accident, to be replaced by a new substance that is the material body of Christ. Believing that Christ's body is the new substance of the Host, the orthodox are exposed to a series of practical questions involving the mastication, and digestion, and excretion of Christ's body (not to mention derivative problems about what happens when a mouse eats the Host or a maggot breeds upon it). These issues were an endless discomfort for the orthodox, yet caused no difficulty for the heretic, who believed in a symbolic rather than material presence. As Wyclif himself exclaims in *De eucharistia:* "We reply... that when such beasts are able to eat the consecrated Host it is the bare sacrament and not the body or blood of Christ.... Nor do we grind ['conterimus']⁴⁷ the body of Christ with teeth, but we receive it spiritually, and whole" (11, 13). Yet this very horror, of crushing or mastication, seems to be carried at an unacknowledged level within Chaucer's passage, when it continues:

> Out of the harde bones knokke they
> The mary, for they caste noght awey
> That may go thurgh the golet softe and swoote.
> (Lines 541–43)

Here Chaucer's passage distantly and derivatively acknowledges a blasphemy that was never far from its core. In its final and most devastating form, this blasphemy is of course excremental, and the later Lollards would take it on a rhetorical and imaginative rampage. (Space does not permit full development of this subject, but I might note that the later Lollards were not loathe to develop this excremental possibility in all its ramifications. Consider, for example, Margery Baxter's cloacal and extravagantly satirical vision of thousands of priests eating thousands of hosts and discharging gods into thousands of fetid pots.[48])

Chaucer's text labors to avoid such blasphemy, offering the Lollard Host as a target of opportunity, a proximate safeguard against blasphemous contamination of its protected center.[49] Resting at the joke's center, enwrapped and imperiled by the threatened blasphemy, is . . . what? A thing at once sacred and social, crucial to the maintenance of late medieval monarchy and the socially diverse but "graded" state; a conception of sacrally instituted and informed transformation, produced in and through the Eucharist alone. Earlier, I suggested that the selection of the Eucharist and eucharistic remainder as the litmus by which Lollards were to be identified and disciplined was in some respects adventitious; that this was one subject among many possibilities on which Wyclif was rather arbitrarily "drawn." I want now, if not to reverse myself, at least to add an additional perspective, according to which the selection of eucharistic belief as the matter of contention may be seen as inevitable and unavoidable.

The centrality of the Eucharist, and its exceptionality, and its critical importance as a sacramental guarantee of spiritual and social transformation may be illustrated in relation to Roger Dymmok's rejoinder to the Lollard contentions of 1395. To the Lollard insistence that absence of material change means Christ's body cannot have entered the Host, he replies that sacramental action constantly affirms and reveals the possibility of inward change without outward change:

> For if this [Lollard] argument should thrive, all the sacraments of the church, all the oaths of kings, and all political exchange should be completely destroyed. . . . I ask, what sensible change do you see in a boy newly baptized, in a man who has confessed, in a boy or man who has been confirmed, in consecrated bread, in a man ordained into the priesthood, in marriageable persons betrothed or joined? All receive a new virtue, except the bread, which simply ceases to exist without any kind of sensible change, and is transubstantiated into the body of Christ. In what way also is the body of a king changed, when he is newly crowned, or anyone similarly advanced? (130)

Dymmok offers a provisional chain of sacramental signification, a chain that is effectively intact for the Lollard (who believes that every sacrament confers a new virtue symbolically) but for the orthodox contains a single discontinuous element ("the bread...which simply ceases to exist...and is transubstantiated"). The Host functions for the orthodox, in Lacanian terms, as that point of irrationality which protects the entire symbolic sequence, the object that is always sought but presents itself only "in a form that is completely sealed, blind and enigmatic."[50] An aspect of its enigma is its unique structural role, which is to function as pure signification (in effect, as "accidens sine subjecto") and also as (the whole and entire) body of Christ.[51]

Interestingly, the Lollard view does not even threaten the sacral (for it would make the sacrament of the altar coextensive with the other sacraments in its symbolic function). What it threatens is the exceptionality of the Host, its function as that point of irrationality which supports or (in Lacanian terminology) "quilts" the entire ideological system. In one sense, the Lollard view threatens very, very little. It would, as Wyclif and the Lollards were frequently to observe, have been perfectly orthodox as recently as the twelfth century.[52] On the other hand, by offering to dissipate the mystery enclosed in that one exceptional kernel whose irrationality guarantees and protects the orthodox sacramental system, Lollard theology was threatening in the ultimate degree.

The Lollard here functions, like the Jew or Muslim at other medieval social moments, as a symptom of repressed unease at and over the imaginative center of the sacramental system. Like any symptom, the caricatured Lollard functions two-sidedly. Most obviously, the Lollard stages a problem for an orthodox but contradictory center. But, at the same time, Lollardy functions protectively, diverting attention from a center that must remain contradictory in order to fulfill its symbolic function but that must employ every kind of concealment to withhold its deepest contradictions from view.[53]

CONCLUSION

I am, of course, speaking for rather than against the claims of history. The point of historicism as I understand it is not simply to assert the determinative claims of history through thick and thin, but to consider texts historically. One can think historically in more than one vocabulary, and without delimiting the questions, and without assigning each question a single answer. The provisionality of theoretically abetted conclusions seems to me a source of challenge and excitement rather than despair; rather than encouraging a dismissal of the past, theory seems to me to offer an opportunity to return to it with new analytical strategies and better-honed tools.

Take, for example, the case of the Lollard joke. I have cultivated a considerable receptivity to multiple reference, undecidability, and, especially, the constant instability of relations between what frames and what is framed. Reversing the relations of hull and kernel, I have moved from a proximate and specific social target to a more general anxiety, touching on embodiment, pollution, and irrational awe. But the fact that the joke contains sources of theological and social anxiety excessive to its topical reference need not diminish the weight or seriousness of its topicality. Whether the Lollard enters the text by virtue of a primary or a secondary process, the fact remains that the availability of the Lollard as a discursive screen for Ricardian social antagonism was to eventuate in very material and serious Lancastrian consequences. Nor is history — a somewhat more generalized or "late medieval" variant — absent from the joke's core, in which a precariously maintained sacral mystery supports a threatened social system.

Let me return for a final moment to this matter of hull and kernel and its complexity and reversibility. I find a similar reversibility in the relation between historical texts and the theories by which we interpret them. No fixed or inevitable principle governs their relations: if you seek history you need theory; if you pursue theory you should want history, too.

12

JOHN'S LOCKED BOX

KINGSHIP AND THE MANAGEMENT OF DESIRE

Despite the possible implications of the "d-word" in my title, my present interest does not lie in broadly encompassing statements about mirrors or mothers, the acoustic or the pre-Oedipal. Certainly, desire is in some respects a transhistorical condition, one that crosses boundaries of time and even species, implicating not only humans of other times and places, but rabbits, fighting fish, and most other complexly evolved denizens of the planet. The trouble is that, so generally conceived, desire is everything and nothing at all, liable to characterization as what Terry Eagleton calls "a nameless hankering, unfulfillable by any of its particular objects."[1] But the point is that, whatever generality desire possesses as an impulse, it nevertheless is directed at particular objects, within specific contexts. Desire interests me most when it is situated and specific. Thus, my interest rests with desire's instantiations, its realizations for particular persons at definite times and places. A rough schema might assign desire's persistent and timeless elements to its point of origin in the subject's imagination, and its local and specific elements to the inevitability of reliance upon the social/symbolic order for desire's objects and objectives. Understanding desire as relational in this sense, I locate my own interest in the social side of the relation, the sense in which desire is not only answered by socially presented objects, but is constituted by and around them.

The social/symbolic order establishes and delimits the possibilities and conditions of desire's implementation, affording opportunities for satisfaction and setting a limit upon possible realiz ion. In fact, far from dwelling on the issue of fulfillments, any consideration of desire must extensively concern itself with the preponderance of situations in which fulfillment is, or is defined as, unachievable. Precluding the realization of desire is what psychoanalysis discovers as the inevitably partial, or substitutive, quality of its aspirational objects, but also the social institutions that assist in enforcement of desire as a limit. Thus, the institutional context of desire may be viewed as regulatory, as it defines desire's privileged objects and as it affords or denies access to their imagined satisfactions.

Here rests a paradox that will set the terms of my present discussion. For the successful regulation of desire does not necessarily consist in ushering the subject into the presence or possession of the desired object. Rather, the state of desire is most consistently satisfied, not by fulfillment, but by the maintenance of a proper distance between the subject and the desired object. Regulatory responsibility may consist, not in pandering to needs and wishes, but in insisting upon their postponement and denial; and the successful management of desire frequently involves a certain aptitude, not for access or enjoyment, but for prohibition.

Responsibility for such regulatory activities is, of course, broadly shared out within any society, including that of the late Middle Ages. But a disproportionate late medieval responsibility rested with the institution of kingship and the role of the king. The successful monarch was one whose actions represented him, or at least permitted him to be imagined, as promising but also as withholding access to objects of desire. Here rests what I consider the king's responsibility to "manage" desire, to prolong the desiring relation and the pleasures it affords.

A DISCOURSE OF DESIRE

Admonition to the king about his managerial responsibilities is the chosen subject of a highly prolific group of medieval writers. Construction of a properly regulatory role for the medieval prince in relation to his subjects' desires is, in effect, the rationale of an entire genre of mirrors, regiments, and books of good counsel. My chosen text is an exemplum broadly popular in the thirteenth to fifteenth centuries, appearing in general moral-didactic collections and (properly adapted) in works of advice to princes. This is the narrative of a prosperous father (eventually named Iohannes Cavaza or John of Ganazath or John of Canacee) who overindulges his children and wastes his substance among them. Now poor, he experiences their ungrateful mistreatment. He obtains a treasure box, well bound and locked, and fills it with stones. Misperceiving the stones as treasure, the children treat him well for the remainder of his life, in order to gain an additional inheritance.[2]

As it appears in moral-didactic compilations,[3] this exemplum focuses on the ungrateful siblings, their greed and their disrespect for their father, and on the stratagem by which they are brought to heel. Misperceiving the stone-filled chest as the object of their desires, they revise their behavior in order to win its enjoyment. They are, in other words, constituted as good family members by an illusory process, which enables them to configure themselves as "good children" and exemplars of socially accepted behavior, even as their motives remain fatally split between unbridled personal greed on the one hand and conformity to public duty on the other.

A possible focus for this essay might, in fact, have been "Misperception and Historical Process," with its emphasis falling upon the senses in which pursuit of confused or mistaken objectives "makes history," is inevitably implicated in the historical process. But then I noticed that, when adapted as advice to princes, the exemplum gains a different focus. It still, certainly, pivots on the siblings' error, but it is now narratively configured around the father, first as he mismanages his material resources, then as he recoups his position by becoming a successful master of the symbolic and impresario of desire. It becomes, in short, an admonitory (and ultimately vindicatory) exemplum about the position of the father as protoprince or prince manqué, first as unsuccessful and then as successful regulator of his subjects' desires. His children's self-deceptions are still present, but now as the pivot by which the father/prince, as manager of misrecognition, enters his new and successful role.

In his vastly influential circa 1300 compilation of advice to princes, popularly called the "Book of Chess" and formally entitled *Liber de moribus hominum et officiis nobilium* or *Solatium ludi scachorum*, Jacobus de Cessolis centralizes and magnifies the role of the father in several important ways. First, he appears as strategist: the canny father deepens his deception by borrowing real gold and displaying it to his ungrateful daughters, allowing them the conclusion that it rests in the locked chest. Second, he proves a virtuoso able to transmute imaginary money into hard cash, requiring the daughters to make benefactions to the religious orders who keep the keys to the chest. Third, he is now the subject of the entire narration. When the daughters open the chest, they not only find it empty of gold, but discover a *clava,* or club, and a written admonition against dispersing one's substance to one's children. The moralization of the anecdote is, in other words, explicitly directed at the father/prince, with a corresponding shift from the children's greed to the father's responsibility to regulate their greedy desires.

In his closely related, but amplified, version from his early-fifteenth-century *De Regimine Principum,* Thomas Hoccleve continues this redirection of interest to the purposes of fatherly/princely admonition. His John of Canacee likewise possesses a high learning curve, developing from one so unversed in desire that he squanders its object in a vain attempt at ingratiation, to one well able to create desire and confidently to regulate its effects. The narration begins with a regulative failure. Although his daughters have made good marriages and do not need his gold, they nevertheless want it. Yielding improperly to their flattery, the father scatters his gold among them:

> Thei held hym vp so with her flaterye,
> That of dispens he was outrageous,
> And of goode thei were ay desirous;
> Al that thei axed, haden thei redy;
> Thei euer weren on hym right gredy.

The predictable result is that he beggars himself, wasting all his substance:

> This sely man contynued his outrage,
> Tyl al his goode was disshid & goone.

Achieving their aim with such disappointing ease, the children promptly grow "wery" of their father. No wonder. No longer gatekeeper and custodian of desire's object, he has squandered the means to interest them. In fact, the further lesson of desire, which we are now about to learn, is that he may even have given cause for annoyance, since, in ceding his rightful role in desire's prohibition, he has deprived them of their rightful enjoyment in desire's prolongation.

His money gone, John enters that state of self-destitution which he shares with his folkloric cousin Lear after the bestowal of his kingdom; dying a form of first death in the resignation of his power, he awaits only the second or bodily death that will end his tale.[4] But the present narrative is comic rather than tragic. John retrieves himself from the brink of destitution by a decisive action that implies a series of interlinked realizations: that power is based on being, or having, an object of desire; that, because desire is imaginary, desire's object may as well be symbolic as material; that desire is heightened by interdiction, and that his own appropriate role is not to satiate desire but to prolong it by inhibiting its attempted realization.[5] Wised up, he initiates the stratagem of the locked chest, as a result of which desire is rekindled, but now carefully held at that remove which allows its persistence.

He now demonstrates his command of desire with a refinement unimagined by John of Cavaza and other precursor fathers: instead of simply allowing inference about the contents of the locked chest filled with stones, or merely dumping the supposed treasure out on a carpet where the ungrateful heirs can see it, this John implicates his daughters in an inflammatory process of illicit observation. Inviting his daughters and sons-in-law to dinner, he stages a dumb show in which they hear and then see him counting it through a "parclose," or partition, with chinks, or "chynnyngs." His genius is not only to provide his children with an object of desire, but with a *frame* through which to view it. John's genius, in other words, consists in the intuitive perception that provision of a fantasy object is not enough, that the object must also enter the subjective frame of the individual's fantasy.[6] Forbidden knowledge, coupled with a certain requisite distance, turns out to be the perfect condition of desire, which in these bad siblings is whetted almost beyond endurance:

> ... for hir hertis depe
> Stak in his bounded cofre, and al hir hope
> Was gode bagges therin for to grope.
>
> (Lines 4331–33)

Desiring the gold, these bad daughters are as happy as they will ever be.[7]

The children's undoing lies, of course, not in the interdiction of the chest but in their ultimate access to it. For the chest cannot (and, as a

desire machine, was never intended to) supply the satisfactions it promises, but contains only disappointment, unwelcome postmortem, and
disenchanted self-knowledge. But, even as it acknowledges the misgov-
erned and ultimately unproductive impulses of the children who would
open the chest, this anecdote does come to rest in an observation about
good rule. Contained in Hoccleve's chest, once opened, is not just the
clava, or club, of Jacobus's version, but an emblem explicitly alluding to
the civil power of the prince, "a passyngly greet sergeantes mace" bearing the inscribed sentiment, "Who berith charge of othir men, & is / Of
hem despised, slayn be he with this." This exemplum is, in short, addressed to that prince, or potential prince, who would assume responsibility for others, would bear their charge, or the responsibility for their
direction. The prince who has first squandered his economic capital, and
thus permitted himself to be despised, must learn to reconstitute his
capital (in this case, symbolically rather than economically). By recreat-
ing his subjects' desires and by maintaining control of those desires, he
can channel their natural recalcitrance into a workable semblance of compelled good conduct. For the father of the anecdote ended his days secure in the enjoyment of his children's good behavior:

> Aftir this day, thei all in oon house were,
> Til the day com of the fadirs deying.
> Goode mete and drynke, and clothes for to were
> He had, and payed nat to his endyng.

This happy household must be seen as a consequence of the children's
calculation, rather than reformation or sincere love. This calculation is,
furthermore, based on an incomplete grip of the circumstances, on a misrecognized object, a fantasy formation. It is, in this sense, unintended
or accidental. But it is good behavior nonetheless. Having learned that
good behavior cannot be anticipated except through self-deception, the
father/prince institutes the requirements for the temporary history of a
happy family/kingdom.

Here, then, a tale about kingship, which begins in kingship's imagined destitution. The prince who empties his chest, and allows its empti-
ness to be seen, has unwisely squandered his economic capital, but has
squandered his symbolic capital as well. His ability to reward and punish—that is, his power—exhausted, his secret known, he is literally and

symbolically stripped, "unclad," vulnerable to his subjects' mistreatment and contempt. It turns out, though, that his secret, his unknowable reserve, was less dependent upon his power than the other way around; for, his secret restored via the locked chest and the fantasies it engenders, his power is restored as well. His power consists, in other words, in the symbolic trappings with which he surrounds himself and in the fantasies they engender: in his deployment or management of misrecognition.

Here I offer the term "misrecognition" in its fuller Lacanian sense of *méconnaissance*—that is, in reference not only to confusion about external reality (as, for instance, about the contents of John's box) but also to confusion about the self and the locus of personal desire. For the desiring subject, marked by misrecognition or *méconnaissance,* is not only confused about externals but is also fatally split in self-perception, locating the completion of desire in an external rather than an internal process. And, to the monarch able to mobilize symbolic resources both to offer and to shield his secret, misrecognition is an infinitely renewable resource. Possessed of desires awakened in relation to external display and self-deluded about possibilities of access to desire, the Lacanian split subject thus lies open to every kind of manipulation by external appearances and manifestations of imaginary plenitude.[8]

SYMBOLIC CAPITAL AND RICARDIAN-LANCASTRIAN KINGSHIP

Thus far, I have been considering this anecdote in a transhistorical sense—or at least in a sense applicable to several centuries of medieval European kingship. But to say that desire is located within varied historical circumstances is not to say that desire is itself transhistorical, for desire never exists separately from its very particular, inevitably historical, instantiations.[9] In emphasizing the historical specificity of desire and desired objects, I mean not to revise Lacan but simply to reiterate a Lacanian truism: that those sublimated objects of our desire, those objects which we establish in place of the Thing, are always established "at a certain historical moment," and the historicity of their insertion and presentation is what opens them to sociological analysis and historical consequence.[10]

It happens that Hoccleve's rendition of this exemplum of desire within the specific setting of his *Regiment of Princes* suggests a very specific contextualization of its meaning. Hoccleve composed this work of pseudoadmonition and extensive ingratiation for Prince Henry, most probably in the years 1411–12,[11] a point at which he was effective ruler of England and waited impatiently to become its next king.[12] Given Hoccleve's virtual elision of the anointed king, the failing Henry IV, in favor of the prince as his very particular dedicatee and addressee, how might the narrative of John of Canacee have been read?

Let me immediately dismiss a temptation, briefly, since I will be returning to it later. This narrative of early profligacy and hoped-for stewardship might seem to apply rather neatly to the curve of Henry V's own career, as understood by Elyot, Hall, Holinshed, and Shakespeare — except that these are all subsequent accounts and that no single scrap of evidence of early profligacy is attached to the historical prince. As economical and satisfying as the assignment of all this narrative's references to the prince's own career might be, they would have been unrecognizable to a contemporary audience. I will argue instead for a more spacious set of references, in which John of Canacee's learning curve embraced three reigns: beginning with Richard II's profligacy, essentially eliding Henry IV with his promised but wholly unfulfilled restoration of the kingship's good credit, and concluding in utopian hope that a canny and self-restrained prince would effect a full restoration of the throne's intrinsic powers.

The collapse of Richard II's kingship turned on a central paradox: that, although he was possessed of rather considerable economic resources at the time of his deposition,[13] he was widely *perceived* as profligate, heedlessly squandering his own resources and those of the realm. The very first article of his deposition opened with "Ffirst it ys to putt agens Kyng Rychard, that ffor his euyll gouernance in yevyng a way to vnworthy persons the goodes and possessions longyng to his Crovne, disparpelyng hem, and other goodes vndiscretly puttyng ['indiscrete dissipando'] also..."[14] To *disparpel* something is, I might add, even worse than just to dissipate it, since the Middle English word has overtones of rout and defeat, headlong confusion, as when an army is disparpelled in battle, or a people disparpelled over the face of the earth.

The resolution of this paradox lies in the fact that, although Richard II had resources at the end of his reign, he was (as Christine Carpenter has pointed out), regarded as having raised them impermissibly and as bestowing them upon unworthy objects.[15] As the fifteenth article complains,

> The same kyng . . . the moste parte off that that longith to his crovne hath yovyn, grauntyd, and done away to dyuers persones ffull vndygne. And fferthermore hath putte so meny charges off grauntes and taxes to his subgetis and liegis, and that almost yere by yere, that ouermych and to excessively he hath oppressed his peple. . . . And the same goodes tht have so be areysed have nat ben spendyd to the profyte ne worship off his Rewme, but to comendacion off his name and pompe and veyn glorie, disparpelyng the same goodes vnprofitably. (31)

Simultaneously squandering the resources he commands and illicitly extorting new ones, this king is unable to do what he should do: "honestly and sufficeantly lyve off the profytes and Revenues of his Rewme and the patrymoyne longyng to his Crovne withoute oppressyng off his peple" (30). John of Canacee gave away his material resources and thus, having laid bare the secret of his inability to reward or punish members of his family, squandered his symbolic resources as well. Without actually depleting his material resources, Richard II gave the impression that he was, or in any event that he was employing them erratically and self-indulgently, and thus achieved a comparable state of destitution.

Worse yet, Richard found himself constantly represented, not as exercising restraint upon desire, but as indulging desire — in most cases, his own. Richard, for example, had his own "chest" episode, in which he simultaneously and disastrously occupied all the subject positions the narrative affords: at once the exemplar of prohibition and restraint *and* the unruly and invasive debauchee of desire. John of Canacee's chest, guarded by "three lokkys," is the place of his imagined hoard, and the keys to the locks rest in the charge of three religious orders, not to be invaded by himself or anybody else during his lifetime. The articles of deposition inform us that Richard likewise installed himself as the guardian of locked chests, persuading the exiled Arundel to place the jewels and ornaments of his chapel in his own keeping:

> And whanne they were sent to the kyng, and he hadde seyne hem, the kyng dydd hem be putte and lokked in certeyn cofres,

and made oon off the Erchebisshopis clerkis to lokke hem. And
kepte the cofris to hym sylff. But he delyuered the keyes to the
Erchebisshopis clerke. And affterwarde he comandyd the same
cofres to be brake. . . . And dydde his ffree wille with the same
goodes. (40)

Widely defamed as a coffer-breaking king, unable to restrain his own
unruly desires, Richard could hardly have hoped to offer himself, in the
terms of our anecdote's denouement, as an exemplar of good governance
and law and a steward of the realm's material and symbolic resources.
     Henry IV's opening campaign for the crown (including his spon-
sorship of the articles of deposition) certainly aims to confine Richard
to the symbolic space of the spendthrift father. At least at the outset, he
was also successful in portraying himself as the reformed father of the
anecdote's second half: the father who restores, recovers, conserves. His
initial stance upon landing in England was that he sought only to "recover" his rightful (that is, Lancastrian) inheritance,[16] and—even after
his goal became the crown itself—recovery and repossession remained
central themes. As he said in his challenge of the throne, the realm was
about to be undone by its defaults of governance and good law, and with
God's grace and the help of his friends he intended "to recouer hit" (Julius
B.II, 43). Restraint and respect for law and custom were Henry's constant themes, as was his intent to subordinate his own "lust" or pleasure to the requirements of lordship. (As Archbishop Arundel, hailing
Henry's full maturity, was to say in his collocation upon Henry's claim
to the throne, "In stede off a childe wilfully doyng his luste, now shall a
man be lorde to the peple" [Julius B.II, 46].)[17] And lordship, of course,
includes the wherewithal of good lordship, the conservation of a patri-
archal patrimony—both material and symbolic.
     Despite Henry's Lancastrian inheritance and sound initial strategies,
chronic underfunding and exceptional expenses for defense of his title
left him economically prostrate throughout his kingship, and especially
during its crucial first eight years. As early as 1401, his treasurer wrote
to inform him that he lacked the means to pay messengers to summon
the king's Council,[18] and as early as 1402 the *Eulogium* continuator reports that "the people begin gravely to criticize the King, and to wish for
King Richard ['desiderare'], saying that the latter conserved rather than
wasted their goods" ("ipse cepit bona eorum et non solvebat").[19] A. B.

Steel has shown that insecurities regarding legitimate expectations about repayments of Crown indebtednesses multiplied enormously in Henry IV's reign,[20] and Jacob has demonstrated that, even before faced with the challenges of rebellion, Henry faced an annual shortfall of some fifty thousand pounds per year.[21] Henry's material straits in turn impeded his efforts at affirmative self-representation. Spending all his time resisting conspiracies, bargaining for loans, and scheming to invent novel subsidies, Henry could hardly be seen as the king who restored England's good credit, either material or symbolic.

Hoccleve makes his choice, virtually omitting Henry IV from mention in the dedicatory passages of his *Regement*, according him less notice than his father John of Gaunt, and shifting the focus to the prospects for the prince's speedy accession:

> Beseche I hym that sitte on hye in trone,
> That, when that charge receyued han ye,
> Swych gouernance men may feele and se
> In yow, as may be vn-to his plesance,
> Profet to vs, and your good loos avance.[22]

That very governance, and self-imposed restraint, expected of Henry IV is now assigned to his son, whose own "gouernance" will produce "profet"—whether material profit for the realm as a whole or symbolic profit founded on his own good repute. Read in the context of Hoccleve's expectations, his anecdote of John's chest is both cautionary and expectant. Richard having squandered the realm's "chest" of good repute and Henry IV having been unable to refill it, Henry V's charge as monarch must be the recapture of his subjects' unruly desires, first functioning in the realm of symbolic self-representation, and then converting symbolic to real profit for the good of the realm.

A brief anecdote might suggest the firm grasp Henry V enjoyed upon the challenge awaiting him. John of Canacee's genius was to manipulate the symbolic in such a way as to convert his children's intangible imaginings into concrete good behavior, and thence to hospitality, bequests, and other solid profits. As king, Henry V likewise promptly showed himself master of the varied forms of "profit," both symbolic and real. Desperately strapped for cash and seeking funds for the invasion of France that culminated in Agincourt, he cut the crown of the realm—the "Lancaster crown" that appeared on his father's funeral effigy—into multiple pieces and pawned it straightaway.[23] This may be seen as the most literal, if by no means the last, moment at which Henry V converted the symbolic status of the king into very concrete profit for his realm.

OEDIPUS DISMEMBERED

To this point, my discussion of desire has been abetted by several Lacanian formalisms, but I would not declare myself to have been "psychoanalytical" yet. I mean now to take a turn toward a Lacanian structuration that, if not exactly psychoanalytical, will at least represent a further stage into my own inquiry into the use of this body of understandings in textual and historical analysis. I wish here to reference and introduce a central Lacanian precept, which is the indispensability of prohibition to the creation of desire.

Everything about John's chest bespeaks prohibition: the screen through which the chest is viewed, its three locks, the keeping of the keys by religious orders, the father's own interdiction of access during his lifetime. And the one thing that has been in the chest all along is not gold or stones but an emblem of discipline and civil rebuke. Yet all this array of prohibitive paraphernalia and threatened rebuke serves finally not to quell desire but to stoke desire; in fact, to reinvent it.

With respect to this reinvention, let me now turn back to Lacan, who observes of desire and its object, "I would not have had the idea to covet it if the Law hadn't said: 'Thou shalt not covet it.' "[24] Elaborating, he says that "The dialectical relationship between desire and the Law causes our desire to flare up only in relation to the Law" (84). The Law—here with a capital "L"—is naturally not just this or that local statute, but rather the Law of the name of the father, the Law of prohibition. But this is also the law of kingship: not just the law of the statutes but the king's position as sponsor of all legality and all law. This is the authority of the king, and it includes the power to rebuke the very desires that arise in the face of its prohibitions. Indispensable to desire, however, is the father-king's assumption of his symbolic function. This function, which is to proscribe excess enjoyment, is, of course, deeply Oedipal in character.

In Freudian-Lacanian terms, our exemplum may be read as a record of a certain Oedipal progression, in which a father first defies, and then accepts, his symbolic function. Amplified in the terms of *Totem and Taboo* (whose fanciful anthropology I naturally jettison, but whose successive definitions of the paternal function are crucial to the post-Lacanian understanding of the father's symbolic mandate), this progression carries us from the primal or obscene father, who defies his symbolic function and who commands excess or profligate enjoyment, to his assassin and successor, the Oedipal father who institutes law and interdicts enjoyment (thus paradoxically guaranteeing its perpetuation, along with other delightful possibilities of treason and transgression).[25] Our exemplum does not deny the persistence of unruly and potentially destabilizing desire, but it nevertheless imagines the institution of order and control, with desire paternally/regally monitored and held at a constant, and productive, distance from its object.

Chaos would ensue only in the event of a reversal or devolution, if the Oedipal father were supplanted by his debased predecessor, the obscene father who refuses his mandate. This is what Žižek, writing of contemporary society, sees as the disturbing precondition of *noir*: "Instead of the traditional father—guarantor of the rule of Law, i.e., the father who exerts his power as fundamentally *absent*, whose fundamental feature is not an open display of power but the threat of potential power—we obtain an excessively *present* father who, as such, cannot be reduced to the bearer of a symbolic function."[26]

I won't claim Richard II as a precursor of *noir*, but I don't hesitate to suggest that, as a sponsor of obscene enjoyments who refuses his symbolic mandate, Richard II poses what can be understood as an Oedipal problem, a problem of regressivity, in which he refuses his proper Oedipal interpellation. But, in proposing the application of an Oedipal patterning to the contested field of late-fourteenth- and early-fifteenth-century English kingship, have I not brought us to the brink of that interpretative chasm into which narratives are drawn, depleted, and (in the polemic of Deleuze and Guattari) forced, reduced, and irrevocably "flattened?"[27] Have I not, that is, brought us to the bad place where textual and historical particularities are overriden, fantasies detached from the social field, collective experiences reduced to a single account of infantile development within the context of the bourgeois family? My position is that these reductions need not occur. We may still employ

Freud's insights into the Oedipal configuration to mark powerful and nonrational investments of prohibition and desire without yielding to its claims for exclusivity or its tendency to suppress variety in order always to discover the same.

Deleuze critiques Lacan for recasting the Oedipal triangle, from a personal and developmental crisis to a symbolic structure, to "a structural Oedipus...that does not conform to a triangle, but performs all the possible triangulations by distributing in a given domain desire, its object, and the law" (52). His complaint is that, in moving "from imaginary figures to symbolic functions, from the father to the law, from the mother to the great Other, in truth *the question merely retreats*" (83). Yet emphasis might alternatively be laid upon what the Lacanian model *permits*. Lacan's structural Oedipalism discovers powerful forces of prohibition and desire within the larger social-symbolic field. It encourages understanding of Oedipal relationality as a play of forces rather than an unvarying template. Loosed from Freud's particular account of familial origins, it discovers new locations and distributions for the prohibitive function, new trajectories of desire, new incarnations of the desired object.

To be sure, Deleuze would then take another step, from Lacan's structuralism to his own poststructuralism, opening the three-pointed Oedipal triangle to all the alternatives and complications ignored or jettisoned at any persistent structure's institution, asserting: "There is no Oedipal triangle: Oedipus is always open in an open social field. Oedipus opens to the four winds, to the four corners of the social field.... A poorly closed triangle, a porous or seeping triangle, an exploded triangle from which the flows of desire escape in the direction of other territories" (96). He finally discovers "the disjointed fragments of Oedipus ... stuck to all the corners of the historical social field" (97). I don't want to give away the whole Oedipal store here, but I would argue that Deleuze's account is a refinement, rather than a refutation, of Lacan's structuration of desire. I have no objection to this modification, to a fractured and decentered Oedipalism, operating in a fragmentary and chronologically disordered way.

Accepting Lacan's "structural Oedipus," and then opening this structure in the ways so eloquently urged by Deleuze, we gain a way of talking about desire, as it is produced through prohibition, within a fractured and contested and very particular social field. Richard II's career may, in this sense, be viewed, not as a coherent Oedipal narrative, but as a

series of suggestive fragments, fitfully but arrestingly illuminated by Oedi-
pally derived insights. In its most crucial failure to afford an ordered
Oedipal narrative, Richard's career invites understanding as a devolution,
a falling away from, rather than an assumption of his Oedipal mandate.

Enjoying the remarkable advantage of legitimacy, as the last regularly descended Plantagenet king, Richard had every opportunity to present himself as guarantor of the law — as the austere and absent father
of prohibition, the father who accumulates and conserves, who possesses
power as a threatened sanction but rarely wields it. His early success in
this function might be figured in approving chronicle accounts of his
defusing of the rebel threat at Smithfield in 1381, when he seemed (but
only strategically) to grant charters of manumission, but ultimately defended traditionally sanctioned relations; when he threatened reprisal
but granted wholesale pardons once his objectives were achieved; when
he appeared publicly only as necessary to his goals and then withdrew
behind the council and other organs of legitimacy. Yet this is also the
Richard who, rather than respecting the law, sought finally and excessively and also in the most wretchedly infantile way (according to the
Lancastrian articles of deposition) to ingest it, to take it into his mouth.[28]
This is the Richard who, rather than maintaining and policing existing
social relations, stuffed his personal chest with extorted blank charters
that he might use to accuse any subject, connived in the murder of his
uncle Gloucester, and sought his Lancastrian cousin's unjust disinheri-
tance. Brief sponsor (1388–90) of a law-and-order campaign, he then became the realm's chief extortionist, in a protracted and greedy quarrel
with the city of London. Analysis of his career in the 1390s finds him too
fully abandoned to his own desires to become a law enforcer in any effective symbolic sense. Any appreciation of Henry IV's early successes must
be supplemented by an account of Richard's affective failure fully to embrace his symbolic mandate as guarantor of the law and father of interdiction. Indulging his rages and personal quarrels, cavorting with his
favorites, unevenly and arbitrarily scattering his rewards, sharing homo-
erotic intimacies with his Cheshire archers — Richard begins dangerously
to devolve from the traditional father who forbids excess enjoyment to
the primal father, the obscene and overpresent father who, defying his
symbolic function, commands indulgence and impossible enjoyment.

Henry IV had the good sense to ground his usurpation on his explicit respect for law, adding, in a codicil to his challenge of the realm,

that "hit is nat my wille that no man thynk that by wey off conquest I wolde disherite eny man off his heritage, ffraunchises, or other Rihtes that him ouht to have, ne putte him oute off that he hath and hath hadde by goode lawes and custumes off the Rewme" (Julius B.II, 46). Yet Henry IV's attempts to represent himself as the law's guarantor were undermined from the start by a debilitating contradiction: as a usurper and hence an impostor king, Henry IV was himself the most conspicuous breaker of the law. His position as a would-be exemplar of maturity and restraint was implicitly mocked by his own blatantly apparent inability to resist the proscribed pleasures of the throne. Understanding Richard as the primal and obscene father of enjoyment and Henry (abetted by temporary allies like Percy and Northumberland) as his murderous son, we must see Henry as too fully compromised by his spectacular transgression to overcome the crisis of legitimation that Richard's deposition and death provoked. Barred by his ineradicable taint from assuming his position as sponsor and guarantor of civil and symbolic law, Henry IV's hopes of legitimation were perforce dynastic rather than personal, and he took early and repeated care to affirm his oldest son as his successor. Henry's guilt-ridden testament and choice of burial in Canterbury rather than in the royal precincts of Westminster and continuing concern to secure his son's inheritance effectively repeat Hoccleve's own choice with respect to his *Regiment*: discreetly setting Henry IV aside, it imagines the prince's full assumption of the parental role.

I am arguing that, despite certain promising early signals in each case, neither Richard II nor Henry IV proved able to secure his position as a father or prohibition and a guarantor of the law, and that Hoccleve's anecdote expresses a hope for Henry V's assumption of that position. So completely, in fact, was Hoccleve's hope repeated in the imaginations of Lancastrian and subsequent commentators that they have defied contrary historical evidence in order to draw into the compass of Henry V's own career as prince and monarch the full curve of the entire late- and post-Freudian paradigm, in which the primal father of exorbitant enjoyment is succeeded by the traditional, and remote, father as legislator and enforcer of the law.

As an assertion with no evidential basis whatever, the narrative of Henry V's transformation has little to tell us about his own character or psychological trajectory but much to tell us about ungoverned interpretative desires — not only those of Henry's near-contemporaries, but our own as well.[29] An early, and comparatively modest, imposition of this pattern occurs in the near-contemporary account of the *Historia Anglicana*, in which Walsingham relates that the new king was transformed "in virum alterum" upon the occasion of his coronation.[30] An elaboration of this account, which develops its implications without departing its boundaries, may be found in Fabyan, a hundred years later:

> The King, before the death of his father, applyed himself unto all vyce and insolency and drew unto himself riotters and wildly disposed persons, but after that he was admitted to the rule of the land anon and sodainely he become a new man, and turned all that rage and wildness into soberness and wise sadness and the vice into constant vertue.[31]

Subsequent accounts, in which the prince disports himself in robbery and other lawbreaking with fictitious low companions, were elaborated in the sixteenth century, as was Thomas Elyot's wholesale fabrication of another imagined confrontation between the prince and the Law, in this case his quarrel with the chief justice of the realm and subsequent imprisonment.[32]

In point of fact, as demonstrated in the nineteenth century by Solly-Flood, in the early years of this century by Kingsford, and more recently by Christopher Allmand,[33] Henry as prince had spent his time in the most blameless ways.[34] What we here encounter is a collision between a highly influential narrative and psychological pattern, on the one hand, and a resistant or at least unhelpful factual record on the other; no surprise that the influential pattern prevails! We can be certain of Elyot's uninterest in revealing Henry V as a proto-Freudian exemplar of the transition from primal father of misrule to Oedipal father and guarantor of the law. Nevertheless, he sponsors a pattern of lawbreaking/lawmaking that sweeps aside more sober and less enticingly arranged documentary testimony.

My argument here is that evidence of implicitly Oedipal patterning should neither be relentlessly pressed on the one hand nor debunked on the other, but that, when employed flexibly and with respect for the resistances of contrary evidence, such patterns can offer shafts of indispensable illumination. The historical record disappoints pattern by refusing Henry IV his chosen role as guarantor of the law and by refusing to acknowledge the young Hal as a libertine. But it nevertheless affords a rich variety of senses in which our several claimants of the throne temporarily occupy different facets of the implicitly Oedipal interpellation conveniently figured in Hoccleve's anecdote, and appear briefly and provisionally as masters of self-imposed restraint and fathers of prohibition. The historical "evidence" of chronicles and other writings is already highly interpretative and hardly allows confident statements about monarchic motivation and behavior. But it may at least be said that, briefly and early, Richard II and Henry IV were able plausibly to sponsor and even to attract to themselves beneficial accounts of their capacity to inhabit a paternal and prohibitive function, and that, as both prince and monarch, Henry V displayed such traits throughout his adult career.

I am describing what I see as a sundered evidential field, in which decentered desires — originating in Oedipal prohibition and frustrated by failed Oedipal interpellation — remain operative, in fragmentary and achronological ways, from each of its "four corners." My use of the vocabulary of desire and prohibition aims, not at a rediscovery of sameness or likeness to us, but at new understandings of how particular medieval texts like Hoccleve's worked in their highly special circumstances. I am willing, in the course of this discussion, to risk or even to seek a certain amount of conceptual anachronism, in order to accomplish a defamiliarization in which late medieval texts and events are allowed to become temporarily strange to themselves, in the conviction that a frontier of additional understanding lies somewhere beyond the terms of these texts' deliberate self-description.

At the same time, I would not want to underestimate the sophistication with which medieval texts handle and process matters of desire. Hoccleve's desiring subjects are already, in Lacan's subsequent sense, "split," seeking satisfaction in erroneously understood and unattainable objects external to themselves; the presented object at the center of their yearning is already a Lacanian "vacuole," a symbolic function empty of real substance, the attainment of which ultimately frustrates rather than grants their desires;[35] John's prohibitions are not only disciplinary but benign in their concern to protect the selfish children from realization of inevitable self-deception. So Hoccleve's discussion of John's locked box is already, in Joan Copjec's phrase, "literate in desire"; fully possessed of its own "pockets of empty, inarticulable desire that bear the proof of society's externality to itself."[36] A task of the historicist critic is to avoid premature analytical closure; to refrain from explaining too much, too rationally, or from overassigning agency and purpose to actors who have as much right as ourselves to be deceived or befuddled about their own objectives. The documents of Lancastrian succession are fully urbane in acknowledging pockets of unarticulated desire. Part of our responsibility as critics is not to efface or hasten past such pockets, but to seek an equivalent urbanity in acknowledging their existence and employing them to enhance historical understanding.

13

MELLYAGANT'S PRIMAL SCENE

A recent diatribe, cited in the introduction to this volume, accuses theoretical practitioners of disingenuousness in using early texts as vehicles for their own more contemporary interests: "It seems to me wrong to seek to advance your career by professing to be concerned with Shakespeare, while actually writing about what happens to interest you more, forcing a limited set of new interests onto the old topic, using that topic as an excuse to write about these more fashionable concerns."[1] A different essay might pause to refute the sour assumption that only career-mongers and fashion victims pursue theory. I wish, however, to address the more substantial accusation that theory encourages effacement of the text. This is obviously a possible consequence of theory ill applied, yet theory holds out the equal and opposite promise that it might foster valued (and otherwise unobtainable) interpretative understandings.

One would be disingenuous to deny theory's possible problems; paramount among them is the power to enforce a reading, to discover in any text exactly what the theory was programmed to find. Against this possible pitfall I would, however, adduce a major benefit, which is the capacity of theory to reveal new and important aspects of a text that might otherwise have escaped notice. My intention in this essay is to weigh these two poles of possibility, by reading a passage in the light of a "strong" theory—strong in such senses as its capacity to discover its own preconditions in the widest variety of texts and its temporal and conceptual distance from the possible intentions of any medieval author, but also strong in its capacity to illuminate unnoticed aspects of a text, allowing us to see them in a new way. I mean, in short, to attempt a kind of "cost-benefit" analysis, between theory that, on the one hand, threatens to interpose itself between reader and text, and theory that, on the other, earns its way by sheer suggestiveness about the text. The occasion will be a scene at once familiar and disturbing to readers of medieval literature: a bloodied bed, in this case, that of Malory's Guinevere. The theory will be drawn from Freud's several discussions of what he came to call the "primal scene."

GUINEVERE'S BLOODY BED

Bloody beds are rife in late medieval literature. The Wife of Bath claims to dream of one.[2] Julian of Norwich imagines herself in a bed bloodied by the wounds of Christ.[3] The Tristan of Béroul opens a wound leaping across a barrier to land, and bleed, in Yseut's bed.[4] Chrétien's Lancelot gets into an analogous scrape, injuring his fingers entering Guinevere's chamber and then notoriously bloodying her bed — even as her ten wounded knights simultaneously bloody theirs.[5] This story reaches Malory via a lost intermediate *Shyvalere le Charyote*,[6] and to his "Knight of the Cart" I turn for the incident that provokes this essay. I choose this instance as a case in which meaning is both ostentatiously exhibited and arrantly withheld, in which a debate about meaning is foregrounded and fully thematized in the text, even as all the most promising interpretative avenues are blocked, rerouted, and systematically disavowed.

Guinevere is semiprisoner in Mellyagant's castle, tending over her wounded knights. Lancelot has arrived in his *charyott*, or cart, and boisterously spent the night with Guinevere, after ripping the bars off her window and wounding his own hands in the process. After "wacching" the night away, he withdraws. The wretched Mellyagant then arrives and opens the bed-curtain:

> And therewithal he opened the curtain for to beholde her. And than was he ware where she lay, and all the hede-sheete, pylow, and over-shyte was all bebled of the bloode of sir Launcelot and of hys hurte honde. When sir Mellyagant aspyed that blood, than he demed in her that she was false to the kynge, and that som of the wounded knyghtes had lyene by her all that nyght. (1132)

In typically craven fashion, he resolves to accuse her of treason before King Arthur.

Both captor and petitioner, Mellyagant finds himself obliged to spy upon the woman whom he would possess, demoted to the role of standby and witness of a situation he had thought to control. We here encounter him as an interpreter of other people's activities, and not even a very good one at that. For this scene hinges on a point of interpretation, becomes a virtual allegory of the necessity and fallibility of the interpretative process. Mellyagant's "deeming" that she has slept with one of the wounded knights represents a misperception of the situation; but, since her wounded knights did in fact spend the night in her chamber and since Lancelot is nowhere to be seen, it is an entirely reasonable misperception. Such, in fact, seems always to have been this sorry character's role. In the same situation in Chrétien's *Lancelot*, his attempts at reasoned assessment are even more labored, and no less wrong:

> I have found
> Blood on your sheets, clear proof ["que le tesmoingne"],
> Since you must be told.
> This is how I know ["par ce le sai"], and this my proof,
> For on your sheets and his I have found
> Blood that dripped from his wounds.
> This evidence ["ansaignes"] is irrefutable![7]

For all the proof he is able to adduce, the secure knowledge he believes he has achieved, the evidence he brings to bear, he is off the mark; Guinevere's companion is neither innocent Kex (in Chrétien) nor any of the equally innocent knights (in Malory) but Mellyagant's actual nemesis Lancelot.

For all his hapless folly, Mellyagant is, in a sense, *our*—that is, the reader's—representative in this scene. He is condemned to an act of interpretation, and carries it forward in the most reasonable and empirical way, only to fall short of anything approaching an account of what has actually transpired. Adding insult to injury, Mellyagant is further chastised for his role in this sorry interpretative scene. For one thing, as Lancelot then makes clear to him, his viewing of the bed constituted an impermissible breach. As befits a man of action, Lancelot offers us an action-oriented interpretation. In the bedchamber, "looking" (as opposed to "doing") is a doubly contemptible pursuit:

"Now truly," seyde sir Launcelot, "ye ded nat youre parte nor knyghtly, to touche a queyns bede whyle hit was drawyn and she lyyng therein. And I daresay... my lorde kynge Arthur hymselff wolde nat have displayed hir curtaynes, and she beyng within her bed, onles that hit had pleased hym to have layne hym downe by her. And therefore, sir Mellyaguance, ye have done unworshypfully and shamefully to youreselff." (1133)

Note, of course, that this wretched bedstead snooper is able only to do things "to himself" and not to Guinevere at all. He is, in this sense, a Peeping Tom, a scopophile, a would-be beholder of events from which he is otherwise excluded. Even the cuckolded Arthur would have known enough to enter Guinevere's bed ready for action, or not to enter it at all, but never just to snoop around. Here, as in every other episode in which we encounter him, Mellyagant displays his incapacity for chivalric norms of behavior, his inability to be properly "knightly." And, to the extent that he is our fellow interpreter, and thus our representative within the world of this tale, we must accept a share in his shame. But the full dimensionality of Mellyagant's shame remains unexpressed. He has, indeed, improperly entered Guinevere's bed, just as he improperly assaulted her knights, detained her, will trick Lancelot, and the like. Yet he is, in spite of all, not *wrong*; something untoward *did* happen in Guinevere's bed that night, and for all Lancelot's success in seizing the offensive, Mellyagant should hardly have to bear the entire burden of shame for its disclosure. Something more, in other words, remains to be said about the character and intensity — and ultimately the source — of Mellyagant's shame.

MELLYAGANT'S "PRIMAL SCENE"

One might — and here I choose to take a theoretical step — elicit additional aspects of this situation that have the effect of guaranteeing Mellyagant's shame by recourse to Freud's discussions of the "primal scene." This is Freud's evocation of the young child's real or imagined witness of parental intercourse, with its accompanying confusion about the event witnessed,[8] uneasy surmise that violence is somehow involved,[9] inevitable feelings of rivalry, and guilty fear of punishment springing from those feelings and from a sense of impermissible viewing.[10] Excluded by the curtained bed, forced boisterously to intrude by thrusting the curtains aside,[11] then required to engage in an after-the-fact reconstruction of an imperfectly understood event, Mellyagant is discovered in a situation similar to that of Freud's young Wolf Man. This is the patient who, tormented by his sense of being veiled from reality,[12] is aided in his own reconstruction of what occurred during the parental siesta one early childhood afternoon.

I must address a frequent misconception by asserting that I do not introduce Freud in order to psychoanalyze the character Mellyagant — or, for that matter, Béroul, Chrétien, Malory, medieval culture, or the original readers of this scene. Mellyagant is, after all, only marks on a page, without depth or specific personal history of the sort that would justify such an analytical enterprise. The conceptual gain in relating this moment to Freud's "primal scene" lies elsewhere; lies, in this case like so many others, with Freud's astounding analytical capacity to identify and describe particular meaning-making structures and effects. In this case, Freud recognizes a particular typology — that of the "primal scene" — that enables him to stipulate particular roles for the various participants. Freud's typology allows us, in other words, certain expectations about which participants are inside the bed and which destined to remain outside; who actually performs the purported deed and who watches or imagines the performance; who is or is not entitled to lay claim to emotions such as anger, fear, or embarrassment; and so on.

Lancelot and Guinevere, after all, enjoy a provisional entitlement to share her bed. I say "provisional" because they are not, in fact, a marital or parental couple, but an adulterous one. Nonetheless, Lancelot occupies the place of the king, and even, when lecturing Mellyagant, presumes to speak on his behalf concerning matters of bedroom decorum, and Guinevere is indeed the Queen. They are, in this sense, a satisfactory metonym for the parental couple, with its full rights of private enjoyment — enjoyment from which, needless to say, Mellyagant is structurally excluded. The role of the child observer of the parental scene is, of course, an abject role, in the sense that it is founded on nonparticipation, disempowerment, necessary exclusion. Occupying the structural role of the child observer of parental enjoyment, Mellyagant must accept the bitter truth that the scene in question is engineered for its immediate participants' enjoyment, that it is not "about" or "for" Mellyagant at all. Confronted in the primal scene is the child's sense of having no rights in the matter; that any participation engineered by the child will probably be unwelcome and cannot occur without demonstrating feelings of rivalry and inviting possible punishment.

To be sure, the narrative already has a good deal to tell us about the impropriety of Mellyagant's behavior and the fecklessness of his attempt to know what transpired there in the curtained bed; we have already seen the passage in which Lancelot fully informs him of the chivalric shortcomings of his curiosity. Here as elsewhere in the narrative, we might conclude that Mellyagant's abjection is already fully commented upon and sufficiently explained. Yet Mellyagant's impropriety is also so flagrant as to be susceptible to more than one kind of explanation, at more than one textual level. Indeed the overly curious Mellyagant is a boorish and coercive and unchivalric lover, and it is no wonder that Guinevere resists his unwelcome importunings; and he is no less deficient in a number of other categories of analysis, some of which are highlighted via a consideration of his role in "primal" and psychological terms. In the first place, Mellyagant's desire to know more about potential rivals in Guinevere's bed is only peripherally related to the progress of his own menacing courtship — may, in a sense, be seen as a distraction from his stated aims — yet his curiosity becomes a principal motive of the narrative. Also prominent within Freud's analysis is a humiliating (but necessary — the Wolf Man was only eighteen months old!) preference for looking over doing. Like the child observer, Mellyagant is perforce a kind of scopophile, with the additional increment of shame attending that role. Like the child observer, Mellyagant is troubled and puzzled by a confusion about the nature of the event that bloodied the bed in the first place. The child of Freud's primal scene surmises the presence of some violent misbehavior, and the violent origins of this blood as a product of struggle and injury are not far to be sought. In the case both of Mellyagant's mistaken theory (in which the blood belongs to one or more of the knights injured in his treacherous ambuscade) and of the true event (in which the blood is the product of Lancelot's forced entry through the barred window), the hypothesis of violence is sustained. Although the latter's violent exploit did not occur in the bed itself, we may see it as only slightly displaced from the bed, since it is motivated by love and the desire to enjoy love's pleasures:

"Than shall I prove my might," seyde sir Launcelot, "for youre
love." And than he sette hys hondis uppon the barrys of iron
and pulled at them with such a myght that he braste hem clene
oute of the stone wallys. And therewithall one of the barres of
iron kutte the brawne of hys hondys thorowoute to the bone.
And than he lepe into the chambir to the quene. (1131)

Mellyagant's confused deeming about the nature of the event in Guinevere's bed is, in a sense, the reaction of a child—who is guaranteed a
full measure of ignorance and agitation about an event not supposed to
have been seen in the first place. Something other than simple sexual
jealousy—some childish sense of broader impropriety—attaches itself
to his response.

Freud's formulation of the primal scene also speaks to the oddly lop-
sided assignment of guilt within the narrative. Although an adulterous
couple, Lancelot and Guinevere feel no guilt at all. Their imperviousness
is undoubtedly associated with qualities of blindness and arrogance implicated in the ultimate fall of Arthur's court, but it may also be associated with the symbolic prestige owed to the parental couple—the couple
in authorized possession of the nuptial bed—within the primal narrative. Similarly, the frustrated Mellyagant, who really is onto something
but is unable to make anyone see it, is dogged by that imputation of guilt
which will always fall upon the unsanctioned or illicit beholder. Lancelot's
behavior throughout suggests that no guilt is to be assigned to himself,
as Arthur's worthy stand-in, but that all guilt rests with the craven onlooker, the supposition-ridden interpreter—*our* representative in the narrative, the hapless Mellyagant.

Furthermore, this typology helps me to understand the assurance
and even serenity with which this text is able to protect its own central
event—the commerce between Lancelot and Guinevere in her bed—
from our, as well as Mellyagant's, gaze. For no sooner has Lancelot left
Guinevere's soiled bed than the text propels itself into a strenuous and
extended program of disavowal. Denied is the possibility that the soiled
sheets testify to much of anything. Certainly to be rejected is Mellyagant's
attempt to place blame on the wounded knights. But the text goes on
more ambitiously to reject any suggestion of untoward behavior of any
kind. For the taint of treason against Arthur, which would ordinarily at-

tach itself to Lancelot's adulterous invasion of his bed, is promptly and decisively withdrawn from the adulterous act and rebounds upon Mellyagant the accuser. Mellyagant first introduces the subject of treason, accusing Guinevere of being "a traytouras unto my lorde Arthur" (1132), yet Mellyagant's "treson" against Lancelot soon overshadows any other possible offense (1137): once "the kynge and queen and all the lordis knew off the treson of sir Mellyagante, they were all ashamed on hys behalffe" (1138). Thus, the burden of shame lies entirely upon Lancelot's accuser, even as Lancelot ends up "more . . . cherysshed than ever he was aforehande" (1140).

A part of the work of this text is to protect its own most ambitious fantasy of proscribed/authorized indulgence between Lancelot and the queen. Mellyagant is a pleasure-seeker, too, yet his desire is degraded by a variety of means, not excluding his infantilization and exclusion from rightful participation via the typology of the primal scene. By this and other means, the text moves treason out from its center to its periphery, away from Lancelot's bloody tumble with his queen and toward Mellyagant's impermissible viewings and base (though not, except technically, erroneous) imputations. I should say that I am not surprised by this textual operation: texts routinely — one might even say inevitably — engage in such self-protective stratagems, whereby their origins, and constitutive exclusions and, especially, central preoccupations are shielded from (rather than exposed to) view.

This text talks constantly about treason and is always assigning blame for treason, but the accusations tend to cluster about Mellyagant rather than to fall where they are most deserved, upon Lancelot's impermissible relation with the queen. Mellyagant's much discussed treasonous behavior is significant as an instance of "overdetermination" — by which Freud describes the effect whereby a dream's preoccupations will be multiply restated (sometimes even in random or incidental ways) within the dream. In this sense Mellyagant functions as a kind of litmus or beacon, attracting to himself multiple evidences of the treason that saturates the entire narrative, at once concealing and broadcasting the ultimate importance of treason *somewhere* within the total narrative scene. This use of Mellyagant's character requires that he be placed at a certain distance from the central action of the seduction scene, a state of acute curiosity unrelieved by any possibility of actual participation. In other words, the typology of the primal scene, and Mellyagant's role in it, well serves the mingled motives of secrecy and disclosure that mark the handling of treason in this tale.

I have thus far made a kind of "soft" or selective use of Freud, in the sense of emphasizing those potentially Freudian insights which rest most easily with the more literal motives and purposes of the narrative. Naturally, a truly "Freudian" reading will also work back against the grain of the text, emphasizing those insights to be gained which are at some level disguised or negated by the text or even actively contest its more literal sense. By way of example, I might return to the case of the young Wolf Man, to elicit another aspect of the primal experience as Freud describes it. For, by way of simplifying a highly complicated exposition, I might simply mention that Freud characterizes his infantile observer as highly uncertain about his particular attachment to the scene he has witnessed — a scene that had the effect of "splintering" his sexual life for years to come. If the obvious point of entry to the scene was identification with the father and desire to enjoy the mother, a strong countertheme as identified by Freud is adoption of a passive attitude toward the father and "to be given sexual satisfaction in the same way as his mother."[13] Yet this satisfaction had its potential cost, for this is a satisfaction "whose attainment seemed to involve the renunciation of [the male] organ." Thus, along with his confusion about object choice, the infant observer also reaped an emphatically unwelcome consequence: "What was essentially new for him in his observation of his parents' intercourse was the conviction of the reality of castration."

Returning to the situation of Mellyagant, whose own sexuality is of a stunted and only partially participatory form, we must notice that the event for which he has paid the greatest price in lost prestige and for which he will ultimately forfeit his life — that is, the rape of Guinevere — has not and never does occur in this narrative. Instead he turns to connivance, the dubious penal pleasures of incarceration, and endless curiosity about the whereabouts and doings of Lancelot. The plot to detain Guinevere, in fact, soon gives way to a plot to detain Lancelot in a kind of thinly disguised "love cave" reminiscent of other favored resorts in medieval romance. Guinevere is permitted simply to return to Westminster — albeit under accusation — as the momentum of the story shifts to the final struggle between Mellyagant and Lancelot.

Here rests an interpretative avenue that I will not fully pursue but that I believe lies open to intelligent investigation, which is the homo-erotics of chivalry and the sense in which Guinevere here as elsewhere serves as a chivalric pretext, enabling a relation of greater intensity between men. I do, however, wish to return to the matter of castration anxiety, which resurfaces in an extraordinary way at the end of the narrative. Here Mellyagant, after characteristic chicanery and evasion, finds himself in combat with Lancelot only to avoid its consequences by yielding in a most craven way. Certainly, in the literal terms of the story, we have here yet one more illustration of Mellyagant's utter incapacity to inhabit exterior chivalric norms. Yet a complementary point can be made at the psychoanalytical level, involving the terms of Mellyagant's identification with Lancelot and the former's faltering ability to recognize himself in the latter—and thus to constitute himself as his proper opponent. It is only when Lancelot offers to accept an impairment—literally to expose one side of his body and tie one arm behind his back—that the combat can resume: "I shall unarme my hede and my lyffte quarter of my body... and I woll lette bynde my lyfft honed behynde me there hit shall nat helpe me, and right so I shall do batayle with you" (1139). This narrative has already been supersaturated with images of castration, including Lancelot's own mangled fingers (a severed finger in Chrétien),[14] and here Lancelot offers to place himself on Mellyagant's plane by accepting an impairment. Literally, he appeals to his opponent's cowardice and opportunism. Psychoanalytically, he accepts the symbolic wound Mellyagant has already received as a result of his infantile demotion within the framework of the primal scene, rendering himself recognizable to Mellyagant, an object of identification and hence an appropriate opponent in the final struggle between the two knights.

COSTS AND BENEFITS

Has looking at Guinevere's bloody bed through the lens of the primal scene done any harm so far? The reader who might think so has probably long since closed this book. I suppose one might argue that, tarrying with Freud, I have failed or neglected to so something else more worthwhile, such as performing a historicist analysis of this scene—in terms, perhaps, of various detained, maligned, and abused fifteenth-century English queens, or fears of ungallantry associated with the rise of the commercial system, or some other presenting topic. But the critic's choice of subject presumably falls within the zone of taste and tactics, rather than some more absolute criterion. No, the *real* issue here is whether Freud is actually necessary to any of the points I have made. I have had the pleasure of debating Freudian criticism with Lee Patterson on several occasions, at a University of Oklahoma forum and elsewhere, and he has more than once observed, with characteristic penetration, "Sure, but did you need Freud for that?"

In this essay, I have.made several "Freudian" observations about my text, and each might have been made at some level without reference to Freud at all. I have noted an emphasis on situations of impermissible looking—of eavesdropping or spying. Yet, from Pandarus to Frocin (in Béroul's *Tristan*) to Agravain (in the *Morte*), medieval texts afford us numerous condemnations of onlookers, snoops, and spies. I have noted that Mellyagant's demeaning role as unsanctioned onlooker repeats the confusion and consternation of the excluded child in the primal triangle. Yet excluded claimants, from Absolon (in the "Miller's Tale") to the Pardoner (in the Prologue to the *Tale of Beryn*), are *always* inherently ridiculous, and liable not only to victimization but to infantilization as well. I have noted that this scene is permeated by guilt and that issues pertaining to guilt's final assignment are illuminated with reference to the guilty anxieties of the child observer in the primal scene. Yet medieval analysts have their own proven strengths in the attestation and assignment of guilt; the fine-tuning of guilt in the closing lines of *Sir Gawain and the Green Knight* overcomes any suggestion that the medievals need Freud's help in that area. Besides, Malory is clearly aware of his own central ironies—that Guinevere really is guilty of treason against Arthur (though not the variety of treason that Mellyagant has claimed) and that Lancelot really is the most guilty party, even though the temporary effect of this episode is to enhance his position and increase his esteem.

Nevertheless, I would resist the suggestion that Freud has nothing at all to add here. Each imaginative text is, to be sure, wholly a product of its own times, articulated at its own moment and within available discursive and explanatory systems. Whatever its debts to the past and hopes for the future, its meanings are refocused around the Now of its composing process. Yet each imaginative text simultaneously records more general strivings and desires, for which contemporary terms of reference provide a grounding and occasion and partial object, but which speak more broadly to matters of persistence and recurrence. I would never go so far as to argue—as Freud at least considered arguing, in the case of the primal scene—that some propensities and desires altogether escape time, to become the birthright of persons in all times and places.[15] Yet I would argue that texts work on both levels: accommodating full renderings of their immediate cultural circumstances and other less intelligible impulses. Thus, to say that Mellyagant is "infantile" in his headstrong desires and readiness to defy chivalric codes and to say that he is "infantile" as a result of his regressive reduction to confusion and passive spectatorship within the presuppositions of the primal scenario is to say two slightly different things—the one dependent on the text's overt instructions and the other more analytically derived. My contention is that both things are worth saying, and that the reading that acknowledges both of them strengthens itself. Always to be preferred is that reading which illuminates the text in several of its dimensions. In this respect, the final obligation of theory is not to permanence or even to truth; the best theory is the most *suggestive* one, the one most completely suggestive of added riches in the text.

PREMATURE KNOWLEDGE

The enemy of good criticism is what might be called "premature knowledge," which I would define as knowledge achieved the easy way, by acceptance of the text's own self-descriptions. In my view Freud's wise caution is to be respected; temporarily adrift in his analysis of little Hans, he observes, "I can only advise those of my readers who have not yet conducted an analysis not to try to understand everything at once, but to give a kind of unbiased attention to every point that arises and to await further developments."[16] Also to be resisted is the subsequent error, which is to become so arrogant about the capacities of one's critical tools that one indiscriminately overrides or reverses what the text seems to be trying to tell us about itself. Returning for a moment to Mellyagant's splintered desires: although the text leaves some leeway for a relation between Mellyagant and Lancelot as object of affective identification, I am reluctant to go so far against its grain as to claim that Mellyagant wishes to be enjoyed by Lancelot, or (thinking of little Hans's long afternoon of spectatorship) that he wishes Lancelot 'o take him violently or from behind.

Preferable either to accepting everything a text says about itself or
to negating its self-descriptions is a middle way that accepts theory as a
partner in inquiry without signing away all our rights in the matter. One
aspect of this middle way, as I have said, is not to be hasty about conclusions. Another is to invest particular confidence in those moments at
which the text's different levels of statement are found to be mutually
reinforcing. Yet another is not to imagine that everything about a text
can be known. Some aspects of the "truth" about what happened in Guinevere's bed can never be known to us. We know that Lancelot "toke hys
pleasaunce and hys lykynge untyll hit was the dawning of the day," and
we are in an excellent position for surmise, but in the end we do not
know or experience a good deal more than the balked and baffled Mellyagant. At the center of every text lies a blind spot—Freud's *omphalos* or
dream navel—that resists full disclosure.[17] This evokes Lacan's vacuole,
the empty place at the center of every signifier, best epitomized in Lacan's
view by the enigmas of desire, the occlusion of the love object, and the
detours and obstacles that constitute the gift of love: "Where, in effect,
is the vacuole created for us? It is at the center of the signifiers—insofar as that final demand to be deprived of something real is essentially
linked to the primary symbolization that is wholly contained in the signification of the gift of love."[18] We have a certain explanatory choice here.
The text's blind spot may be unreadable because, in the Freudian system,
it is overfull, overimplicated in too many different kinds of inextricable
meanings. Or it may be unreadable because, in the Lacanian system, it
is an "empty place," hollowed out, awaiting colonization only by our own
inferences and desires. Either way, we are not finally to know everything
about Guinevere's bloody bed and what happened there.

Whether because of its inherent richness or the inexhaustible creativity of our own object-seeking desires, this bed must remain a hot
spot of alternative interpretation. For example, the blood in Guinevere's
bed may be read as another kind of symptom altogether: as a symptom
of woman's secrets, the obscurity and terror of her gynecological functions, the inviolable and unknowable character of her private space. It
may, in other words, be read as an occasion and symptom of male baf-
flement—in which not only the hapless Mellyagant, but also the ten
knights and Lancelot himself must be supposed to share.

The right use of theory is not to "settle things." Quite the contrary:
its use is to *un*settle things, first by evading the text's own self-serving

simplifications, and second by displaying the multiplicity (or silence) at the text's core. In this I would recommend to the critic some of the inscrutability maintained by Arthur himself about the precise character of relations between his best knight and his queen. At the opening of the *Morte,* when the literal minded Agravain thinks he knows the one and only true thing about Lancelot and Guinevere, Malory comments,

> For, as the Freynshe booke seyth, the kynge was full lothe that such a noyse shulde be uppon sir Launcelot and his quene; for the kynge had a demyng of hit, but he wold nat here thereoff, for sir Launcelot had done so much for hym and for the quene so many tymes that wyte you well the kynge loved hym passyngly well. (1163)

A certain "deeming" — partly knowing without claiming fully to know — certainly turns out to be the best thing for the maintenance of Arthurian society. Only when Arthur lets himself be drawn into the camp of those literalists who claim emphatically to know do the real troubles begin. I propose Arthur's posture as a chastening model for the critic, who forms certain inferences and suppositions about the concealed act at the text's center... but should not claim overrapid or overcomplete knowledge of all that has happened there.

NOTES

INTRODUCTION

1. I. A. Richards, *Practical Criticism: A Study of Literary Judgment* (London: Kegan Paul, 1930).

2. Jacques Derrida, *Of Grammatology*, trans. Gayatri Spivak (Baltimore, Md.: Johns Hopkins University Press, 1976), 158.

3. Edward Said, *The World, the Text, and the Critic* (London: Faber, 1984).

4. See Barthes's enormously influential "From Work to Text," in *Image, Music, Text* (New York: Hill and Wang, 1997), 155–64.

5. On "text" as a production of theory, see John Mowitt, *Text: The Genealogy of an Antidisciplinary Object* (Durham, N.C.: Duke University Press, 1992), esp. chap. 1.

6. "To know the work, we must move outside it"; Pierre Macherey, *A Theory of Literary Production* (London: Routledge, 1978), 90. One of my problems with the world of theoretical studies is the haste with which some valuable books are briefly cried up and then abandoned; this provocative study continues to inform my sense of the literary and its practice.

7. Pleased with the convenience of this formulation, I didn't suppose when I wrote it that I was being very original, but I wasn't sure exactly whom to credit. Since then, I have come across a close variant, though (ironically) conceived by a couple of self-styled antitheorists. In "Against Theory 2," Steven Knapp and Walter Benn Michaels argue against the proposition that "a text can mean something other than what its author intends" and in favor of their contention that "meaning is determined by intention." Medievalists, of course, have their own reasons to doubt this contention, owing to their frequent contact with anonymous, plagiarized, overwritten, and lapidary texts and textualities. But, even in their own terms, Knapp and Michaels appear to have committed themselves to a position that could be rescued only by a sustained theoretical exercise, in and around the meaning of "intention" and how intention might be nonnaively understood. Their essay appears in *Critical Inquiry* 14 (1987): 49–68.

8. David Aers, "Magpie Theory," a presentation at the New Chaucer Society Congress, University of Kent at Canterbury, 1990.

9. "Repression," for example, means something entirely different in the Marxist system (where it refers to the active use of dominant institutions and agencies to interdict oppositional action) and the Freudian system (where it operates as an unconscious and subjective process, to prohibit impermissible thoughts). And "misrecognition" has utterly different implications for Bourdieu (where it refers to an institutionally guaranteed reprocessing of coerced or interested relations as elective ones) and Lacan (where it names the

"fundamental function of the *ego*," which is to refuse recognition either of the self or the objects of one's desire). I attempt to observe such differences when they occur, holding superficially homologous terms apart when they do not actually concur and paying proper attention to their context and proper use.

10. Writing on "resistance to theory," even archdevotee de Man argued that theory is not only resisted by nonpractitioners, and within theory's own terms, but is also resisted by the text itself, which eludes grammatical, historical, and even rhetorical "decoding." See Paul de Man, *The Resistance to Theory* (Minneapolis: University of Minnesota Press, 1986), 15–17.

11. Frank Kermode, "Writing about Shakespeare," *London Review of Books*, 9 December 1999, 3–8.

12. So, Jameson on history: "History is *not* a text, not a narrative, master or otherwise, but . . . as an absent cause, it is inaccessible to us except in textual form." See Fredric Jameson, *The Political Unconscious: Narrative as a Socially Symbolic Act* (Ithaca, N.Y.: Cornell University Press, 1981), 35. Jameson's formulation has often been discussed, and trenchantly critiqued, particularly by Robert Young, *White Mythologies: Writing History and the West* (London: Routledge, 1990), esp. 100–101, in which Jameson is found to instate history as "a final cause beyond knowledge." For my part, I rest content with the concept of an extratextual and material history measurable in its textual effects.

13. Some ground is given in this debate, even within the writings of the extratextual world's presumed archopponents. Consider, in this respect, Derrida's arguments on iteration and recontextualization as determinants of a text's enlarged field of implication, in *Limited Inc* (Evanston, Ill.: Northwestern University Press, 1988), esp. 136.

1. THREE LONDON ITINERARIES

Very different versions of this essay were presented at the Villanova Patristics Conference in 1997 (for which it was commissioned), the University of Connecticut in 1998, and Cambridge University in 1999.

1. Henri LeFebvre, *The Production of Space*, trans. D. N. Smith (Oxford: Blackwell, 1991), 31.

2. Pierre Bourdieu, *Outline of a Theory of Practice* (Cambridge: Cambridge University Press, 1977), 78.

3. Michel de Certeau, *The Practice of Everyday Life* (Berkeley: University of California Press, 1984), 99–103.

4. See Bronislaw Geremek, *The Margins of Society in Late Medieval Paris*, trans. J. Birrell (Cambridge: Cambridge University Press, 1987).

5. On Walter Benjamin's concept of the *flâneur*, see Susan Buck-Morss, *The Dialectics of Seeing* (Cambridge, Mass.: MIT Press, 1991), esp. 185–87, 304–7.

6. *Hoccleve's Works*, ed. F. J. Furnival, EETS, e.s., 72 (London, 1897).

7. Here, cited from N. H. Nicolas, ed., *The Scrope and Grosvenor Controversy*, 2 vols. (London: S. Bentley, 1832), 1:178; also available in M. M. Crow, *Chaucer Life-Records* (Oxford: Clarendon Press, 1966), 370–74.

8. John Stow, *The Survey of London* (London: Purslowe, 1618), 668. Although Ekwall, citing occurrences of the name since the twelfth century, thinks it might alternatively have been based on a personal name, such as OE *Frigdaeg*. See Eilert Ekwall, *Street-Names of the City of London* (Oxford: Clarendon Press, 1954), 85.

9. His mayoral term having recently come to an end, Brembre had returned to his customary post of alderman representing Bread Street Ward, a post he would occupy until his ouster (and subsequent death) at the hands of the aristocratic appellants in the following year; *Calendar of Letter Books . . . of the City of London,* ed. R. R. Sharpe (London: Corporation Record Office, 1899–1912), *Letter-Book H,* 283, 304.

10. Also adjacent to, or touching, Friday Street were the boundaries of two other parishes: Saint Mildred Breadstreet and Saint Nicholas Cole Abbey.

11. Jacques LeGoff, "Merchant's Time and Church's Time," in *Time, Work, and Culture in the Middle Ages* (Chicago: University of Chicago Press, 1980), 29–42.

12. M. M. Bakhtin, "Forms of Time and Chronotope in the Novel," *The Dialogic Imagination* (Austin: University of Texas Press, 1981), esp. 156–58.

13. After the critique of Susan Reynolds, *Fiefs and Vassals: The Medieval Evidence Reconsidered* (Oxford: Oxford University Press, 1994).

14. Caroline Barron, "Centres of Conspicuous Consumption: The Aristocratic Town House in London, 1200–1550," *London Journal* 20 (1995): 1–16, esp. 12.

15. Here accepting Crow's "nenyl" over Nicholas's "neuyl."

16. "Appeal of Thomas Usk against John Northampton," in *A Book of London English, 1384–1425,* ed. R. W. Chambers and Marjorie Daunt (Oxford: Clarendon Press, 1931), 22–31.

17. E. Powell and G. M. Trevelyan, eds., *The Peasants' Rising and the Lollards* (London: Longman's, Green, 1899), 27–35. The immediate text might be taken to apply to a single meeting, though several meetings are implied; the jury presentment implies that these meetings might have occurred on several occasions ("quolibet tempore").

18. He may have been the son of Nicholas and Agnes Uske, who were living in the parish of Saint Michael Queenhithe in 1368 (*Calendar of Wills . . . in the Court of Husting,* ed. R. R. Sharpe [London, 1890], 2:111); correspondence from Caroline Barron, 31 October 1988.

19. In the fourteenth and fifteenth centuries a street actually named "Bowe Lane" existed to the south, in Dowgate Ward. But the parish would seem to be the scene of the Northampton faction's comings and goings; the Latin presentment clearly situates the faction's agitations "in parochia beate Marie atte Bowe" and indiscriminately places John More's house "apud le Bowe" and "in parochia beate Marie atte Bowe."

20. *Hoccleve's Works: The Minor Poems,* ed. F. J. Furnivall, EETS, e.s., 61 (London, 1892), 25–39.

21. Westminster boasted two other gates as well: one at the abbey, one at the palace. On King Street taverns, see Gervase Rosser, *Medieval Westminster, 1200–1540* (Oxford: Clarendon Press, 1989).

22. Vanessa Harding, "The Port of London in the Fourteenth Century: Its Topography, Administration, and Trade" (Ph.D. diss., Saint Andrews University, 1983), 68–74. The *OED* (3.6) has "bridge" in the fifteenth and sixteenth centuries as "a fixed or floating landing-stage, jetty or pier." *Lauenderebridgge* is used in this sense in 1324, and *Tempelbrygge* in 1373–74. See Harding, "The Port of London," 70–71; *Calendar of Letter Books . . . of the City of London, Letter-Book G*, 322, 325.

23. John J. Gross, *The Rise and Fall of the Man of Letters* (New York: Macmillan, 1969), locates the "rise" in the eighteenth century.

24. Peter Clark's typology divides drinking establishments into inns (respectable food, drink, and chambers), taverns (ale and wine, means and lodging), and alehouses (only ale; variable lodging). Clark observes that these distinctions did not fully solidify until the sixteenth century, yet finds them incipient in the fourteenth century. See the first three chapters of *The English Alehouse: A Social History, 1200–1830* (London: Longman, 1983).

25. On the tavern as a seat of seditious activity, see Barbara Hanawalt, "The Host, the Law, and the Ambiguous Space of Medieval London Taverns," in *"Of Good and Ill Repute": Gender and Social Control in Medieval England* (New York: Oxford University Press, 1998), 113.

26. For the stimulus to add this section to my essay I am indebted to a comment by Professor Robert Hasenfratz of the University of Connecticut.

27. Though Hanawalt additionally observes that clerics would normally have lodged at religious establishments ("The Host," 103–4). Great nobles would, presumably, have lodged at their own mansions, or those of their families or friends.

28. Hanawalt's characterization possesses a certain expansiveness that I have thought appropriate to capture here, although it likewise possesses a rather fanciful dimension, of the sort characteristically owed to less-than-critical uses of literary sources; see the animadversions of Ralph Hanna III, "Brewing Trouble: On Literature and History—and Alewives," in *Bodies and Disciplines*, ed. Barbara Hanawalt and David Wallace (Minneapolis: University of Minnesota Press, 1996), 1–17.

29. The more than two hundred deponents on behalf of Scrope represented the cream of English chivalry, from John of Gaunt on down, including only some forty persons below the rank of knight. Moreover, most of those forty were "ancient" esquires, possessors of hereditary titles based on landed status, whereas Chaucer had achieved his title as a result of exertions "en service." On this last point, see Strohm, *Social Chaucer* (Cambridge, Mass.: Harvard University Press, 1989), 10–13, 21–23.

30. Maurice Keen has aptly described his testimony as that of "one who had seen honourable war service and could recall what old knights and squires worthy of credence in points of chivalry had retailed in his hearing." See "Chaucer's Knight, the English Aristocracy, and the Crusades," in *English Court Culture*, ed. V. J. Scattergood and J. W. Sherborne (New York: St. Martin's Press, 1983), 50.

31. Derek Brewer reminded me of the latitude of this term when I presented an earlier version of this essay to the Cambridge Medieval English Research Seminar in May 1999.

32. John Burrow, "The Title Sir," *Essays on Medieval Literature* (Oxford: Clarendon Press, 1984), 70.

33. Ibid., 70–74.

34. When he was unable to be present, the same task would be assumed by Willingham, evidently also a scrivener, and one Marchaund, a clerk.

35. *Scriveners' Company Common Paper, 1357–1628*, ed. Francis Steer (London Record Society, 1968), 1–5.

36. *Calendar of Plea and Memoranda Rolls*, 6 vols., ed A. H. Thomas (Cambridge, 1926–61), 2:221, 257.

37. Caroline Barron, personal correspondence, 31 October 1988.

38. *Westminster Chronicle*, ed. L. C. Hector and B. Harvey (Oxford: Clarendon Press, 1982), 90–91.

39. Thomas Walsingham, *Historia Anglicana*, Rolls Series (London, 1863), no. 28, pt. 1, 1:216.

40. "Appeal," 25–30.

41. *Calendar of Letter-Book H*, 317; *Rotuli Parliamentorum* (hereafter, *RP*), ed. J. Strachey, 6 vols. (London, 1783), 3:234; *Historia Mirabilis Parliamenti*, ed. May McKisack, *Camden Miscellany* 14 (1926): 19.

42. As a casual scanning of references in the *Middle English Dictionary* (ed. Hans Kurath and Sherman Kuhn) will quickly confirm, the same term is often applied to social inferiors in medieval romance.

43. Lee Patterson, *Chaucer and the Subject of History* (Madison: University of Wisconsin Press, 1991), 194–96.

44. Solidified in texts like Brembre's 1383 Proclamation against congregations, conventicles, and assemblies (Record Office, Corporation of the City of London, Letter-Book H, fol. clxxii).

45. John G. Bellamy, *The Law of Treason in England in the Later Middle Ages* (Cambridge: Cambridge University Press, 1970).

46. Thomas Usk, *Testament of Love*, bk. 1, chap. 6, in *The Complete Works of Geoffrey Chaucer*, vol. 7, ed. Walter W. Skeat (Oxford: Clarendon Press, 1897).

47. Rosser, *Medieval Westminster*, 161.

48. The panel in question, involving presentations by Kathryn Kerby-Fulton, Steven Justice, and Anne Middleton, sought to argue (improbably, in my view) that Chaucer, Langland, and Usk were members of a single "coterie," associated on the basis of their common belief in the priority of aesthetic production.

2. WALKING FIRE

This essay was originally given as a paper at Duke University on 10 March 1998.

1. I thank Susan Crane for pointing out the relevance of state sponsorship to the parallelism I mean to construct here.

2. H. G. Richardson, "Heresy and the Lay Power under Richard II," *English Historical Review* 51 (1936), 1–28; Peter McNiven, *Heresy and Politics in the Reign of Henry IV* (Woodbridge, Suffolk: Boydell, 1987); Margaret Aston, "Lollardy and Sedition, 1381–1431," *Past and Present* 17 (1960): 1–44. A more general essay on the solidification of sentiment for persecution among the medieval laity, especially by operation of decree and statute, is Peter D. Diehl, "Overcoming Reluctance to Prosecute Heresy in Thirteenth-Century Italy,"

Christendom and Its Discontents: Exclusion, Persecution, and Rebellion, 1000–1500, ed. Scott L. Waugh and Peter Diehl (Cambridge: Cambridge University Press, 1996), 47–65.

3. See Wendy Scase, *"Piers Plowman" and the New Anticlericalism* (Cambridge: Cambridge University Press, 1989), 125–60.

4. Peter of Blois, epistle 113 (*Patrologia Latina*, ed. J.-P. Migne, vol. 207).

5. See Miri Rubin, *Corpus Christi: The Eucharist in Late Medieval Culture* (Cambridge: Cambridge University Press, 1991), 312–16. Also see Margaret Aston, "Corpus Christi and Corpus Regni: Heresy and the Peasants' Revolt," *Past and Present*, no. 143 (1994): 27–31, and Anthony K. Cassell, *Dante's Fearful Art of Justice* (Toronto: University of Toronto Press, 1984), 100–103.

6. X.5.7.10, in *Corpus Iuris Canonici*, ed. A. Friedberg (Leipzig: B. Tauchniz, 1879), vol. 2, cols. 782–83.

7. *Clem.* 5.3.3, ibid., cols. 1183–84.

8. Register Arundel (Ely), Ely Diocesan Records, Cambridge University Library, G/1/2, ff. 41v–42r.

9. Text and translation from *Knighton's Chronicle*, ed. G. H. Martin (Oxford: Oxford Medieval Texts, 1996), 306–7.

10. *RP*, 3:459.

11. *Knighton's Chronicle*, 312. Sympathizers, especially John of Gaunt, are said to have interceded with the bishop to seek a lighter sentence ("ut penam eius transferret in aliam penatenciam"; 312). The account is, of course, fanciful, since no heretics had been officially burned in England, and because such a penalty would in any event have been a matter for secular rather than ecclesiastical determination. Martin translates this phrase as "[he was] adjudged fuel for the flames," and considers it a formal sentence: "This observation, made c. 1390, seems not to have been noted in discussions of the death penalty for heresy in England" (313). My own inclination is to treat it as an opinion as to Swinderby's deserts, although, as I am arguing here, the line between speech acts and corporeal acts grows increasingly dim.

12. Cited in H. G. Richardson and G. O. Sayles, "Parliamentary Documents from Formularies," *Bull. Inst. Hist. Research* 11 (1933–34): 147–62.

13. Roger Dymmok, *Liber contra XII Errores et Hereses Lollardorum*, ed. H. S. Cronin (London: Wyclif Society, 1922), 5.

14. I am grateful to Andrew Cole, who brought the subject of Lollard response to my attention on the occasion of my Duke lecture, and who suggested several of the passages discussed in this paragraph and the next. "Leaven of Pharisees" is from *The English Works of Wyclif*, ed. F. D. Matthew, EETS, o.s., 74 (London, 1880), 16. See also 88, 124, 246.

15. *English Wycliffite Sermons*, ed. Anne Hudson (Oxford: Clarendon Press, 1983), 1:375.

16. On the performative aspects of speech, I have been influenced by (and employ terminology from) J. L. Austin, *How to Do Things with Words* (Cambridge, Mass.: Harvard University Press, 1967); "Performative Utterances," in *Philosophical Papers*, 3rd ed. (Oxford: Oxford University Press, 1979), 233–52; and John R. Searle, "What Is a Speech Act?" in *Philosophy in America*, ed. Max Black (Ithaca, N.Y.: Cornell University Press, 1965), 221–39.

17. On the subject of "action-seeking" utterances I have been guided by Danilo Marcondes de Souza Filho, *Language and Action* (Amsterdam: Benjamins, 1984).

18. Austin, *How to Do Things with Words*, 117.

19. Richard's lack of adamancy in this regard is persuasively set forth by Richardson, "Heresy and the Lay Power," 1–28.

20. D. Wilkins, ed. *Concilia Magnae Britanniae et Hiberniae* (London, 1737), 3:260.

21. *RP*, 3:459.

22. *RP*, 3:466–67; *Statutes of the Realm*, 2 Henry IV, 125–28.

23. Austin, "Performative Utterances," 123.

24. Austin, *How to Do Things with Words*, 109.

25. *Eulogium and Continuatio Eulogii*, Rolls Series, no. 9, pt. 3 (London, 1863), 388.

26. Here echoing the language of Michel Foucault, *Discipline and Punish* (New York: Vintage Books, 1979), 48.

27. *RP*, 3:459.

28. A subject in literature or in life who offers himself or herself as an example, might, as Larry Scanlon puts it in the case of Chaucer's Parson, "become exemplary precisely by transforming his or her actions into a moral narrative"; *Narrative, Authority, and Power: the Medieval Exemplum and the Chaucerian Tradition* (Cambridge: Cambridge University Press, 1994), 34. Or a subject like Sautre might *be* transformed, willy-nilly, into a moral narrative.

29. King Henry was not alone in assigning exemplary value to Sautre's burning. A commons petition framed in obvious reference to Sautre's case and submitted to the parliament then sitting urged that "anyone" taken in Lollardy and held in prison should receive the judgment he has reserved, "as an example to others of that evil sect" ("en ensample d'autres de tiel male secte"; *RP*, 3:473). So, too, does *De heretico comburendo* argue that burning occurs in order that the deed might inspire fear in the minds of others ("ut hujusmodi punicio metum incuciat mentibus aliorum"; *Statutes of the Realm* [London: Dawsons, 1810], 2:128). Chronicle accounts, likewise, underscore the spectacle's exemplary value, stressing the impetus it provided toward recantation among Sautre's fellows. Thus the *Eulogium* continuation argues, "After this terrible example other of his accomplices personally recanted their heresies at the cross of Saint Paul" (*Continuatio Eulogii*, 388).

30. As discussed in Strohm, *England's Empty Throne: Usurpation and the Language of Legitimation, 1399–1422* (London: Yale University Press, 1998), chap. 2.

31. As specified in the Kent Heresy Proceedings. See Norman Tanner, "Penances Imposed on Kentish Lollards by Archbishop Warham, 1511–12," in *Lollardy and the Gentry in the Later Middle Ages*, ed. Margaret Aston and Colin Richmond (Stroud: Sutton, 1997), 247.

32. *The Book of Margery Kempe*, ed. S. Meech, EETS, o.s., vol. 212 (London, 1940), 1:28.

33. Michel Foucault, *Discipline and Punish* (New York: Pantheon Books, 1977), 34–47.

34. In the formulation of Slavoj Žižek, *The Sublime Object of Ideology* (London: Verso, 1989), 58–62.

35. Anne Middleton, "Acts of Vagrancy: The C Version 'Autobiography' and the Statute of 1388," in *Written Work: Langland, Labor, and Authorship* (Philadelphia: University of Pennsylvania Press, 1997), 284.

36. Mary Douglas, *Purity and Danger* (London: Routledge, 1966), 40.

37. Ibid., 39.

3. Coronation as Legible Practice

The original of this essay was given as a plenary address to the Illinois Medieval Conference, 24 February 1996. In preparing this version for publication, I have borrowed several sentences from a related conference commentary, separately published as an afterword to *Bodies and Disciplines*, ed. Barbara Hanawalt and David Wallace (Minneapolis: University of Minnesota Press, 1998), 223–32. That commentary proposes practice theory as an "intersection" among the contributed papers at that conference.

1. I am indebted to John Mowitt's observation that symbolic objects are "constructs of the interaction between a signifying practice and a methodological field," and that we bear a particular obligation to the question of "how what eludes us in our interpretation has to do with the limits imposed upon our construction by the field in which it is executed." See his *Text: The Genealogy of an Antidisciplinary Object* (Durham, N.C.: Duke University Press, 1992), 45–46.

2. A provisional and very incomplete list might include the Freudian/Lacanian analysis of the text's (and textual subject's) unacknowledged designs and desires; the feminist and postcolonialist analysis of steps necessary to hear the suppressed voice of the "other"; gender as an analytical category, the emergent sense of hybridity as the zone of what gender excludes or leaves out; and structuration theory as it extends the boundaries of personal and social performance.

3. Diane Elam, "Ms. en Abyme: Deconstruction and Feminism," *Social Epistemology* 4 (1990): 293–308.

4. Intelligently surveying the origins of practice theory and critiquing some of its assumptions is Sherry B. Ortner, "Theory in Anthropology since the Sixties," *Comparative Studies in Society and History* 26 (1984): 126–66.

5. Pierre Bourdieu, *Outline of a Theory of Practice* (Cambridge, 1977), 54. Unless otherwise indicated, all Bourdieu references are to this work.

6. Ian Hacking, *The Social Construction of What?* (Cambridge, Mass.: Harvard University Press, 1999), 33–34.

7. A corollary is that not all knowledges are discursive, that people know more than they can say they know. See Anthony Giddens on the distinction between discursive and practical consciousness, in *Central Problems in Social Theory* (Berkeley: University of California Press, 1979), 25 and passim.

8. See Sherry B. Ortner and Marshall D. Sahlins, "Theory in Anthropology," in *Culture/Power/History*, ed. N. Dirks, G. Eley, and S. Ortner (Princeton, N.J.: Princeton University Press, 1994), 400–401. They offer an independent account of the inherently unruly aspect of representation that Judith Butler calls the "swerve," the sense in which a subversion of identity becomes possible "*within* the practices of repetitive signifying." See *Gender Trouble: Feminism and the Subversion of Identity* (London: Routledge, 1990), 145. I find *Gender Trouble* an enormously useful and satisfying book, but have wondered whether some of its points could not have been more efficiently established via the argumentative trajectory afforded by practice theory.

9. Unless otherwise specified, page references to medieval coronation documents are to Leopold G. W. Legg, *English Coronation Records* (Westminster, 1901).

10. Thomas Walsingham, *Historia Anglicana*, Rolls Series (London, 1863), no. 28, pt. 1, 2:332–39.

11. Adam of Usk, *Chronicon*, ed. E. M. Thompson (London, 1904), 34.

12. John Dymmok died in the fourth year of Richard's reign. An undated petition on behalf of his wife Margaret to the Council suggests that he had not received the customary fees for this service (including the best available horse and armor) at the time of his death. Susan Crane has suggested, in correspondence, that fees may have been withheld because he was not called upon to serve in his capacity. See H. Nicolas, ed., *Proceedings and Ordinances of the Privy Council of England* (London: Commissioners of Public Records, 1834), 1:87.

13. *Westminster Chronicle*, ed. L. C. Hector and Barbara Harvey (Oxford: Clarendon Press, 1966), 414–17, with minor alterations. These same points are made in the *Liber regalis*, a coronation *ordo* of Westminster provenance, of which the fourth recension may have been followed in the coronation of Richard II. There, the king is to be divested of his principal regalia immediately after the service, and, taken to a closed place near the altar, he is divested of his tunic and shoes and sandals ("caligas regales et sandaria"; 106), the latter to be delivered to the abbot of Westminster. Then, clad in other vestments, he is to exit the abbey through the choir (Legg, *English Coronation Records*, 127).

14. Certainly, Richard was made to feel his omission, since in March 1390 (his first regnal year of majority) he sent to the monks of Westminster a new pair of sandals, or *sotularia*, blessed by Pope Urban VI. (This act, in turn, triggered the chronicler's tirade.)

15. Adam of Usk, *Chronicon*, 200–202.

16. Ibid., 32, 185.

17. See Strohm, "Saving the Appearances," in *Hochon's Arrow* (Princeton, N.J.: Princeton University Press, 1992), 75–94.

18. "Nothing that goes before, and nothing which follows, can approach the anointing in significance. Without it the King cannot receive the royal ornaments, without it, in a word, he is not King.... the King is vested and adorned with the *regalia* because he is anointed;... he is not anointed in order that he may receive the *regalia*" (Legg, *English Coronation Records*, xxxiv).

19. Ibid., 49. As printed in *Chronicles of London*, ed. Charles Kingsford (Oxford: Clarendon Press, 1905). Possibly corroborative of the suggestion that Henry's anointment was open to view is the early-fifteenth-century *Forma et Modus*, which omits mention of the *pallium* and says only that "surgat Rex de cathedra et vadat ad altare et deponet vestes suas... vt recipiat vnccionem" (Legg, *English Coronation Records*, 175).

20. Legg translates the phrase "recuperabit sine vi" as "shall recover by force," on the apparent assumption that Henry IV wanted to represent himself as a conquering king. In fact, the Lancastrians proposed to effect this recuperation as an easy and beneficent side effect of their ascent to the throne. Before and during Richard's negotiation of the peace treaty of 1396, the English feared the alienation of Aquitaine through its reversion

to the duchy of Lancaster; with the crowning of Henry IV, Aquitaine would once again become Crown land.

21. The manipulation of Richard as unsuccessful claimant is carried one step farther in the *Continuatio Eulogii*, which first relates his discovery (in the "stripped," Lancastrian version), then passes on to other subjects, then returns to it in recounting Henry's coronation with the previously mentioned oil ("cum oleo aquilae innotatae"; 380, 384). The oil here functions as a prophetic object, carried around unwittingly by Richard II until its meaning is retrospectively conferred. Opening a temporal and narrative division between the oil's discovery and its use, this account preserves the innocence of its own corroborative scheme.

22. Pierre Bourdieu, *Language and Symbolic Power* (Cambridge, Mass.: Harvard University Press, 1991), 115.

23. Frederick Devon, *Issues of the Exchequer* (London, 1837), 296.

24. *Annales Henrici Quarti*, ed. H. T. Riley, Rolls Series, no. 28, vol. 3 (1866), 350.

25. A good reproduction may be viewed in *Pageant of the Birth, Life, and Death of Richard Beauchamp, Early of Warwick K.G., 1389–1439*, ed. Viscount Dillon and W. H. St. John Hope (London, 1914). On the ramifications of these symbolic inflections, see John Carmi Parsons, "Ritual and Symbol in the Medieval English Queenship to 1500," in *Women and Sovereignty*, ed. Louise O. Fradenburg (Edinburgh: Edinburgh University Press, 1992), 61–66.

26. Gui Lobineau, *Histoire de Bretagne* (Paris, 1707), 2:878; *Histoire d'Artus III, duc de Bretaigne*, ed. D. Godefroy (Paris, 1622), 11–12.; A. R. Myers, "The Captivity of a Royal Witch," *Journal of the John Rylands Library* 24 (1940): 263–84.

27. As daughter of the notorious and well-heeled Charles le Mauvais, king of Navarre, Joanne did bring a dowry to a marriage, when her father promised the remarkable sum of 120,000 gold livres and 6,000 livres annually in rents for her 1386 marriage to the elderly, headstrong, and truculent John IV, duke of Brittany. John, for his part, responded with an equally munificent dower, including the rents of the city of Nantes, and other substantial properties; Pierre-Hyacinthe Morice, *Histoire ecclésiastique et civile de Bretagne*, vol. 1 (Paris, 1750), 395. After the duke died in 1399, Joanne served as regent of Brittany until 1401, when her twelve-year-old son was instated in office. Negotiations for marriage with Henry IV were begun in March 1402 and consummated with considerable rapidity, considering that the marriage required a papal dispensation on consanguinity, a 3 April 1402 proxy ceremony in England, a further dispensation from the pope to live among schismatics, and arrangements for the bestowal and governance of her lands. On 20 December 1402 Joanne set out from Nantes, with the marriage finally occurring at Winchester on 8 February 1403 and a ceremony of coronation on 26 February at Westminster. Speculation about Henry IV's interest in marriage to Joanne cannot avoid the subject of this wealthy widow's dower from the duke of Brittany. The chronicler of Saint-Denys says that first awareness of the marriage negotiation sparked a rumor to the effect that she had shipped her treasure and jewels abroad; *Chronique de religieux de Saint-Denys*, ed. M. L. Bellaguet (Paris, 1841), vol. 3, 40. Writing at the end of the seventeenth century, Lobineau lists an interest in the dower prominently among possible considerations: the likelihood of her continuing influence in duchy affairs, the possibility of an English-Breton alliance against France, access to Continental ports, and "le gros douaire

qu'elle avoit en Bretagne, auquel le feu Duc avoit adjousté trois ou quatre ans avant que de mourir"; *Chronicon Briocense,* in Lobineau, vol. 1, cols. 500–501. If this was indeed Henry's list, he must have been a disappointed man. Joanne left the young duke and her other sons under the hostile guardianship of the duke of Burgundy, the Bretons were in arms against the British within months after the wedding, and Joanne was thwarted in her attempt to raise ready cash by selling the governorship of Nantes to Olivier de Clisson for 12,000 crowns. The dower and its disposition appear also to have eluded whatever hopes Henry might have entertained.

In fact, the ever financially hard-pressed Henry IV was to endure a squadron of monetary disappointments in his alliance with the wealthy countess, at least when the financial aspects of his marriage are compared with generally accepted medieval norms. First, no record exists of any dowry that came to Henry as a result of the marriage. A second area of more promise would seem to be the large dower from her previous marriage that Joanne brought with her to England, and to which medieval precedents would have granted Henry administrative control and enjoyment during his lifetime; Pollock and Maitland, *The History of English Law,* 2nd ed. (Cambridge: Cambridge University Press, 1952), 2:407–8, 427. On dower in the fourteenth and fifteenth centuries, see Judith M. Bennett, *Women in the Medieval English Countryside* (Oxford: Oxford University Press, 1987), 110–14, and Diane Owen Hughes, "From Brideprice to Dowry," *Journal of Family History* 3 (1978): 282. Henry, however, seems to have achieved no control whatever over his wife's inherited revenues and funds. Rather, in another costly decision, he followed a different medieval precedent, acting promptly to assure Joanne of a second dower, from the English treasury and from lands under his control, together with certain guarantees from the income of the Lancaster estates: on 8 March 1403, a month after the marriage, a sum of 10,000 marks annually was granted to the queen, to be paid from the exchequer, pending satisfaction of the sum by rents from possessions later to be assigned; *Calendar of Patent Rolls* (Stationer's Office, 1901–), 1401–5, 231. This massive sum, amounting to some ten per cent of the annual income of the royal government, was roughly half again as large as the £4500 granted to English queens in dower over the preceding two centuries.

28. *Calendar of Patent Rolls,* 1401–5, 473.

29. London and New York: Routledge, 1990.

4. "LAD WITH REVEL TO NEWEGATE"

In January 1992 I spoke at the Oxford University Early Modern History Seminar, arranged by Robin Briggs and Miri Rubin, on "Chronicle Evidence and the Rebel Voice," since published as a chapter in *Hochon's Arrow.* I found a number of comments after the talk, particularly those by my two hosts, quite stimulating, and this paper embodies my "after the fact" reconsiderations. It has been previously published in *Art and Context in Late Medieval English Narrative,* Essays in Honors of Robert Worth Frank Jr., ed. Robert R. Edwards (Cambridge: Brewer, 1994), 163–76. I wish to add thanks to Sheila Lindenbaum for several historical suggestions and to Kimberly Keller for assistance in research. For this version, several notes have been added and several sentences rewritten.

1. All quotations from Chaucer's writings will be taken from *The Riverside Chaucer*, ed. Larry D. Benson, 3d ed. (Boston: Houghton Mifflin, 1987).

2. I agree with Lee Patterson's observations about the rejection of Perkyn's "riotous excess that threatens the social order as a whole," but I do not agree that the Cook himself is "the voice of lower-class criminality." At this point in the *Tales* the Cook's is very much the voice of middle-class moralization; only later, in the "Manciple's Prologue," will the Cook be reinscribed as the representative of revelry gone stale and be subject to rejection in his own right. See his *Chaucer and the Subject of History* (Madison: University of Wisconsin Press, 1991), 278–79.

3. *The Westminster Chronicle, 1381–94*, ed. L. C. Hector and Barbara Harvey (Oxford: Clarendon Press, 1982), 2.

4. See *Westminster Chronicle*, 4. On Corpus Christi as a time of potential disorder, see Miri Rubin, *Corpus Christi: The Eucharist in Late Medieval Culture* (Cambridge: Cambridge University Press, 1991), 263–64. On the potential relation of festivity and revolt, see Yves-Marie Bercé, *Fête et Revolté* (Paris: Hachette, 1976), esp. 72–77. For explicit connection between festivity and the Rising of 1381, see Christopher Dyer, "The Rising of 1381 in Suffolk: Its Origins and Participants," *Proceedings of the Suffolk Institute of Archaeology and History* 36 (1988) 281. Published in the same year as the present essay was Margaret Aston, "Corpus Christi and Corpus Regni: Heresy and the Peasants' Revolt," *Past and Present* 143 (1994): 3–47. Although Aston's final interest rests with the disputed theology of the eucharistic text and the possibility that heretical views of the Eucharist were bound up in the oppositionality of revolt, her account also raises issues of popular practice, ceremonial access, and wished-for closure that I am addressing here. Although Corpus Christi was hardly a day of carnival, it was nevertheless a feast day and day of festivity, in which celebration occurred and issues of participation and control inherent in any such occasion came to the fore. She observes, "I am not the first...to see a connection between popular risings and church festivals....Corpus Christi celebrations sparked brawls and dissension on numerous occasions" (10). She additionally notes that the rebels' letters include tags and figures which participate "in the worlds both of fact and folk festival" (25–26).

5. Thomas Walsingham, *Historia Anglicana*, vols. 1 and 2, ed. H. T. Riley, Rolls Series, 28 (London, 1863, 1864), pt. 1, 1:462.

6. *Anonimalle Chronicle*, ed. V. H. Galbraith (Manchester: Manchester University Press, 1970), 145.

7. Walsingham, *Historia Anglicana*, 1:459; *Anonimalle Chronicle*, 147–48; Henry Knighton, *Chronicon*, ed. Joseph R. Lumby, 2 vols., Rolls Series 92 (London, 1895), 2:137, 131.

8. See Andrew Prescott, "London in the Peasants' Revolt: A Portrait Gallery," *London Journal* 7 (1981): 131–33.

9. Perry Anderson, *Passages from Antiquity to Feudalism* (London: New Left Books, 1974), 205.

10. Perkyn's associational tendencies, their rebuke by the Cook's antiassociational rhetoric, and the wider implications of this ideological field are evoked and productively analyzed in David Wallace, "Chaucer and the Absent City," in *Chaucer's England: Literature in Historical Context*, ed. Barbara Hanawalt (Minneapolis: University of Minnesota Press,

1992), esp. 71–81; since republished in Wallace's *Chaucerian Polity* (Stanford, Calif.: Stanford University Press, 1997), 156–81.

11. R. B. Dobson, *The Peasants' Revolt of 1381* (London: Macmillan, 1970), 291.

12. Reginald Call, "'Whan he his papir soghte,'" *Modern Language Quarterly* 4 (1943): 167–76. On conditions governing apprentices in the thirteenth and fourteenth centuries, see A. H. Thomas, ed., *Calendar of Plea and Memoranda Rolls, 1364–81* (Cambridge: Cambridge University Press, 1929), xxxi–xlvii. The form of a sixteenth-century agreement, still possibly incorporating some standard features, emphasizes the responsibility of the apprentice to avoid dice and other unlawful games as well as taverns and playhouses, and to be readily available for his master's service; see P. E. Jones, *The Corporation of London: Its Origin, Constitution, Powers, and Duties* (London: Corporation of London, 1950), 90.

13. A splendid discussion of the importance of writing and exclusion from writing and the sometimes touching faith among the rebels that early charters might confirm their liberties is Susan Crane's essay "The Writing Lesson of 1381," in *Chaucer's England: Literature in Historical Context*, 201–21.

14. Robert Darnton, *The Great Cat Massacre* (New York: Vintage Books, 1985), 75–104.

15. Roger Chartier, "Text, Symbols, and Frenchness," *Journal of Modern History* 57 (1985): 688.

16. Robert Darnton, "History and Anthropology," in *The Kiss of Lamourette* (New York: Norton, 1990), 333.

17. As noted by Harold Mah, "Suppressing the Text: The Metaphysics of Ethnographic History in Darnton's Great Cat Massacre," *History Workshop Journal* 31 (1991): 1–20.

18. Roger Chartier, *The Cultural Uses of Print in Early Modern France*, trans. Lydia G. Cochrane (Princeton, N.J.: Princeton University Press, 1987), 7–11.

19. Representative instances of such punishments appear in *Liber Albus*, ed. H. T. Riley, 3 vols., Rolls Series, no. 12 (London, 1862), 1:458–59. See also Arthur Griffiths, *The Chronicles of Newgate* (London: Chapman and Hall, 1884), 34–39. I am grateful to Sheila Lindenbaum for calling my attention to these references.

20. Walsingham's reliance on tragedy would seem to vindicate Hayden White's suggestion that quasi-literary "emplotment" lends meaning to a historical narrative by suggesting that it is a story "of a particular kind"; see, for instance, his *Metahistory* (Baltimore, Md.: Johns Hopkins University Press, 1973), 7–11. Readers of the remainder of this essay will, however, see that I find the organizing principles of historical narrative as no less likely to originate in the frames opportunistically or adventitiously employed to make sense of our everyday or practical experience than in the more formalized renderings that have been stabilized as literary genres.

21. So, too, are the rebels bearing down on London said by the Westminster chronicler to have raved or revelrously debauched themselves *(debachabantur;* 2). The Westminster chronicler introduces the concept of bacchanal at the outset rather than at the end of his narration, though it still seems intended to suggest a "brief frenzy," headed for a predictably early demise.

22. A similar view is expressed at somewhat greater length in my *Hochon's Arrow* (Princeton, N.J.: Princeton University Press, 1992), esp. 54–56. Not subscribing to this view is Steven Justice, *Writing and Rebellion* (Berkeley: University of California Press, 1994),

173. I might add that, in my observation that the rebels lacked a comprehensive revolutionary ideology, no derogation of rebel creativity is intended; their apparent redirection of revel strikes me as inspired improvisation. But that they continued, *faute de mieux*, to (mis-)place their principal trust in the king's goodwill and powers of redress seems to me beyond doubt. For particular emphasis on the diversity of rebel motives, see Andrew Prescott, "The Judicial Records of the Rising of 1381" (Ph.D. diss., University of London, 1984).

23. David Carr, *Time, Narrative, and History* (Bloomington: Indiana University Press, 1986), 61, 68. Carr's emphasis on the practical origins of narration in the production of everyday actions, as opposed to Paul Ricoeur's assumption that experience is only retrospectively organized via narrative configuration, is conveniently set forth in his review of *Temps et récit*, vol. 1, in *History and Theory* 23 (1984): 357–70.

24. A different but parallel point, involving sermon rhetoric rather than narrative as such, is Margaret Aston's description of official attempts to regain control of the theology and social meaning of Corpus Christi, in "Corpus Christi and Corpus Regni," 37–39.

25. A tendency may be noticed among twentieth-century commentators, and especially literary people interested in "historical backgrounds," to treat the Rising (along with the Black Death and, optionally, the Hundred Years' War) as an unprecedented and traumatic moment of rupture, the importance and singularity of which are enhanced by its discontinuity with events before or since. In this treatment, they show themselves influenced by medieval source-narratives that treat the Rising as a sudden and overwhelming phenomenon that subsided as rapidly as it occurred. Some historians have, on the other hand, asserted their urbanity and sense of diachronic process by disallowing a sense of rupture and insisting instead that the Rising had little effect and changed little or nothing. An extreme rendition of this view is that of F. M. Powicke, with his dismissal of the Rising as "an 'incident' of no enduring importance." See his *Medieval England, 1066–1485* (London: Oxford University Press, 1931), 214. The latter view may still be conditioned by the lingering effect of medieval narratives of flare-up and subsidence in its assumption that the Rising can be isolated or bracketed for limited analysis and an enumeration of its effects. An approach somewhat more resistant to the rhetoric of narrative closure would return the events of 1381 to the stream of history, recasting them in a narrative open, rather than closed, at the far end. This analytical effect is, for example, achieved — possibly inadvertently — by Charles Oman when, seeking to minimize the long-term significance of the Rising, he returns it to a longer-term account of landlord-tenant struggles: "For the next ten years the archives of England are full of instances of conflict between landlord and tenant precisely similar to those which had been so rife in the years immediately preceding the rebellion." See Charles Oman, *The Great Revolt of 1381*, new ed. with intro. and notes by E. B. Fryde (Oxford: Clarendon Press, 1969), 154. A brief treatment that reveals a disposition to treat the events of 1381 as an episode in a struggle of longer duration is V. H. Galbraith, "Thoughts about the Peasants' Revolt," in *The Reign of Richard II*, ed. F. R. H. Du Boulay and Caroline M. Barron (London: Athlone Press, 1971), 55–57; also see Fryde's introduction to Oman, *The Great Revolt of 1381*, xxxi–ii.

26. On the civic regulation of brothels and the involvement of prominent citizens like William Walworth in their ownership and management, see Ruth Mazo Karras, "The

Regulation of Brothels in Later Medieval England," *Signs* 14 (1989): 399–433. This *wyf* was operating in defiance of a number of ordinances, including the stipulation that a prostitute should be associated with a brothel and should not be attached to any one man (422, 425). Ruth Karras has commented, tellingly, that attempts at regulation were intensified by the threat posed by prostitution in creating "a group of women outside of male control" ("Common Women: Prostitution and Sexuality in Medieval Culture," a lecture delivered at Indiana University in March 1992). On the characteristics that prostitution holds in common with other later medieval forms of women's work, including its temporary nature and lessened requirements for capital investment, see Karras, "The Regulation of Brothels," 414 and n. 60.

27. Michel de Certeau, *The Practice of Everyday Life* (Berkeley and Los Angeles: University of California Press, 1984), esp. 39.

5. FICTIONS OF TIME AND ORIGIN

This essay was first given as a plenary address at the Notre Dame graduate medieval conference on Critical Genealogies, September 1999, and was repeated, with extensive revisions, at the Centre for Medieval Studies, University of York, November 1999.

1. *The Riverside Chaucer,* ed. Larry D. Benson, 3rd ed. (Boston: Houghton Mifflin, 1987), I.35–39.

2. Bloch's views on this subject are most conveniently available in "Nonsynchronism and the Obligation to Its Dialectics," *New German Critique* 11 (1977): 22–38.

3. Ernst Bloch, *The Principle of Hope* (Cambridge, Mass.: MIT Press, 1995), 1:9.

4. On the Plowman's economic opportunities, see R. H. Hilton, *The Decline of Serfdom* (London: Macmillan, 1969), esp. 32–43.

5. For a particularly authoritative presentation of this view, see Jill Mann, *Chaucer and Medieval Estates Satire* (Cambridge: Cambridge University Press, 1973), 55.

6. Karl T. Hagen, "A Frere Ther Was...," in *Chaucer's Pilgrims,* ed. Laura C. and Robert T. Lambdin (Westport, Conn.: Greenwood Press, 1996), 90–91.

7. Lawrence S. Cunningham, *Saint Francis of Assisi* (Boston: Hall, 1976), 29.

8. Thomas of Celano, *First Life,* cap. 1, para. 2; *St. Francis of Assisi: Writings and Early Biographies,* ed. Marion A. Habig (Chicago: Franciscan Herald Press, 1972), 230 (hereafter, *Writings*); *Analecta Franciscana,* 10 (1941): 6–7 (hereafter, *Analecta*); *Fontes Franciscani* (Assisi: Edizioni Porziuncola, 1995), 278 (hereafter, *Fontes*).

9. Roland Barthes, *Camera Lucida* (1982; reprint, Vintage Books, 1993), 26–27, 41, 65.

10. Charles A. Mercier efficiently surveyed the rise and decline of the medieval leper populace, based upon records of founding and maintenance of leper houses, concluding that the high point in numbers (with accompanying charitable impulses) was the second half of the twelfth century, and that numbers in England had dwindled to near-insignificance by the second half of the fourteenth century. Interestingly, he adduces records of

Edward III that suggest that the decline predated the Black Death; although that cata-
strophic event was undoubtedly influential in its own way. See *Leper Houses and Mediaeval
Hospitals* (London: H. K. Lewis, 1915), 17–20, 32–33. R. I. Moore also notes the upsurge of
restrictive and segregative legislation in the second half of the twelfth century and the beginning of the thirteenth century. See *The Formation of a Persecuting Society* (Oxford: Blackwell, 1987), 50–60.

11. This point is made by Penn R. Szittya, *The Antifraternal Tradition in Medieval Literature* (Princeton, N.J.: Princeton University Press, 1986), 223–27. But see David Knowles,
The Religious Orders in England (Cambridge: Cambridge University Press, 1955), 2:261–
62; John R. H. Moorman, *The Franciscans in England* (London: Mowbrays, 1974), 75–76.

12. Jill Mann, *Chaucer and Medieval Estates Satire*, 37–54, esp. 53–54.

13. Gary Shapiro, "Foucault, Derrida, and *The Genealogy of Morals*," in *Nietzsche as
Postmodernist: Essays Pro and Contra*, ed. Clayton Kolb (Albany: SUNY Press, 1990), 40.

14. Michel Foucault, "Nietzsche, Genealogy, History," in *Language, Counter-Memory,
Practice*, ed. D. Bouchard (Ithaca, N.Y.: Cornell University Press, 1977), 142.

15. "Testament," in *Writings*, 67; original text in *Fontes*, 227.

16. Bonaventure, reworking the same passage in his *Legenda maior*, describes the
kind of reaction these lepers can ideally provoke: "He had never been able to stand the
sight of lepers, even at a distance, and he always avoided meeting them, but now *in order
to arrive at perfect self contempt* he served them devotedly with all humility and kindness";
cap. 2, para. 6; *Writings*, 639; *Analecta*, 10 (1941): 562–63; *Fontes*, 786. The point is less
what he can do for them, in the way of charitable works, than what they can do for him,
in the way of self-abasement and restraint of pride. This same motive is expressed in expanded form in the *Legenda minor*, when Bonaventure reiterates Francis's horror of lepers
and adds that, as a result of grace, "he devoted himself to waiting on their needs with
such humility of heart that he washed their feet and bound their sores, drawing out the
pus and wiping away the corrupt matter. . . . He would expose himself to every kind of in-
dignity, that he might bring his rebellious lower nature into subjection to the rule of the
spirit; so he would gain complete control of himself and be at peace, *once he had subdued
the enemy that was part of his own nature*"; *Legenda minor*, cap. 1, para. 8; *Writings*, 797–98;
Analecta, 657–58; *Fontes*, 970–71.

17. Thomas of Celano, *Second Life*, cap. 36, para. 66; *Writings*, 418; *Analecta*, 170–
71; *Fontes*, 505.

18. The disappearance of the leper, around whom so many of Francis's doctrines
originally "firmed up," may reasonably be taken as an example of the general softening of
Francis's original doctrines noted by so many commentators — most recently, and trenchantly, by Eamon Duffy, "Finding St Francis: Early Images, Early Lives," in *Medieval Theology and the Natural Body*, ed. Peter Biller and A. J. Minnis, York Studies in Medieval Theology 1 (York: York Medieval Press, 1997), esp. 193–201.

19. Thomas of Celano, *First Life*, cap. 7, para. 17; *Writings*, 242–43; *Analecta*, 16; *Fontes*,
292.

20. Thomas of Celano, *Second Life*, cap. 5, para. 9; *Writings*, 370–71; *Analecta*, 136;
Fontes, 451.

21. On Bonaventure's compositional influence, see Alastair Smart, *The Assisi Problem and the Art of Giotto* (Oxford: Clarendon Press, 1971), 17–29.

22. *Writings*, 39; *Fontes*, 194.

23. Thomas of Celano, *Second Life*, cap. 64, para. 98; *Writings*, 442–43; *Analecta*, 188–89; *Fontes*, 533. So, too, do the aggressivity and aversion that had never really left Francis's vision—which were in fact central to it—gradually reassert themselves. Bonaventure's *Legenda maior*, for example, reports that Francis had a dream in which those friars who refuse to obey him (by eating a bread he has forged from the crumbs of the gospel) are visited with leprosy. A voice then interrupts his prayer to explain that "those crumbs . . . are the words of the Gospel. The single piece is the rule and the leprosy is wickedness"; *Legenda maior*, cap. 4, para. 11; *Writings*, 661–62; *Analecta*, 576–77; *Fontes*, 812–13.

24. Hugh of Floreffe, *The Life of Yvette of Huy*, ed. and trans. Jo Ann McNamara (Toronto: Peregrina, 1999), 60–62. Written after Yvette's death in 1227, this account may, of course, be partially influenced by later devotional fashions.

25. Jacques de Vitry, *Vita Mariae Oigniacensis, Acta Sanctorum*, June 23 (1867) 5: 550.

26. Ernest W. McDonnell, *The Beguines and the Beghards in Medieval Culture* (New Brunswick, N.J.: Rutgers University Press, 1954), 50–51. Pointing out that Mary of Oignies endowed Willambroux over a period of fifteen years, McDonnell observes the strong parallels between her conduct and that of Francis: "Her ecstatic experiences, accompanied with mortification of the flesh, renunciation of an early marriage and dedication to the eucharist, ardent and spontaneous pursuit of apostolic poverty in a manner reminiscent of Francis of Assisi, and complete and self-effacing humility, together with a lively interest in the neighboring leper-house, are all symptomatic of the more ascetic side of beguine life" (120–21).

27. See A. Mens, "L'Ombrie italienne et l'Ombrie brabançonne! Deux courants religieux parallèles d'inspiration commune," *Études Franciscaines*, annual supplement 17 (1967): 44–47.

28. "Des Cäsarius von Heisterbach Schriften über die hl. Elisabeth von Thüringen," *Annalen des historischen Vereins für den Niederrhein*, vol. 86 (Cologne, 1908), 33, 32. I wish to thank Dyan Elliott for drawing the case of Elisabeth of Hungary to my attention and for generously sharing views and materials on leprosy and female spirituality in central Europe and the Lowlands.

29. A. Huyskens, ed., *Quellenstudien zur Geschichte der hl. Elisabeth Landräfin von Thüringen* (Marburg, 1908), 158–59.

30. Dietrich von Apolda, *Die Vita der heiligen Elisabeth*, ed. Monika Rener (Marburg: Elwert, 1993), 40–41.

31. Friedrich Nietzsche, *The Genealogy of Morals*, in *Basic Writings of Nietzsche*, trans. Walter Kaufmann (New York: Modern Library, 1992), essay 2, sec. 12, 513.

32. Foucault, "Nietzsche, Genealogy, History," 139–64.

33. Ernst Bloch, *The Principle of Hope*, 1:158–59.

34. "To articulate the past historically does not mean to recognize it 'the way it really was' (Ranke). It means to seize hold of a memory as it flashes up at a moment of danger"; Walter Benjamin, "Theses on the Philosophy of History," in *Illuminations* (New York: Schocken Books, 1969), 255.

6. CHAUCER'S *TROILUS* AS
TEMPORAL ARCHIVE

This essay retains features of its original airing, as the inaugural lecture for the J. R. R. Tolkien Professorship at Oxford University, on 13 May 1999.

1. Jacques Derrida, *Archive Fever*, trans. Eric Prenowitz (Chicago: University of Chicago Press, 1996).

2. I allude to Julia Kristeva's discussion of the "futur antérieur," that sense in which a text is always "avant ou après" its moment, is always at once "écho et précurseur." See *La révolution de langage poétique* (Paris: Éditions du Seuil, 1974), 364–68.

3. Moreover, the poem produces even its provisional present as a product of artifice, illusion, sleight of hand. A previously noted element of Chaucer's achievement is his success in disguising some major narrative incommensurabilities, by the device of recasting a story that happens, with major starts and stops and lacunae, over a period of three or four years into a single year or seasonal cycle of love—by arranging incident and selecting imagery in such a way as to suggest a single, figurative "year" of progress from winter to the springtime of consummation and back to winter again. See Henry W. Sams, "The Dual Time-Scheme in Chaucer's *Troilus*," *Modern Language Notes* 56 (1941): 94–100.

4. Ernst Bloch, "Nonsynchronism and the Obligation to Its Dialectics," *New German Critique* 11 (1977): 22–38. Bloch's nonsynchronous temporalities are all finally reunited in their dialectical relations with the Marxist teleological narrative of class struggle. In this sense, a given temporality is viewed as precocious or belated in relation to a presupposed norm of political development. My own intention here is to deploy his terminology analytically, but divorced from any necessary developmental narrative—a narrative that is certainly part of Bloch's own total system, but upon which his concept of nonsynchronicity need not depend. My remarks here are stimulated by the observations of Thomas Foster, " 'The Very House of Difference': Gender as 'Embattled' Standpoint," *Genders* 8 (1990): esp. 31 n. 3.

5. Some of these matters are explored in my *Social Chaucer* (Cambridge, Mass.: Harvard University Press, 1989), 118–23.

6. *Any* text that encompasses a variety of perspectives or styles in a process of extended narration inevitably becomes a "patchwork." I borrow this term from Barry Windeatt, "The Text of the *Troilus*," in *Essays on Troilus and Criseyde*, ed. Mary Salu (Cambridge: Brewer, 1979), 1–22. Or, in the terminology I have adopted here, it may be seen as an "archive"— of different historical origins and temporal identifications. Because of the historical nature of language and the temporal morphology of literary forms—as well as the likelihood of generic interpenetration—the single text cannot help but embrace different segments or passages with radically incommensurate textual prehistories. One textual option is to emphasize this diversity. Helen Cooper (*The Structure of the Canterbury Tales* [London: Duckworth, 1983]) has shown the extent to which an accentuation of internal diversity is an aspect of Chaucer's accomplishment in the *Canterbury Tales*. Alternatively, a text might disguise or override the potential cacophony of its constituent parts, trading upon the apparent integrity of its own present-time reading surface in order to offer an impression of unity; I refer here, for example, to the fusion of narrative and lyric modes in the

Filostrato (the principal source of Chaucer's *Troilus*). Or, as in Chaucer's poem, different sources and temporalities might be acknowledged, but within a supervening narrative structure.

7. On this point see Thomas C. Stillinger, "Sailing to Charybdis: The Second *Canticus Troili* and the Contexts of Chaucer's *Troilus*," in *The Song of Chaucer: Lyric Authority in the Medieval Book* (Philadelphia: University of Pennsylvania Press, 1992), 172 and passim.

8. In the case of the aube, Chaucer works from a different kind of source, marked not by its novelty but its historical depth. He takes hints provided by Boccaccio but also realizes his effect within a tacitly understood tradition of French, Provençal, and German letters, causing Criseyde to chide the vanishing night and Troilus the approaching day. "O nyght," exclaims Criseyde,

> allas, why nyltow ovr us hove
> As longe as when Almena lay be Jove?

And Troilus, straining his lady in his arms, likewise apostrophizes the day:

> Envyous day, what list the so to spien?
> What hastow lost? Why sekestow this place?
> Ther God thi light so quenche, for his grace!

R. E. Kaske, who most deeply studied this matter, concludes that no one very close source exists, but that these lines are informed by a several-hundred-year-old tradition, forming a backdrop against which they would have been understood. Moreover, this is a tradition that points the significance, and the comedy, of the lovers' situation. For, as Kaske observes, certain features of Criseyde's subsequent words (including her vows of faithfulness) and certain of Troilus's (including his irreconcilability to separation and his anxiety about love's continuance) are products of deliberate role reversal and would have been recognized as risible misassignments. See Kaske, "The Aube in Chaucer's *Troilus*," published in R. Shoeck and J. Taylor, *Chaucer Criticism* (South Bend, Ind.: University of Notre Dame Press: 1961), 2:167–79. Thus, we here encounter a complexly realized temporal effect: although (like most of the constituent forms of *Troilus*) rather exorbitantly anachronistic in the sense of not reaching back to the imagined time of Troy, the aube is nevertheless by several centuries antecedent to the composition of Chaucer's poem. It represents an unacknowledged (but tacitly recognizable) effect of temporal depth, in which a preexistent textual tradition is employed in order to shape and inflect present meaning. Meaning is, in obvious and accessible ways, abetted by past familiarity.

9. Stéphane Mallarmé, "The Impressionists and Edouard Manet," in *The New Painting: Impressionism, 1874–1886* (Fine Arts Museums of San Francisco, 1986), 27–36.

10. I borrow the terms "residual" and "emergent" in homage to Raymond Williams, *Marxism and Literature* (Oxford: Oxford University Press, 1977), 121–27. Like Bloch, Williams deploys these terms in relation to a teleological or purpose-driven interpretation of history, yet their force applies as well to more local and particular interpretative moments.

11. Émile Zola, writing in *Le sémaphore de Marseille*, 18 April 1874; quoted in *The New Painting*, 126.

12. Jules Antoine Castagnary, quoted in Richard Schiff, "The End of Impressionism," in *The New Painting*, 61–89. Mallarmé, two years later, uses the term with confidence ("Impressionists and Manet").

13. *The Complete Works of Thomas Watson*, ed. Dana F. Sutton, vol. 1 (Lewiston, Pa.: Mellen Press, 1996). "And it may be noted, that the Author in his first halfe verse of this translation varieth from that sense, which Chawcer vseth in translating the selfe same" (157).

14. My original, or lecture version, of this material contained the phrase "parodic reiteration" in place of the present "playful elaboration." I have, in the interim, been much influenced by a comment from Derek Pearsall: "I'm not sure about 'parodic reiteration' in Jean de Meun's oxymorons of love.... I have the feeling that medieval poets and audiences could take almost any amount of exaggerated playfulness without falling into the overdeterminations of parody" (correspondence, 24 May 1999).

15. Gordon Braden speaks of a sixteenth-century development in which "specifically Petrarchan topics and conventions were systematized, altered, and supplemented ... to create an international poetic idiom corresponding to no particular writer's own *parole*." See "Shakespeare's Petrarchanism," in *Shakespeare's Sonnets: Critical Essays*, ed. James Schiffer (New York: Garland, 1999), 164. Chaucer's own facility at Petrarchan *langue* is suggested by the relative ease with which the later, Bannatyne editor of the "Canticus Troili" augmented it by merging the three Petrarchan stanzas with the immediately following stanza of Chaucer's own composition. See *The Bannatyne Manuscript*, ed. W. Tod Ritchie (Edinburgh: Blackwood, 1928), 3:304–5.

16. Joel Fineman, *Shakespeare's Perjured Eye: The Invention of Poetic Subjectivity in the Sonnets* (Berkeley: University of California Press, 1986), esp. 10, 85, 193, 198.

17. *The Bannatyne Manuscript*, 304–5. That the compiler worked from a manuscript of the larger poem is suggested by the fact that an additional two stanzas are copied, with the transitional "And to the god of luve thus said he" first copied and then crossed through with a horizontal line, in order to give the sense of a continuous utterance.

18. Jean-François Lyotard, *The Postmodern Condition: A Report on Knowledge* (Minneapolis: University of Minnesota Press, 1989), 79; and *The Postmodern Explained to Children* (London: Turnaround, 1992), 21–22.

19. On the apophatic method, see M. M. Bakhtin and P. M. Medvedev, *The Formal Method in Literary Scholarship* (Cambridge, Mass.: Harvard University Press, 1985), 92.

20. Thus, returning to Ernst Bloch's observations on the temporal instability of the present: the future does not just succeed the present, or answer the invitation of the present, but is already "present" within the present. It is there as extra or nonutilized signification (14), as sign or meaning unexhausted in the terms of the moment in which it appears, as an excess out of which the future can be made. Bloch's present includes the possibility of "the future in the past" (9), or a divisible moment fractured between what Augustine calls "the present of the past" ("praesens de praeteritis") and "the present of the future" ("praesens de futuris"); *Confessions*, book 11, chap. 20.

21. For recent discussion, see Sylvia Federico, "A Fourteenth-Century Erotics of Politics: London as a Feminine New Troy," *Studies in the Age of Chaucer* 19 (1997): 121–56.

22. C. S. Lewis, "What Chaucer Really Did to *Il Filostrato,*" *Essays and Studies* 17 (1932): 56–75.

23. Thomas S. Kuhn, *The Structure of Scientific Revolutions* (Chicago: University of Chicago Press, 1970).

24. *Oxford Book of Late Medieval Verse and Prose,* ed. Douglas Gray (Oxford: Clarendon Press, 1985).

25. Anne Hudson, "*Visio Baleii:* An Early Literary Historian," in *The Long Fifteenth Century,* ed. Helen Cooper and Sally Mapstone (Oxford: Clarendon Press, 1997), 329.

7. PROHIBITING HISTORY

1. Michel de Certeau, *The Writing of History* (New York: Columbia University Press, 1988), 250–51.

2. Ruth Morse, "Telling the Truth with Authority: From Richard II to *Richard II,*" *Common Knowledge* 4 (1995): 128. In this regard see also Derek Pearsall, "Interpretative Models for the Peasants' Revolt," in *Hermeneutics and Medieval Culture,* ed. Patrick J. Gallacher and Helen Damico (Albany: SUNY Press, 1989), 63–70.

3. John Capgrave, *The Book of the Illustrious Henries,* trans. F. C. Hingeston (London, 1858), 107.

4. On the premodern historian's elliptical relation to matters of proof, see Paul Veyne, *Did the Greeks Believe in Their Myths?* (Chicago: University of Chicago Press, 1988), esp. 5–15.

5. *Annales Henrici Quarti,* ed. H. T. Riley, Rolls Series, no. 28, pt. 3 (London, 1866), 330–31. For the derivative passage in Walsingham, *Historia Anglicana,* see H. T. Riley, ed., Rolls Series, no. 28, pt. 1 (London, 1864) 2:245–46.

6. *Chronicque de la Träison et Mort,* ed. Benjamin Williams, English Historical Society (London, 1846), 94–96.

7. As in Waurin, *Chroniques et anchiennes istoires,* ed. William Hardy, Rolls Series, no. 39 (London, 1868), 36–38.

8. *Historia Vitae et Regni Ricardi Secundi,* ed. George B. Stow (University of Pennsylvania Press, 1977), 166.

9. Although Chris Given-Wilson does translate the phrase as "he was miserably put to death by starvation there"; *Chronicles of the Revolution, 1397–1400* (Manchester: Manchester University Press, 1993), 241.

10. Jean Froissart, *Chroniques,* ed. Kervyn de Lettenhove (Brussels: Devaux, 1872), 16:233.

11. John Capgrave, *Chronicle of England,* ed. F. C. Hingeston, Rolls Series, no. 1 (London, 1858), 276.

12. That decade's climate of rumor and speculation regarding Richard has recently been discussed in several essays: Peter McNiven, "Rebellion, Sedition, and the Legend of Richard II's Survival," *Bulletin of the John Rylands Library* 76 (1994): 93–117; Philip Morgan, "Henry IV and the Shadow of Richard II," in *Crown, Government, and People in the*

Fifteenth Century, ed. Rowena Archer (London: Alan Sutton, 1995), 1–31; and Paul Strohm, "The Trouble with Richard: The Reburial of Richard II and Lancastrian Symbolic Strategy," *Speculum* 71 (1996): 87–111.

13. It bore a dedication to the reigning Henry VI. As Karen Winstead has shown, its Lancastrian devotion is qualified by telling omissions and by oblique admonitions; "Capgrave's Saint Katherine and the Perils of Gynecocracy," *Viator* 25 (1994): esp. 367–71. Nevertheless, it quotes extensively from the documents of Lancastrian legitimation, including an emphasis upon Richard's voluntary resignation and the full rationale of Henry's assumption of the throne, and it even includes the discredited story of ancestor Edmund Crouchback's frustrated claim. Henry IV, in this rendition, assumed the throne "providente Deo," by the providence of God.

14. See, in this regard, Derrida's discussion of iteration/recontextualization as the means by which the *hors-texte* imposes itself upon the text, in *Limited Inc* (Evanston, Ill.: Northwestern University Press, 1988): "[T]he question can be raised, not whether a politics is implied (it always is) but which politics is implied in such a practice of contextualization. . . . One of the definitions of what is called deconstruction would be the effort to take this limitless context into account, to pay the sharpest and broadest attention possible to context, and thus to an incessant movement of recontextualization" (136). In this case, the "recontextualization" is twofold: both that accomplished by Capgrave, with respect to his new Yorkist orientation, and also that adduced as an aspect of my own interpretation of the passage.

15. "A ce que len suppose quil est . . ."; *Proceedings and Ordinances of the Privy Council,* ed. H. Nicolas (London: Commissioners of Public Records, 1834), 1:208.

16. "En cas que Richard nadgairs Roy . . . soit uncore vivant quil soit mys en seuertee aggreable . . . et sil soit alez de vie . . . soit il monstrez overtement au poeple au fin quils ent puissent avoir conissance" (ibid., 111–12).

17. "Cuius corpusper loca celeberrima quae interjacent a dicto castello usque Londonias, ubi contigit pernoctare, monstratum est post Officium Mortuorum"; Walsingham, *Historia Anglicana,* 2:246. An entry in the Issues of the Exchequer for 17 February allocates 100 marks for clerk of the wardrobe Thomas Tuttebury for expenses owing to transport of Richard's body from Pontefract to London ("super expensis faciendis super cargaio corporis Ricardi nuper regil anglie de villa de Pomfrait vsque London"; Public Record Office (PRO), E403/564). Adam of Usk, probably present at the funeral, reports that his face was not covered but was shown openly to all ("non velate facie sed publice cuique ostensa"). See *Chronicon Adae de Usk,* ed. E. M. Thompson (London, 1904), 44–45. Froissart claims that twenty thousand people saw him, his face uncovered, on that occasion. See *Oeuvres,* ed. de Lettenhove (Brussels, 1872), 16:233.

18. PRO, Issues of the Exchequer, E403/564. In addition to the entry on Swynford's valet, these items include expenses for William Loveney, a trusted clerk of the wardrobe, to travel with his men from London to Pontefract and back on secret business of the king ("in secretis negociis ipsius domini Regis") — also 20 March; esquire Robert Hethecote sent to the north ("versus partes boriales") on secret business — 20 March; "To a certain other valletus sent from London by the King's Counsel to Pontefract Castle for the protection and custody of the body of Richard the Second, late King of England" ("tutoribus &

custodibus corperis Ricardi nuper Regis Angliae secundi") — 6s. 8d.; distribution of alms at Richard's funeral (a measly 20 shillings!) and provision for a thousand funeral masses — 20 March; and final charges for expenses incurred in the carriage of Richard's body from Pontefract to London for the funeral — 7 April. See F. Devon, *Issues of the Exchequer* (London, 1837), for translations of several of these items.

19. This item is noted by Given-Wilson, *Chronicles of the Revolution*, 90 n. 1.

20. Note, too, a further curiosity that links the two texts: in each case, the destination is not Westminster, as we might suppose, but London, whether the Tower or some other location within the city.

21. Swynford's father had been one of John of Gaunt's most esteemed and highly compensated retainers from 1382–99. See Simon Walker, *The Lancastrian Affinity, 1361– 1399* (Oxford: Clarendon Press, 1990), 282. The younger Thomas, as son of Gaunt's third wife (and, incidentally, Chaucer's nephew by marriage), was himself a particularly trusted retainer, receiving an annuity as one of Henry's first royal actions, and a grant for life of the castle of Somerton in October 1399; *Calendar of Patent Rolls, 1399–1401*, 295.

22. Translation and text from Chris Given-Wilson, ed. and trans., *The Chronicle of Adam Usk* (Oxford: Oxford Medieval Texts, 1997), 88–91.

23. Andrew Prescott, "Writing about Rebellion: Using the Records of the Peasants' Revolt of 1381," *History Workshop Journal* 45 (1998): 1–27.

24. Veyne, *Did the Greeks Believe in Their Myths?* 59–78.

25. Jean-François Lyotard, "Le Meurtre de Pierre Overney," in *Des Dispositifs Pulsionnels* (Paris, 1973), 205.

26. Ned Lukacher, *Primal Scenes* (Ithaca, N.Y.: Cornell University Press, 1986), xii.

8. Trade, Treason, and the Murder of Janus Imperial

This essay was originally composed for delivery in September 1993 in a lecture series entitled "London in Europe/Europe in London," organized by Julia Boffey and Pam King at Queen Mary and Westfield College, University of London. It subsequently appeared in revised form in *Journal of British Studies* 35 (1996): 1–23.

1. Unless otherwise identified, all the Imperial documents are cited from the splendid collection and edition of G. O. Sayles, *Select Cases in the Court of King's Bench*, Selden Society, vol. 88 (London: Bernard Quaritch, 1971), 14–21, 40–41. English translations are based upon those of Sayles, though with occasional light modification.

2. Bernard William McLane notes of earlier fourteenth-century trial juries that "jurors generally may have had a 'live and let live' policy toward accused killers, especially in cases where the homicides were alleged to have been the unexpected outcome of an argument or a fight that had begun in a tavern or some other public place"; "Juror Attitudes toward Local Disorder," in *Twelve Good Men and True*, ed. J. S. Cockburn and Thomas A. Green (Princeton, N.J.: Princeton University Press, 1988), 36–64. On jury leniency, see also Green, *Verdict according to Conscience* (Chicago: University of Chicago Press, 1985), 3–102.

3. Both Newgate and the first trial venue of Saint Martin le Grand were enclaves of royal justice within the City (Helen Cam, "The Law-Courts of Medieval London," in *Law-Finders and Law-Makers* [London: Merlin Press, 1962], 92–93), and the Tower was, of course, such a precinct adjacent to it. The Crown gained control of felony and treason cases prior to 1400, and once a case was declared treasonous in nature the jurisdiction of the king's bench was absolutely foregone; Edward Powell, *Kingship, Law, and Society* (Oxford: Oxford University Press, 1989), 49–50, 54–55. Even though no record of a complaint to the king's Council survives, an additional precedent for royal involvement is the responsibility of the king's Council to receive complaints of injury to foreign subjects; on the role of the Council in such cases, and its close collaboration with the king's bench, see Alice Beardwood, *Alien Merchants in England* (Cambridge, Mass.: Mediaeval Academy of America, 1931), 86–104.

4. This was not, according to J. B. Post, an unusual circumstance in itself; "Jury Lists and Juries in the Late Fourteenth Century," in *Twelve Good Men and True: The Criminal Trial Jury in England*, ed. Cockburn and Green (Princeton, N.J.: Princeton University Press, 1988), 67–68. But it is indicative of the atmosphere surrounding the case.

5. J. B. Post comments that persons acquitted by juries may be remanded in custody for a wide range of reasons. Such mundane matters as fees to be paid or peace bonds to be assured might entail a temporary return. But persons might be remanded for longer periods of time by justices unhappy with a jury verdict, on grounds as general as "bad repute." "Justices," he adds, "may have felt entitled to use remand in custody as a punitive sentence" (76–77). In view of the open-endedness of the confinement, this may presumably be considered such a case.

6. Kirkby and Algor were switched from Newgate to the Tower between 27 September and 3 March (Sayles, *Select Cases*, 18), from the Tower to Nottingham Castle on 24 June 1380 (*Calendar of Close Rolls [CCR]* [Stationer's Office, 1892–], 1377–81, 389), and from Nottingham to Northampton on 29 November 1380 (*CCR*, 1377–81, 412).

7. Frederick C. Hamil, "The King's Approvers," *Speculum* 11, 1936: 238–58.

8. *RP*, 3:75.

9. For the text of the statute, see *Statutes of the Realm* (London: Basket, 1810), 1:319–20. For a discussion of its provisions, as they touch on the present case, see J. G. Bellamy, *The Law of Treason in the Middle Ages* (Cambridge, Mass.: Harvard University Press, 1970), 180–81.

10. *RP*, 3:75.

11. E. B. Fryde, *Studies in Medieval Trade and Finance* (London: Hambledon, 1983), 305; Alwyn A. Ruddock, *Italian Merchants and Shipping in Southampton, 1270–1600* (Southampton: Southampton Records Series, 1951), 40, 46.

12. *RP*, 3:48.

13. Thomas Walsingham, *Historia Anglicana*, 1:408.

14. *CCR*, 1377–81, 389.

15. For a summary of his career, see Sylvia Thrupp, *The Merchant Class of Medieval London* (Ann Arbor: University of Michigan Press, 1948), 361.

16. *Calendar of Plea and Memoranda Rolls*, ed. A. H. Thomas (Cambridge: Cambridge University Press, 1926), 1:281; *Calendar of Letter-Books: Letter-Book H*, 218.

17. PRO, C54/218/8d; *CCR*, 1377–81, 244. Imperial's actual titles are given as *ambassiator* and *sindicus* (or official advocate). The Genoese pleaded that the ship had been taken unlawfully and without resistance by English subjects (or, as the rolls put it, "per ligeos nostros") and offered to post an indenture pending a demonstration that their assertions were true. The entry does not name the English subjects who were to profit from the seizure, but does suggest that (consistent with the pattern of conflicting loyalties emerging in this case) the Crown was to receive a share.

18. E. E. Rich, "The Mayors of the Staples," *Cambridge Historical Journal* 4 (1932), 120–42.

19. Based on T. H. Lloyd, *The English Wool Trade* (Cambridge: Cambridge University Press, 1977), 251–52; a sack equals 364 lb.

20. E. Carus-Wilson and Olive Coleman, *England's Export Trade* (Oxford: Clarendon Press, 1963), 49.

21. E. Power, *The Wool Trade in English Medieval History* (Oxford: Oxford University Press, 1941), 97–103.

22. *RP*, 3:48.

23. Based on *RP*, 2:326; Lloyd, *The English Wool Trade*, 226; Sayles, *Select Cases*, 18; *RP*, 3:48; *CCR*, 1377–81, 244.

24. Far from being a matter of indifference to the wool-shipping Londoners, the rise of the cloth-making industry in southwestern England may be supposed their greatest nightmare. For a trade in finished woolens would foster a competition for domestic raw materials and would challenge the very Continental cloth-making industries that provided the foreign demand for the raw English product. The centrality of Southampton to a Genoese-English cloth trade is tellingly chronicled by E. B. Fryde: "At the time when the Genoese were beginning to use Southampton as their chief harbour in England an English woollen industry capable of manufacturing for export was developing in the southwestern region for which Southampton provided one of the best outlets. The Genoese specialized in the distribution of alum, dyes and other chemicals indispensable to the textile industry.... In March 1372 a Genoese ship called Christopher landed at Southampton 52 bales of woad, 26 of alum, 20 of madder and 6 of brazil. These were only the small beginnings of a trade that grew steadily.... Gradually the Genoese and other Italians also became interested in exporting some of the cloths produced in the hinterland of Southampton" (346–47). In 1379, this two-way trade in cloth-making chemicals and finished woolens existed mainly as a threatening possibility; by 1381–82, the death of Janus Imperial notwithstanding, it had become a reality.

25. Not only (in the terms of detective fiction) is it Kirkby who "takes the fall," but the record suggests that he might have been everybody's pigeon all along, recruited as an acceptable sacrifice from both the city's and the royal council's point of view. Kirkby's last hope was a plea of clerical standing and request for an ordinary, but that recourse was both anticipated and blocked as early as the January/February 1380 parliamentary confirmation of treason, when the framers went out of their way to declare that, since the crime was treason, no one involved in it should be permitted to enjoy benefit of clergy ("en quel cas y ne doit allouer a nully d'enjoier privilege de Clergie"; *RP*, 3:75).

26. On the subject of investigative procedure, assignment of responsibility, and diffuse enjoyment, see Slavoj Žižek, *Looking Awry* (Cambridge, Mass.: MIT Press, 1991), 48–66. Readers of Žižek will recognize my broad indebtedness to his treatment of these concepts.

27. *Plea and Memoranda Rolls*, 114; *Calendar of Letter-Book H*, 218; Thomas Usk, "Appeal... against John Northampton," in *A Book of London English, 1384–1425*, ed. R. W. Chambers and M. Daunt (Oxford: Clarendon Press, 1931), 22–31.

28. Pamela Nightingale has argued that the middle and late 1370s were a time in which a hegemonic body of London capitalists still operated in relative harmony. According to her analysis, the groups that would eventually separate as the Brembre and Northampton factions in and after 1381 still cooperated across a broad front in the 1370s, as when they joined their influence in the Parliament of 1376 to win concessions for the Calais staple (high on the agenda of the wool merchants) and for the London franchise (important to the lesser guildsmen and domestic traders). She regards the interim period 1376–81 as one in which the different agendas of the two groups had begun to emerge, but in which an attitude of mutual conciliation and a political common front still prevailed; "Capitalists, Crafts, and Constitutional Change," *Past and Present* 124 (1989): 16–36.

29. M. M. Postan, *Medieval Trade and Finance* (Cambridge, 1973), 211.

30. Power tellingly observes of the Calais staple that "the king was satisfied by an arrangement whereby the Company provided the mechanism by which he could raise loans. The custom and subsidy on the export of wool was the best possible security which he could offer, and a chartered company enjoying the monopoly of the trade was a much safer source of loans than the series of firms and syndicates which had, one by one, gone bankrupt in the early years of the Hundred Years' War" (*Wool Trade*, 99).

31. Opinion was, in fact, abroad in the Good Parliament of 1376 that the Calais staple had been a parliamentary creation in the first place, and the reinstitution of the staple in that parliament was a cornerstone of its reform agenda (Lloyd, *English Wool Trade*, 221–24).

32. Again, Power: "The staple monopoly... narrowed the channels of export, and, in order to enable the Staplers to shoulder the enormous export tax and make the king his loans, it secured for [the growing English cloth industry] low prices in England and high prices abroad. It is not difficult to see at once that this immense margin between the domestic and the foreign prices of wool provided the most effective protection for an infant industry." (*Wool Trade*, 101)

33. Žižek, *Looking Awry*, 48–66.

34. The ultimate intraindebtedness of English society is suggested in the fact of Algor's royal pardon, dated 15 July 1384 (Sayles, *Select Cases*, 1), at a time when Brembre and Philipot and the other wool-merchant opponents of the royal council and justiciary in 1379 had now become Richard II's most stalwart allies, in London and possibly in the kingdom as a whole.

35. These are, according to Ernesto Laclau and Chantal Mouffe, *Hegemony and Socialist Strategy* (London: Verso, 1985), moments that reveal "the limits of society, the latter's impossibility of fully constituting itself" (125).

36. On the recognition of alien merchants as a financial asset and on the reiteration of this view in statutes, petitions, and customs rolls, see Beardwood, *Alien Merchants in England,* 39 and notes 2–4.

37. Walsingham's rendition offers an additional interpretative temptation, and one that might subsume all the rest: that of seeing this crime as one of those sacrificial moments of "unanimous victimage," preferably visited upon an outsider or stranger, through which a community affirms its hierarchies and values; René Girard, *"To double business bound"* (London: Athlone Press, 1978), 207. And, to be sure, I do not deny that this crime encouraged a closing of ranks within the city of London and perhaps even the nation as a whole. But, while recognizing the explicitly sacrificial language of the chronicle account, I would nevertheless draw another lesson from all these portrayals of our slain merchant. As an outsider, a foreigner, he remains a kind of "blind spot" in the record, an effectively unaffiliated individual without rights or standing, and hence a symbolic dumping ground for virtually any sort of signification any commentator wishes to place upon him.

38. We need hardly be reminded that, less than two years after Imperial's death, native rivals took advantage of the disturbances accompanying the Rising to slaughter dozens, and perhaps scores, of Flemish weavers and to pile heaps of their headless bodies in the streets. Or that *Beuis of Hamptoun* imagines its hero doing the same for the London Lombard community; in the milder fourteenth-century version he slays thirty thousand, and in the bloodier-minded fifteenth-century version we read that, in the wake of his encounter,

> In euery strete men myght se
> Lumbardys on hepys dede there lye,
> Hedys and quarters lye in pecys
> And leggis cutt of by the knees,
> Hedus with helmys strayling aboute,
> Handys and armes cutt oute and oute,
> Dede bodyes quarterrid in thre. (213)

Or that periodic xenophobic outbursts would follow, culminating in the next century in the anti-Italian riots of the 1450s and the forced exodus of many of London's Italian inhabitants in 1457. See *Beues of Hamtoun,* ed. E. Kölbing, EETS, e.s., 46, 48, 65; and Ruddock, *Italian Merchants and Shipping in Southampton,* 25–29, 162–68.

39. Robert S. Lopez, "Venise et Gênes," in *Su e Giù per la Storia de Genov* (Genoa: University of Genoa, 1975), 35–42; Benjamin Z. Kedar, *Merchants in Crisis: Genoese and Venetian Men of Affairs and the Fourteenth-Century Depression* (New Haven, Conn.: Yale University Press, 1976), 9–13.

40. Lopez, "Market Expansion," in *Su e Giù per la Storia de Genova,* 43–62; Kedar, *Merchants in Crisis,* 1–20.

41. E. Carus-Wilson, *Medieval Merchant Venturers* (London: Methuen, 1967), 261–62.

42. *CCR,* 1377–81, 224; PRO, C54/218/mem. 8d.

43. Chaucer was, of course, no stranger to merchants like Imperial, having worked with several of our protagonists on the wool quay, and having in fact himself taken part in a precursor mission in 1372–73 to discuss opening English ports to Genoese tarits; M. M.

Crow, *Chaucer Life-Records* (Oxford: Clarendon Press, 1966), 32–40; Chaucer text from *The Riverside Chaucer* (Boston: Houghton Mifflin, 1987).

9. SHAKESPEARE'S OLDCASTLE

This essay was originally the second of two William Matthews lectures, delivered at Birkbeck College, University of London, in May 1997. Materials from the first lecture, on Oldcastle's absence from the revolt that bears his name, have subsequently been published in *England's Empty Throne: Usurpation and the Language of Legitimation* (London and New Haven, Conn.: Yale University Press, 1998), 65–86. My present title, like that of the original series, alludes to William Matthews's own distinguished medieval scholarship, in this case his provocative biographical study of Malory, *The Ill-Framed Knight*.

1. William Shakespeare, *The Complete Works*, ed. Stanley Wells and Gary Taylor (Oxford: Clarendon Press, 1986).

2. F. Solly-Flood, "The Story of Prince Henry of Monmouth and Chief-Justice Gascoign," *Transactions of the Royal Historical Society*, n.s., 3 (1886): 72, 74, 75.

3. As contemporaneously mentioned by Walsingham, *Historia Anglicana*, Rolls Series (London, 1863), no. 28, pt. 1, 2:286 (hereafter, *Historia*). See also W. T. Waugh, "Sir John Oldcastle," *English Historical Review* 20 (1905): 445.

4. Solly-Flood, "The Story of Prince Henry," 140. See T. Rymer, *Foedera*, 20 vols. (London, 1735). 9:46.

5. J. H. Wylie, *The Reign of Henry V* (Cambridge: Cambridge University Press, 1914), 1:245–46; PRO, Issues of the Exchequer, 406/21 mem. 23.

6. The present text is drawn from *Concilia Magnae Britanniae*, ed. D. Wilkins (London, 1737), 3:353–54.

7. *Gesta Henrici Quinti*, ed. F. Taylor and J. Roskell (Oxford: Clarendon Press, 1975), 2–3 (hereafter, *Gesta*).

8. *Statutes of the Realm* (London: Basket, 1763), 1:320.

9. Jean de Waurin, *Recueil des Croniques . . .*, ed. W. Hardy, Rolls Series, no. 39, vol. 5, 177–79

10. *The Chronicle of Adam Usk*, ed. and trans. Chris Given-Wilson (Oxford: Oxford Medieval Texts, 1997), 246.

11. Walsingham, *Historia*, 2:282.

12. Peter McNiven, *Heresy and Politics in the Reign of Henry IV* (Woodbridge, Suffolk: Boydell Press, 1987), 199–219.

13. Michel de Certeau, *The Writing of History* (New York: Columbia University Press, 1988), 156–57. De Certeau is speaking of the early modern period; yet, as is so often the case, no distinct boundary separates late medieval from early modern practice.

14. See Jeremy Catto, "Religious Change under Henry V," in *Henry V: The Practice of Kingship*, ed. G. L. Harriss (Oxford: Oxford University Press, 1985), 115; Patrick J. Horner, "The King Taught Us the Lesson," *Mediaeval Studies* 52 (1990): 220.

15. *The Famous Victories of Henry V*, printed in *The Oldcastle Controversy*, ed. P. Corbin and D. Sedge (Manchester: Manchester University Press, 1991), scene 5, line 30.

16. Titus Livius compares Henry to Saint Thomas of Canterbury, "chaunged into a newe man" ("mutatus est in virum alium"), upon assumption of the throne (18). The notion of the *novus homo* is ultimately reliant upon the epistles of Paul, such as Colossians 3:9–10 ("expoliantes vos veterem hominem cum actibus eius et induentes novum") and Ephesians 4:22.

17. Titus Livius, *The First English Life of King Henry the Fifth*, ed. C. L. Kingsford (Oxford: Clarendon Press, 1911), 8. The language is that of the early-sixteenth-century English translator, but this passage represents the words of Titus Livius, rather than (as elsewhere) the translator's elaborations.

18. R. Fabyan, *The New Chronicles of England and France*, ed. Henry Ellis (London, 1811), 577.

19. These sixteenth-century elaborations are conveniently summarized in C. L. Kingsford, *Henry V* (New York, 1901), 87–93.

20. Paul Veyne, *Did the Greeks Believe in Their Myths?* (Chicago: University of Chicago Press, 1988), 41–51.

21. Christopher Allmand, *Henry V* (Berkeley: University of California Press, 1992), 16–58.

22. David Carr, *Time, Narrative, and History* (Bloomington: Indiana University Press, 1986).

23. British Library, Cotton MS Claudius A.8, fol. 17.

24. Sigmund Freud, *Totem and Taboo* (New York: Norton, 1950), 140–46.

25. K. B. McFarlane, *Lancastrian Kings and Lollard Knights* (Oxford, 1972), 123.

26. Wilkins, *Concilia*, 3:353.

27. Hoccleve, "To Oldcastle," in *Hoccleve's Works: The Minor Poems*, ed. F. J. Furnivall, EETS, e.s., 61 (London, 1892), line 10.

28. Seldon Society, 88:244–46.

29. My argument here parallels David Wallace's observation on Oldcastle and Lollard textuality: "His fleshliness may issue from a strange literalization of a long-established critique of Lollards: that they are literal, hence fleshly, readers"; *Chaucerian Polity* (Palo Alto, Calif.: Stanford University Press, 1997), 382.

30. In an essay that successively adopts — and never quite rejects — all of the possible theories entertained in this section of my discussion, Gary Taylor suggests that Shakespeare's Oldcastle is a "deliberate lampoon" of his historical original, that Shakespeare abandoned his name in order not to offend the Cobhams of his own day, and that, finally (and most convincingly), "the controversy over whether Shakespeare intended to satirize the Cobhams has obscured the much more important fact that he portrayed a Protestant martyr as a jolly hypocrite." See "The Fortunes of Oldcastle," *Shakespeare Survey* 38 (1985): respectively, 99, 86, 98.

31. This explanation was originally offered by seventeenth-century antiquarian Richard James in his manuscript "edition" of Hoccleve's poem against Oldcastle: "In Shakespeares first shew of Harrie the fift, the person with which he undertook to playe a buffone was not Falstaffe, but Sr John Oldcastle, and that offence being worthily taken by personages descended from his title" (British Library, MS Addit. 33785) the change was made. This suggestion has been augmented by subsequent commentary; the Oxford

Shakespeare has it that "Shakespeare changed his surname as the result of protests from Oldcastle's descendants, the influential Cobham family, one of whom . . . was Elizabeth I's Lord Chamberlain from August 1596 till he died on March 1397" (509).

32. A theory mentioned in the capable survey of Rudolph Fiehler, "How Oldcastle Became Falstaff," *Modern Language Quarterly* 16 (1955): 27. On the Protestant/Puritan divide, see Jonas Barish, *The Antitheatrical Prejudice* (Berkeley: University of California Press, 1981), 82, esp. n. 5. Owing to the courtesy of David Kastan, I have recently seen a lively and persuasive essay that concurs with mine in many respects, differing only in a conclusion about the valence of Shakespeare's attack, precisely in respect to the "Protestant/Puritan divide." My own analysis discovers the target of Shakespeare's extended jibe in those mainstream Protestants like Munday, who had not forsworn the theater, but who wished to moralize and reform it. Kastan takes the other path, discovering in Shakespeare's lampoon the mark of a more specifically anti-Puritan bias, "providing evidence of the very fracture in the Protestant community that made the accommodation of the Lollard past so problematic." See David Kastan, "'Killed with Hard Opinions': Oldcastle, Falstaff, and the Reformed Text of *1 Henry IV*," forthcoming in *Textual Topography*, ed. Thomas Berger and Laurie Maguire. Although I am leaving my own text unrevised with respect to the conclusion embraced in my Matthews lecture — that Shakespeare's target was the more moderate party of moralizing and "theatrical" Protestants rather than harder-line Puritans — I regard Kastan's suggestion as a strong alternative possibility, in the light of the Puritan embrace of Foxe's martyrs, Oldcastle included. Whichever of these groups was Shakespeare's particular target, Kastan and I agree that Shakespeare's interest lay in the politics of his immediate present rather than the past.

33. On these varied shadings, see Elbert N. S. Thompson, *The Controversy between the Puritans and the Stage* (1903; reprint, New York: Russell and Russell, 1966), 54–61, 86–92.

34. John Northbrooke, *A Treatise against Dicing, Dancing, Plays, and Interludes* (London: Shakespeare Society, 1843), 94–95.

35. Printed in Corbin and Sedge, eds., *The Oldcastle Controversy*, 40.

36. Jacques Derrida, *Specters of Marx* (New York and London: Routledge, 1994), xix.

37. Walter Benjamin, "Theses on the Philosophy of History," *Illuminations* (New York: Harcourt Brace, 1968), 253–64.

10. Postmodernism and History

1. The conference was organized by D. Vance Smith and Michael Uebel and hosted by Martin Irvine. Proceedings of the conference, though without Carolyn Dinshaw's address, which appears in her book *Getting Medieval: Sexualities and Communities, Pre- and Post-Modern* (Durham, N.C.: Duke University Press, 1999), 143–82, are available at www.georgetown.edu/labyrinth/conf/cs95. Conference papers by Steven F. Kruger, Jeffrey Jerome Cohen, Sarah Stanbury, Andrew Galloway, Robert L. A. Clark and Claire Sponsler, and Leslie Dunton-Downer have since been published (and joined by other contributions) in a special issue of *New Literary History* 28 (1997), edited by D. Vance Smith and Michael Uebel, together with a downsized and rather chastened preface by Michael Uebel.

2. Stephen Greenblatt, "Fiction and Friction," in *Shakespearean Negotiations* (Berkeley: University of California Press, 1988), 72.

3. Diane Elam, *Romancing the Postmodern* (London: Routledge, 1992), 15.

4. Jean-François Lyotard, *The Postmodern Condition* (Minneapolis: University of Minnesota Press, 1984), 79. This same passage resurfaces as an object of partial critique in my lecture "Chaucer's *Troilus* as Temporal Archive." My objection there is not to Lyotard's contention, which seems to me completely right, but rather to his uneven and hesitant exemplification of his own insight.

5. Compare Freud's parallel observation, in "Notes upon a Case of Obsessional Neurosis": "The results of such an illness are never unintentional: what appears to be the *consequence* of the illness is in reality the *cause* or *motive* of falling ill." See *Standard Edition* (London: Hogarth Press, 1958), 10:199.

6. Dinshaw, *Getting Medieval*, 151 and passim.

7. Fredric Jameson, *Postmodernism; or, The Cultural Logic of Late Capitalism* (Durham, N.C.: Duke University Press, 1991), 9.

8. Julia Kristeva, *Powers of Horror* (New York: Columbia University Press, 1982), 4.

9. Paul Strohm, *England's Empty Throne: Usurpation and the Language of Legitimation* (London: Yale University Press, 1998), 128–52.

10. Freud, "Notes on . . . a Case of Paranoia" (Schreber), *Standard Edition*, 12:66–68.

11. Paul Freedman and Gabrielle Spiegel, "Medievalisms Old and New: The Rediscovery of Alterity in North American Medieval Studies," *American Historical Review* 103 (1998): esp. 699–704.

12. For a considerably more subtle rendering of this same idea, see David Aers, "A Whisper in the Ear of the Early Modernists," in *Community, Gender, and Individual Identity: English Writing, 1360–1430* (London: Routledge, 1988).

13. Michel Foucault, "Revolutionary Action: 'Until Now,'" in *Language, Counter-Memory, Practice* (Ithaca, N.Y.: Cornell University Press, 1977), 233.

14. Jean Baudrillard, *Symbolic Exchange and Death* (Beverly Hills, Calif.: Sage, 1993), 50.

15. For a critique of the New Historicist "anecdote," see Joel Fineman, "The History of the Anecdote: Fiction and Fiction," in *The New Historicism*, ed. H. Aram Veeser (New York: Routledge, 1989). This is not an insolvable dilemma. The problem of movement between the anecdote and homologous structures has, for example, been constructively addressed by J. G. A. Pocock, "Texts as Events: Reflections on the History of Political Thought," in *Politics of Discourse*, ed. K. Sharpe and S. Zwicker (Berkeley: University of California Press, 1987), 21–34.

16. Ernesto Laclau and Chantal Mouffe, *Hegemony and Socialist Strategy* (London: Verso, 1985), 3.

17. Ibid., 113.

18. Michel Foucault, "Nietzsche, Genealogy, History," in *Language, Counter-Memory, Practice*, 148.

19. These remarks are offered in refutation of Steven Justice's embrace of ironized detachment, in "Inquisition, Speech, and Writing: A Case from Norwich," in *Criticism and*

Dissent in the Middle Ages, ed. Rita Copeland (Cambridge: Cambridge University Press, 1996), esp. 318–19.

  20. Dinshaw, *Getting Medieval*, 169–72.

  21. Foucault, "Nietzsche, Genealogy, History," 160–61.

  22. This might be seen as Dinshaw's answer to the question challengingly posed (in relation to identification within psychoanalysis) by Diana Fuss: "How can the other be brought into the domain of the knowable without annihilating the other as other—as precisely that which cannot be known?" See *Identification Papers* (New York: Routledge, 1995), esp. 1–17.

11. WHAT CAN WE KNOW ABOUT CHAUCER THAT HE DIDN'T KNOW ABOUT HIMSELF?

Given as the New Chaucer Society's Biennial Chaucer Lecture on 24 July 1994, this essay was later published as "Chaucer's Lollard Joke: History and the Textual Unconscious," *Studies in the Age of Chaucer* 17 (1995): 23–42. Prior to the lecture, I received valued advice from Rita Copeland, Carolyn Dinshaw, Dyan Elliott, Jonathan Elmer, Miri Rubin, and David Wallace. Subsequent to the lecture, I enjoyed a fruitful correspondence with Fiona Somerset on substance, accidents, and the "stakes" of the joke, one portion of which is quoted below.

  1. Terms for construction of such a correlation may be derived from Freud's "Repression" and "The Unconscious," both published in *The Standard Edition* (London: Hogarth Press, 1957), 14:147–48 and 180–85, respectively. Entry into textuality may be thought to create the conditions for Freud's "primal repression" (148). The text's reliance upon idea over affect, time over timelessness, and words over things (153, 187, 201) guarantees the denial of full expression to certain impulses. My emphasis on repression owes much to a talk given by Sarah Stanbury at Kalamazoo, Michigan, in May 1994, in which she proposed a common ground between historicism and psychoanalysis, based on a shared assumption that the subject—whether the analysand or the historical text—cannot know itself because of its implication in strategies and practices of repression. For a discussion in which primary repression is fruitfully treated as the effective founding moment of a textual unconscious, augmented through processes of secondary repression, see Elizabeth J. Bellamy, *Translations of Power* (Ithaca, N.Y.: Cornell University Press, 1992), 38–81.

  2. Ralph Waldo Emerson, *Collected Works* (Harvard: Belknap Press, 1979), 2:185.

  3. Myra Jehlen, "Archimedes and the Paradox of Feminist Criticism," in *The Signs Reader* (Chicago: University of Chicago Press, 1983), 69–95.

  4. The phrase is taken from Derrida, *Of Grammatology* (Baltimore, Md.: Johns Hopkins University Press, 1976), 158. I do not claim originality for this observation. It has been made, and practiced, in a number of recent studies in our field. I am thinking, for example, of Ralph Hanna's recent critique of a glossing practice that "perpetuates uncritically Chaucer's own ideological labor," in "Pilate's Voice/Shirley's Case," *South Atlantic*

Quarterly 91 (1992): 806, or Sarah Beckwith's critique of functionalist anthropology's tendency merely to "reiterate the very clerical project it seeks to articulate," in *Bodies and Disciplines*, ed. Barbara Hanawalt and David Wallace (Minneapolis: University of Minnesota Press, 1996), 65.

5. Because I am impatient with limitations on textual/historical understanding, I have no hesitation in answering a question that has surfaced in several recent medieval discussions: of whether one can apply "post-Cartesian" models to "pre-Cartesian" systems. Although normally posed in terms of anxious solicitude and apparent indecision, this question seems actually to invite a negative answer. My own, affirmative, reply involves an assumption about textuality itself, pre- or post-Cartesian: that textual defenses need to be unsettled, and that such agitation is precisely theory's task.

6. I am indebted to Judith Butler's deft formulation: "Every text has more sources than it can reconstruct within its own terms." See *Gender Trouble* (New York: Routledge, 1990), xii.

7. The relation between *De contemptu mundi* and this passage is indicated by F. N. Robinson, *The Works of Geoffrey Chaucer*, 2nd ed. (Boston: Houghton Mifflin, 1957), 731. The supposition that Chaucer translated this work is based on his own assertion (*Legend of Good Women*, G 415). Although, as Robert E. Lewis has pointed out, his translation of this work must be considered a probability rather than a certainty, and the intertextual relation of *De contemptu* and the "Pardoner's Tale" might have occurred in other ways. See Lotario dei Segni, *De miseria condicionis humane*, ed. Robert E. Lewis, the Chaucer Library (Athens: University of Georgia Press, 1978), 17–30.

8. Lotario dei Segni, *De miseria condicionis humane*, ed. Lewis, 164–65.

9. Sigmund Freud, *Jokes and Their Relation to the Unconscious, Standard Edition*, 8:121.

10. Lewis observes that the original work was dedicated to fellow cardinal Peter Galloccia and that it represents an excited (if preliminary) immersion in the scholastic concepts of the day (2–3).

11. I am here reversing Freud's observation about the double entendre as words "full and empty" (41).

12. E.g., "in sacramento corporis accidens non est in substantia, sed substantia consistit sub accidente"; *Patrologia Latina*, vol. 217, bk. 4, chap. 11, col. 863.

13. "Berengar, identifying form with accident, sees no real distinction between accident and subject and hence no separability. . . . Later, when it was discovered that, in pure Aristotelian doctrine, the accident is not identical with substantial form, [they] could easily reason from this real distinction of substance and accident to the[ir] separability"; Raymond G. Fontaine, *Subsistent Accident in the Philosophy of Saint Thomas and in His Predecessors* (Washington, D. C.: Catholic University Press, 1950), 34–35.

14. Personal correspondence, 29 April 1995.

15. *Sacrorum Conciliorum Nova et Amplissima Collectio*, ed. G. Mansi (Graz: Akademische Druck, 1961), 22:981.

16. Miri Rubin, *Corpus Christi: The Eucharist in Late Medieval Culture* (Cambridge: Cambridge University Press, 1991); Gary Macy emphasizes "the tradition of diversity" in *The Theologies of the Eucharist in the Early Scholastic Period* (Oxford: Clarendon Press, 1984).

Other works I have found useful include R. W. Southern, "Lanfranc of Bec and Berengar of Tours," in *Studies in Medieval History Presented to F. M. Powicke* (Oxford: Oxford University Press, 1948), 27–48, and Raymond G. Fontaine, *Subsistent Accident*).

17. With apologies for the haste of this rough summation, I refer the reader to previously cited works by Macy and Fontaine, and also to David Burr, *Eucharistic Presence and Conversion in Late Thirteenth-Century Franciscan Thought*, Transactions of the American Philosophical Society 74 (Philadelphia: American Philosophical Society, 1984).

18. These voices are further subdivided in the climate of locally intensified debate, when "substance" and "accident" became fighting words in a renewed eucharistic controversy: Innocent is alternatively seen as the irresponsible innovator and antichristus of Lollard condemnation and as the font of eucharistic orthodoxy. See *Fasciculi Zizaniorum*, ed. W. W. Shirley, Rolls Series (London, 1858), 5:383–84 (hereafter, *FZ*). Berengar is both the contrite subject of the "confession" in which Wyclif sought a grounding for his views and the wild raver from whose dreams Tyssyngton claimed Wyclif roused his heresies. See Wyclif, *De eucharistia*, ed. Johann Loserth (London: Wyclif Society, 1892), 30–31; *FZ*, 5:134. Also see Anne Hudson, *The Premature Reformation* (Oxford: Clarendon Press, 1988), 286–87.

19. Cf. Rubin: "Power and aesthetics turned the eucharist into the battleground where the new vision of Christian society would be won or lost" (*Corpus Christi*, 22).

20. In this spirit, see Peggy Knapp's observation that, despite the condemnation of certain of Wyclif's views, the subversive content of his opinions remained undecided during his lifetime: *Chaucer and the Social Contest* (London: Routledge, 1990), 63–67.

21. My argument in the remarks that follow has been conditioned by my reading of H. G. Richardson's superb "Heresy and the Lay Power under Richard II," *English Historical Review* 51 (1936): 1–28. See also Margaret Aston, "Lollardy and Sedition, 1381–1431," *Past and Present* 17 (1960): 1–44.

22. Henry Knighton, *Chronicon*, ed. Joseph Lumby, Rolls series, no. 92 (London, 1895), 2:163, 178–89. Knighton uses the term "Lollardi" in his write-up of 1382, but somewhat retrospectively, since his account may have been written as late as 1390. The term was, nonetheless, in use in 1382; Henry Crump, master of theology, was suspended in mid-1382 by the chancellor of Oxford for calling Wyclif's followers "Lollardi"; *FZ*, 5:311–12.

23. *RP*, 3:124–25.

24. See Herbert B. Workman, *John Wyclif* (Oxford: Clarendon Press, 1926), 2:271.

25. Workman identifies him as a courtier, pensioner of the Crown, and frequent debtor, saltily observing that he seems not to have been "given either to lollardy or to seeing visions, unless they made for his own advancement" (ibid., 2:272–73).

26. *FZ*, 105.

27. *FZ*, 277–78.

28. *RP*, 3:141. The king assented to the counterpetition ("Y plest au Roi"), but the statute was never rescinded.

29. Knighton, *Chronicon*, 193; *FZ*, 340. The petitions seem ultimately not to have been successful, but one is struck by the optimism underlying the fact that they were launched at all.

30. Richardson ("Heresy and the Lay Power") offers evidence (21) that they even sent a copy to the pope!

31. The Latin version appears in *FZ*, 360–69; the English in Anne Hudson, *Selections from English Wycliffite Writings* (Cambridge: Cambridge University Press, 1978), 24–29.

32. *FZ*, 408–10.

33. Roger Dymmok, *Liber contra XII Errores et Hereses Lollardorum*, ed. H. S. Cronin (London: Wyclif Society, 1922). The tendency of this debate to rely on crude stereotyping is exemplified by Dymmok's absurd imputation that the anti-imagistic Lollards were somehow to be considered guilty of idolatry.

34. See H. G. Richardson and G. O. Sayles, "Parliamentary Documents from Formularies," *Bulletin of the Institute of Historical Research* 11 (1933–34): 152–54.

35. See *RP*, 3:459, 466–67.

36. *Continuatio Eulogii*, Rolls Series, 9:3, 387–88.

37. Although, as David Lawton pointed out in his subsequent comment on these remarks, the capacity of at least some segments of the fifteenth-century public for decidedly uninnocent enjoyment of such matters must not be underestimated. Hoccleve's wish that all those who believe as Badby did should be burned as he was (*Regiment*, lines 327–29) and his strident "Remonstrance against Oldcastle" (esp. lines 357–58) leave little doubt of his capacity to enjoy a good Lollard joke, the fates of Sautre, Badby, Oldcastle and the rest notwithstanding. I have chosen to present this essay essentially in the form in which it was delivered; a revision or extension would devote more attention to the varieties of likely fifteenth-century response.

38. See Derek Pearsall, "The *Troilus* Frontispiece and Chaucer's Audience," *Yearbook of English Studies* 7 (1977): 68–74; V. J. Scattergood, "Literary Culture at the Court of Richard II," *English Court Culture in the Later Middle Ages* (New York: St. Martin's Press, 1983); and Paul Strohm, "Chaucer's Audience," *Literature and History* 5 (1977): 26–41.

39. Assertions about a closely knit group of "Lollard knights" (most of whom, like Clifford, Clanvowe, and Neville, were also associates and friends of Chaucer) were first advanced by the contemporary chroniclers Knighton (in relation to events of 1382) and Walsingham (in 1387 and 1395). First weighed and substantially discounted by W. T. Waugh, the same charges were more recently reviewed by K. B. McFarlane, who (augmenting them with several pieces of new evidence, including Neville's apparent protection of Lollard preacher Nicholas Hereford) found them to be warranted, with respect at any rate to seven central members of the group. See Waugh, "The Lollard Knights," *Scottish Historical Review* 11 (1914): 55–92, and McFarlane, *Lancastrian Kings and Lollard Knights* (Oxford: Clarendon Press, 1972), 139–226. McFarlane rather considerably overstates his evidence; he argues, for example, that Clanvowe's protest that those who live meekly in the world are regarded as "lollers and losels" amounts to a "confession" of personal Lollardy (205, 207), and in his effort to detect a Lollard voice in three of the knights' wills he goes so far as to suggest Lollard influence on Archbishop Arundel, Repingdon, and Henry IV! But he draws closer to a more tenable assessment of the situation when he leaves off his effort at proof and observes that English religious life in the later fourteenth

century was characterized by "the growth of moral fervour among the laity" (224). This is likewise the conclusion of Anthony Tuck, who, pointing out the varieties of fervent experience cultivated by courtiers of Richard II, observes that "a wide range of religious attitudes is discernible at Richard II's court, from sympathy with some of the ideas of Wycliffe and the Lollard preachers among one group at one extreme to the patronage of the Carthusians among another group close to the king." See "Carthusian Monks and Lollard Knights: Religious Attitude at the Court of Richard II," *Studies in the Age of Chaucer, Proceedings* 1 (1984): 149–61. Both groups, he observes, were attracted to strong appeals to private religiosity, and such religiosity might be expressed in different, and even in superficially contradictory ways.

40. Recall, in this connection, several pieces of debatable but indicative evidence that cannot be brushed away: Neville's keeping (and apparent protection) of Lollard preacher Herefore in Nottingham Castle in 1387, and a 1388 writ to Sir William Latimer requiring him to appear before the appellant-dominated council with the heretical books and pamphlets he had in his custody. On the first instance, see McFarlane, *Lancastrian Kings and Lollard Knights*, 198–99, and Richardson, "Heresy and the Lay Power," 13; on the second, see F. Devon, *Issues of the Exchequer* (London, 1837), 236; see also relevant discussions in Waugh ("The Lollard Knights"), McFarlane, and Tuck ("Carthusian Monks and Lollard Knights").

41. Consider, in this regard, Freud's comment on the use of alternative forms of speech, including dialect, to shield a sequence of thought from criticism (*Jokes*, 108). If all the valences of the joke were ascribed to the Pardoner's character, then Chaucer's "shield" might be said to have worked.

42. On the relations of the preconscious to the unconscious and the augmentation of the unconscious by processes of secondary repression, see Freud, "Repression" and "The Unconscious," *Standard Edition*, 14:147–48 and 180–85, respectively. The particular historical circumstances of a text may be linked with secondary repression (148), in which derivatives or local representatives of the repressed materials are likewise denied admission to the text—although their situation in what might be considered a textual "preconscious" opens the way to their possible retrieval and verbalization (191). Also see Jean Laplanche and Serge Leclaire, "The Unconscious: A Psychoanalytic Study," *Yale French Studies* 48 (1972): 118–75. I am also influenced by Bellamy, *Translations of Power*, 38–81.

43. Although I will not labor the point here, these are all key differentiations of conscious from unconscious effects — effects, that is, accompanying the movement from the unconscious to the conscious — within the Freudian system. See, in particular, Freud's comments on the attachment of words to things, and the predominance of temporality; "The Unconscious," 201, 187.

44. See, for instance, McFarlane's use of such testimentary language as a litmus for Lollard belief in *Lancastrian Kings and Lollard Knights*, 207–20. I want to thank Miri Rubin for pointing out the affiliation of this passage's language with that of Lollard wills.

45. I am not so much interested in intent here as in textual effect, but I might note that, as an indication of possible intention, Chaucer here offers a rearrangement of Lotario's text, removing lines 534–36 from his seventeenth chapter, and placing it ahead of the cooks of his sixteenth chapter.

46. This point has been made with considerable persuasive verve by Samuel Weber, *The Legend of Freud* (Minneapolis: University of Minnesota Press, 1982), 84–117. Disputing the notion that the joke has a "proper meaning," stabilized by the hull/kernel relation, Weber argues in terms of one representative Freudian passage that "the outer garment of verbal play reveals itself to be the inner nucleus of the joke, while the semantic material that usually makes up the interior domain is here only a facade. The prohibited game returns in and as this smearing of oppositions that are seemingly clear-cut" (106). Weber elsewhere observes a telling mistranslation in the *Standard Edition*, in which Freud's "the best performances may use the most substantial thoughts as their guise" is rendered as "the best achievements in the way of jokes are used as an envelope for thoughts of the greatest substance" (89).

47. Suggestively rendered by Spinka as "crush"; *Advocates of Reform*, Library of Christian Classics, vol. 14, ed. Matthew Spinka (Philadelphia: Westminster Press, 1953), 63.

48. *Heresy Trials in the Diocese of Norwich, 1428–31*, Camden Society, 4th series, vol. 20 (London, 1977), 44–45.

49. As John Mowitt says of Barthes, "If one keeps in mind the methodological character of the text, then it is easier to see that Barthes has designed it around the tactical assumption that one can disclose the center... , and thus make it available for criticism, by getting at how it manages that which the center construes as a threat"; *Text: The Genealogy of an Antidisciplinary Object* (Durham, N.C.: Duke University Press, 1992), 121.

50. Jacques Lacan, *The Seminar*, book 7 (New York: Norton, 1992), 70.

51. As Žižek observes of this privileged signifier and sublime object of desire, "[T]he element which only holds the place of a certain lack, which is in its bodily presence nothing but an embodiment of a certain lack, is perceived as a point of supreme plenitude"; *The Sublime Object of Ideology* (London: Verso, 1989), 99.

52. In, for example, Berengar's "confession," as dictated by the most orthodox party of his day, and to which Wyclif was perfectly prepared to subscribe. See *De Eucharistia*, 30–31.

53. The sheer utility of the heretical Lollard to the support of late-fourteenth-century orthodoxy is registered in the refusal of the sacerdotal establishment to let Lollards off the hook. Having been discursively framed as heretics, the Lollards were simply not permitted to extricate themselves argumentatively. Some of their self-justifying treatises possessed considerable persuasive and conciliatory power, as in their demonstration that their view of the Eucharist had prevailed in the Church for nearly a millennium, prior to the introduction of the novel and post-Aristotelian concept of transubstantiation, or in their effective willingness to create and subscribe to a compromise view amounting to consubstantiation. But such reasonable arguments were of no avail, and the Lollards were progressively less and less able to extricate themselves from the position of a group chosen to fulfill an unreasonable need. Ideologically speaking, the late-fourteenth-century Lollard was beginning to function as an available antagonism that, in the Lacanian-Žižekian formulation, permits the symbolic order to conceal its own inconsistencies and hence to suture itself; see Žižek, *The Sublime Object of Ideology*, esp. 11–53. This is the "irrational" kernel that, in its ascribed difference, must either change society or become society's victim.

12. John's Locked Box

The original version of this essay was given at a 22 March 1996 University of Oklahoma Conference on Psychoanalysis and Medieval Literature, arranged by George Economou. The other participants were Nancy Partner and Lee Patterson, respectively representing traditional Freudian and anti-Freudian positions. Since its original presentation, this essay has branched in two different directions. The present version more closely approximates the original by approaching Hoccleve's John of Canacee from a post-Freudian and Lacanian, hence psychoanalytical, perspective; its absent partner is "The Amnesiac Text," a chapter in *England's Empty Throne* (London and New Haven, Conn.: Yale University Press, 1998), 196–214, in which I consider the same narrative in more consistently historical terms, as a withholding but ultimately revealing social and political document. I thank Linda Charnes for a lively reading and helpful critique of the present version.

1. Terry Eagleton, "Good Dinners Pass Away," review of *Death, Desire, and Loss in Western Culture*, by Jonathan Dollimore, *London Review of Books*, 16 April 1998, 13.

2. References to numerous versions (under the rubric "Chest full of stones") are found in Frederic C. Tubach, *Index Exemplorum* (Helsinki: Suomalainen Tiedeakatemia, 1969), 78. Versions of thirteenth-century English and fifteenth-century Italian provenance are found, respectively, in British Museum MS Royal 7 D. I and MS Addit. 27336; see J. A. Herbert, *Catalogue of Romances in the British Museum* (London, 1910), 3:486, 653. A particularly influential version is that of Jacobus de Cessolis, in *Liber de Ludo Scaccorum*, composed ca. 1300. The standard edition is that of Ernst Köpke, *Mittheilungen aus den Handschriften der Ritter-Akademie zu Brandenburg A.H.*, vol. 2, Iacobus de Cessolis (Brandenburg, n.d.). Jacobus's work is one of the first translated and printed by Caxton, in 1474, for which see William Axon, ed., *Caxton's Game and Playe of the Chesse* (London, 1883), 148–51. Thomas Hoccleve's version, based on Jacobus, appears in his *Regement of Princes*, EETS, e.s., 72 (London, 1897), 151–57. For Hoccleve's indebtedness to Jacobus, and for additional bibliographical information, see Friedrich Aster, *Das Verhältniss des altenglischen Gedichtes "De Regimine Principum" von Thomas Hoccleve zu seinen Quellen* (Leipzig: Oskar Peters, 1888), 47–50.

3. Examples are the thirteenth-century British Library MS Latin Royal 7.D.I or the fifteenth-century Italian British Library MS Addit. 27336.

4. On this state of destitution, with particular reference to Lear, see Jacques Lacan, *The Seminar*, book 7 (New York: Norton, 1992), 305–8.

5. My present point of reference is Lacan's establishment of the search for the desired object under the aegis of the pleasure principle, and his perception that this search remains pleasureful only so long as it is maintained at a proper distance from its object: "The pleasure principle governs the search for the object and imposes the detours which maintain the distance in relation to its end" (ibid., 58). The prohibitive father, in this case, acts in accord with the dictates of the pleasure principle.

6. So, Slavoj Žižek: "How does an empirical, positively given object become an object of desire; how does it begin to contain some X, some unknown quality... [which] makes it worthy of our desire? By entering the framework of fantasy, by being included in

a fantasy-scene which gives consistency to the subject's desire"; *The Sublime Object of Ideology* (London: Verso, 1989), 119.

7. Freud, we must recall, places the conscious under the domain of the unconscious, the reality principal under the domain of the pleasure principle. The aim of the pleasure principle is not to satisfy our needs, but to hallucinate their satisfaction—a process of hallucination monitored, but not governed, by the reality principle. The hallucination of satisfaction consists in the search for an object of desire, or at least a suitable stand-in or "partial object," and the art of desiring is to maintain one's search, "at a certain distance from that which it gravitates around" (Lacan, *The Seminar*, bk. 7, 58). The bad siblings' desire for gold is governed by the pleasure principle, only incidentally monitored by the reality principle. The monitoring effect of the reality principle may be observed in the verifications that the father offers to his daughters, and on which they place their hope: we heard (they can tell themselves) the clink of the gold, saw it counted and placed in the box, observed it locked with three keys. Yet these palliatives to the daughter's desire not to be duped in this transaction turn out to be wholly unreliable; turn out, in fact, to be part and parcel of a secondary effect, important only insofar as they permit the daughters an unimpeded access to pleasure's embrace. The pleasure here consists, not in the enjoyment of the gold, but in the expectation of its enjoyment. So long as the box is maintained as a fantastic object of desire—so long, that is, as the daughters are not allowed to penetrate to the center of the box and confront its ruse—they must be accounted happy people.

8. Lacan posits a spectacular origin for the ego, an origin in which the ego is constituted in relation to observed objects outside its own bounds. The ego's relation to this object involves inevitable misrecognition or *méconnaissance*. The central misrecognition is, of course, of other for self, oneself as a more integrated and competent other. (Often reiterated within Lacan's work, these points are conveniently gathered in *The Seminar*, book 1: *Freud's Papers on Technique* [New York: Norton, 1988], 165, 53, 155.) The most celebrated instance of Lacanian misrecognition is, of course, the infant's misrecognition of a reflection in a mirror as a simulacrum of his or her own coherence. See *Écrits* (London: Tavistock, 1977), esp. 15–20, 41–42. I am, frankly, more inclined to regard Lacan's account of the "mirror stage" as a suggestive allegory, a sort of twentieth-century "Mirror of Narcissus," than as a developmental account. Nevertheless, it succinctly registers a mechanism—of imaginary identification—that both attaches and separates the viewer from what is observed. This split state of attraction/alienation is here treated as applicable, not just to the misrecognized self, but to *all* objects of attraction, with which the subject experiences a relation of inevitably frustrated desire. Thus, the wicked children's desire for the imaginary gold participates in all desire of and for the other: unfulfilled and unfulfillable, it is desire for a simulacrum or imaginary construct, the fruits of which are finally to be enjoyed *by another*; see *Écrits*, 42.

In claiming that the Lancastrians were masters of misrecognition, I imagine them as manipulators and beneficiaries of certain effects, without claiming for them any pre-Lacanian analytical precocity! In this case, as in so many others, a successful effect is subject to description in all sorts of vocabularies, Lacanian and other.

9. Desire may, it is true, remain unsatisfied with respect to the objects afforded to it within a particular historical situation; such is our condition as "split subjects," always imagining the fulfillment of our longings within the symbolic order, but never fully satisfied by the partial or incomplete objects of desire the symbolic order affords us. So much the worse. But the objects of our striving are historical, and the consequences of our strivings are thus historically and materially registered.

10. Lacan, *The Seminar*, book 7, 112. Copjec reiterates this view, drawing from it a somewhat sparer conclusion than I aim to pursue: the desire (and object-cause of desire) "that causes the subject has historical specificity (it is the product of a specific discursive order), but no historical content. The subject is the product of history without being the fulfillment of a historical demand"; *Read My Desire: Lacan against the Historicists* (Cambridge, Mass.: MIT Press, 1994), 56. My demurral is simply that the partial objects of desire presented to us within the symbolic not only preexist desire's temporary focus, but play their own role in the incitement and deployment of desire. Whatever inchoate desires precede the subject's historical insertion cannot finally be discussed or measured independently of the historical objects in relation to which they are summoned and to which they attach themselves.

11. J. A. Burrow, *Thomas Hoccleve*, vol. 4 of *Authors of the Middle Ages* (Aldershot: Variorum, 1994), 17–18.

12. See especially Peter McNiven, "Prince Henry and the English Political Crisis of 1412," *History* 65 (1980): 1–16. See also K. B. McFarlane, *Lancastrian Kings and Lollard Knights* (Oxford: Clarendon Press, 1972), 102–13; Christopher Allmand, *Henry V* (Berkeley and Los Angeles: University of California Press, 1992), 39–58.

13. A. J. Gross, "The Fallibilities of the English Kings," *The McFarlane Legacy*, ed. R. H. Britnell and A. J. Pollard (Stroud: Sutton, 1995), 59.

14. From MS Julius B.II, in *Chronicles of London*, ed. C. L. Kingsford (Oxford: Oxford University Press, 1905), 24.

15. Christine Carpenter, *Locality and Polity* (Cambridge: Cambridge University Press, 1992), 5 n. 22.

16. See John Hardyng, *Chronicle*, ed. Henry Ellis (1812; reprint, New York: AMS, 1974), 349.

17. On representation of Henry as a man, in contrast to Richard's presumed youth, despite the fact that Richard was literally, by several months, the older, see Daniel Rubey, "The Five Wounds of Melibee's Daughter: Revenge, Mercy, and the Hundred Years War," paper delivered at the International Medieval Congress, Kalamazoo, Michigan, May 1996.

18. M. D. Legge, ed., *Anglo-Norman Letters and Petitions* (Oxford: Anglo-Norman Text Society, 1941), no. 396.

19. *Eulogium and Continuatio Eulogii*, Rolls Series, no. 9, pt. 3, 389.

20. A. B. Steel, *The Receipt of the Exchequer, 1377–1485* (Cambridge: Cambridge University Press, 1954), 114–15.

21. E. F. Jacob, *The Fifteenth Century, 1399–1485* (Oxford: Oxford University Press, 1961), 87–88.

22. Thomas Hoccleve, *Works*, EETS, e.s., 72 (London, 1897), lines 2159–63.

23. For records of pieces and their recipients, see J. H. Wylie, *The Reign of Henry V* (Cambridge, 1914), 1:471.

24. Lacan, *The Seminar,* book 7, 83.

25. On the murder of the primal father and the deferred forms of Oedipal obedience observed by his successor sons, see Sigmund Freud, *Totem and Taboo, Standard Edition,* 13:140–46. With respect to the Oedipal or "ideal" father, Copjec observes that his prohibitions actually foster a form of limited enjoyment in their own right: "[H]is *interdictions* give the subject a whiff of hope; it is they that suggest the possibility of transgression. In forbidding excess enjoyment, they appear to be its only obstacle; the subject/prisoner is thus free to dream of their removal and of the bounty of pleasure that will then be his." See *Read My Desire,* 156.

26. Slavoj Žižek, "Why Are There Always Two Fathers?" in *Enjoy Your Symptom!* (New York: Routledge, 1992), 158.

27. Gilles Deleuze and Félix Guattari, *Anti-Oedipus: Capitalism and Schizophrenia* (Minneapolis: University of Minnesota Press, 1983).

28. "He seyd opynly...that his lawes weren in his mouthe...And that he allone myht chaunge the Lawes off his Rewme and make newe"; Julius B.II, 31.

29. The evidence of Henry's wild years was extensively investigated, and totally refuted, by F. Solly-Flood, in "The Story of Prince Henry of Monmouth and Chief-Justice Gascoign," *Transactions of the Royal Historical Society,* n.s., 3 (1886): 47–152. That stories of his early involvement with "low and riotous company" are consistently revived—even by such respected analysts as K. B. McFarlane (*Lancastrian Kings and Lollard Knights,* 123)—is testimony to our own persistent desires for a satisfying narrative configuration.

30. Rolls Series, no. 28, pt. 1, 2:290.

31. Cited in Solly-Flood, "The Story of Prince Henry ," 118–19.

32. This anecdote was promptly embraced by chroniclers Hall and Holinshed, biographer Redmayne, and the dramatist of *The Famous Victories of Henry V,* not to mention Shakespeare's own willing use of it. These sixteenth-century elaborations are conveniently summarized in Charles L. Kingsford, *Henry V* (New York: Putnam, 1901), 87–93.

33. Christopher Allmand, *Henry V* (Berkeley: University of California Press, 1992), 16–58.

34. I omit further discussion of these matters, but the reader interested in their elaboration may consult chapter 9 of the present volume and chapter 8 ("The Amnesiac Text") of *England's Empty Throne.*

35. Lacan, *The Seminar,* book 7, 150.

36. Copjec, *Read My Desire,* 14.

13. MELLYAGANT'S PRIMAL SCENE

1. Frank Kermode, "Writing about Shakespeare," *London Review of Books,* 9 December 1999, 3.

2. "The Wife of Bath's Prologue," III.577–79.

3. *A Book of Showings to the Anchoress Julian of Norwich*, ed. E. Colledge and J. Walsh (Toronto: Pontifical Institute, 1978), long version, chap. 12, 343.

4. Béroul, *The Romance of Tristan*, ed. Alfred Ewert, vol. 1 (Oxford: Blackwell, 1977), lines 693–826. See also his valuable commentary on these lines and their analogues, vol. 2 (Oxford: Blackwell, 1970), 125–27. As noted by Ewert, Gottfried von Strassburg and others repeat versions of this episode. The prose Tristan, followed by Malory, shifts the bloodied bed to the wife of Segurades, who confesses that the blood was Tristan's; see Malory for his spectacularly bloody effusion in the bed of Segwarydes' wife: "and so sir Trystrames bledde bothe the over-shete and the neyther-sheete, and the pylowes and the hede-shete." See *The Works of Sir Thomas Malory*, ed. E. Vinaver (Oxford: Clarendon Press, 1967), 1:394.

5. In Malory and elsewhere, Tristan and Iseult are repeatedly likened to Lancelot and Guinevere, and the four regularly indulge in congratulatory recognition of their own similitude. Thus, it is no surprise to find a scene highly similar to that of the Béroul Tristan in Chrétien's *Lancelot*, where (as in Malory) Lancelot injures his fingers forcing entry to Guinevere's chamber, and her obtrusive admirer Meleaganz reaches the reasonable but erroneous conclusion that she has slept with Kay, a bedtime bleeder in his own right. See *Lancelot*, ed. and trans. W. Kibler, vol. 1 (New York: Garland, 1981), lines 4633–986.

6. Malory, *Works*, ed. Vinaver, 3:1592. Subsequent quotations from Malory's "Knight of the Cart" are taken from this volume.

7. *Lancelot*, ed. Kibler, lines 4768–74.

8. As with the issue of the seduction fantasy, Freud takes different positions at different times on the question of whether the primal scene is real, a product of fantasy, or — for that matter — even phylogenetic. Speaking of primal, among other severe childhood experiences, Freud observed in 1916–17, "If they have occurred in reality, so much to the good; but if they have been withheld by reality, they are put together from hints and supplemented by phantasy"; *Introductory Lectures on Psycho-Analysis, Standard Edition* (London: Hogarth Press, 1957), 16:370 (hereafter, *Standard Edition*). See also *From the History of an Infantile Neurosis, Standard Edition*, 17:48–60.

9. "If [the child] finds traces of blood on his mother's bed . . . he takes it as a sign that she has been injured by his father"; *Introductory Lectures on Psycho-Analysis, Standard Edition*, 1: 318–19. See also *From the History of an Infantile Neurosis, Standard Edition*, 17:45.

10. "What was essentially new for him in his observation of his parents' intercourse was the conviction of the reality of castration"; *Standard Edition*, 17:45. Within Freud's system the castration fear may be explained in part by the introjection of a sense of deserved punishment, owing to feelings of hostility and rivalry toward the father. See, for a pertinent analytical moment, the case of little Hans, *Analysis of a Phobia in a Five-Year-Old Boy, Standard Edition*, 10:42.

11. On the child's propensity for interruption, see Freud, *Infantile Neurosis, Standard Edition*, 17:80.

12. Ibid., 17:74–75. However, Freud later (99–100) draws an utterly nonliteral conclusion from this preoccupation.

13. *Standard Edition*, 17:45–48.

14. "de l'autre doi se trancha / la premerainne jointe tote"; lines 4642–43.
15. See note 8, on phylogenetic properties.
16. Freud, *Analysis of a Phobia, Standard Edition,* 10:65.
17. Freud, *Interpretation of Dreams,* Standard Edition, 5: 525.
18. Lacan, *The Seminar,* book 7, 150.

MEDIEVAL CULTURES

INDEXES

PROTAGONISTS, EVENTS, AND SELECTED MEDIEVAL TEXTS

Theoretical Concepts

Absent cause: material world as, xv–xvi, 216n12. *See also* Textuality: and the extratextual

Action, 58; prior rehearsal and, 21–27, 31–32; structure and, 62; symbolization and, 21

Allegory, 17–18, 55

Anachronism (defended), 199

Antagonism, 73, 128–30, 175–81, 251n53; symbolism and, 128. *See also* Action; Violence

Anthropology, 149

Audience, xvi, 173–75

Binaries, 35

Capital: economic, 187, 192–93; symbolic, 35–36, 46, 187,192–93. *See also* Practice theory

Closure: aspiration to, 82; premature, 199–200; rhetoric of, 63–64. *See also* Narrative

Commentary, 52; as "respectful doubling," xii, 166

Coronation, 38–47, 140; queenly, 45–47; regalia, 41; unction, 42–45

Corroboration, 108; and evidential register, 108–9

Counterfeit, 143, 146, 155–56

Culture, 149; vs. cultural materialism, 150; cultural studies, 150

Deconstruction, 34, 105

Defamiliarization, 199

Desire, 141, 182–88; historicity of, 188, 254nn9,10; literacy in, 199; objects and,

182; regulation of, 144, 183, 193–95, 253n7; unarticulated, 199

Disciplinarity, 33, 35; antidiscipinarity, 33–34, 47–48; "antidisciplinary remainder," 35, 47–48; interdisciplinarity, 33–34

Discourse, 53–56, 144, 150, 169, 175

Drama: social, 14–15; theatricality, 137

Enjoyment, 196

Environment, representational, 55

Essentialism, 57

Euphemization, 38–41. *See also* Practice theory

Event, the, 31, 67, 109–10, 112–13, 130; postmodern theory of, 151–52

Exemplarity, 29, 221nn28,29

Fantasy frame, 186, 252n6

Formalism, xii

Framing, 62, 186

Genealogy, 72, 77

Genre, 3, 15, 18, 93, 129; "appeal," 16, 116; aube, 85, 233n8; chronicle, 101–106; complaint, 82, 85; dream vision, 16; exchequer issue, 106–8; historia, 59; sonnet, 90–91; tragedy, 59

Guilt, 125–27; intersubjectivity and, 127

Heterogeneity, 161; and the postmodern, 151–57. *See also* Time

Historical truth, 139; as average or mean, 103; belief and, 133; eclipse of, 149–51; lies and, 105–6; locus of, 100, 140, 142; partial, 110; reconstruction and, 112–13;

Paul Strohm is J. R. R. Tolkien Professor of English at the University of Oxford. He previously taught at Indiana University. His publications include *Social Chaucer; Hochon's Arrow: The Social Imagination of Fourteenth-Century Texts;* and *England's Empty Throne: Usurpation and the Language of Legitimation.*